D0982984

The History of Financial Planning
Planning

The History of Financial Planning

The Transformation of Financial Services

E. DENBY BRANDON, JR.

H. OLIVER WELCH

WILEY

John Wiley & Sons, Inc.

Copyright © 2009 by E. Denby Brandon, Jr. and H. Oliver Welch. All rights reserved.

Published by John Wiley & Sons, Inc., Hoboken, New Jersey.
Published simultaneously in Canada.

No part of this publication may be reproduced, stored in a retrieval system, or transmitted in any form or by any means, electronic, mechanical, photocopying, recording, scanning, or otherwise, except as permitted under Section 107 or 108 of the 1976 United States Copyright Act, without either the prior written permission of the Publisher, or authorization through payment of the appropriate per-copy fee to the Copyright Clearance Center, Inc., 222 Rosewood Drive, Danvers, MA 01923, (978) 750-8400, fax (978) 646-8600, or on the web at www.copyright.com. Requests to the Publisher for permission should be addressed to the Permissions Department, John Wiley & Sons, Inc., 111 River Street, Hoboken, NJ 07030, (201) 748-6011, fax (201) 748-6008, or online at http://www.wiley.com/go/permissions.

Limit of Liability/Disclaimer of Warranty: While the publisher and author have used their best efforts in preparing this book, they make no representations or warranties with respect to the accuracy or completeness of the contents of this book and specifically disclaim any implied warranties of merchantability or fitness for a particular purpose. No warranty may be created or extended by sales representatives or written sales materials. The advice and strategies contained herein may not be suitable for your situation. You should consult with a professional where appropriate. Neither the publisher nor author shall be liable for any loss of profit or any other commercial damages, including but not limited to special, incidental, consequential, or other damages.

For general information on our other products and services or for technical support, please contact our Customer Care Department within the United States at (800) 762-2974, outside the United States at (317) 572-3993 or fax (317) 572-4002.

Wiley also publishes its books in a variety of electronic formats. Some content that appears in print may not be available in electronic books. For more information about Wiley products, visit our web site at www.wiley.com.

Library of Congress Cataloging-in-Publication Data:

Brandon, E. Denby, 1927–
 The history of financial planning : the transformation of financial services / E. Denby Brandon, Jr., H. Oliver Welch.
  p. cm.
  Includes bibliographical references and index.
  ISBN 978-0-470-18074-7 (cloth)
 1. Financial planners–History. 2. Financial services industry–History.
 I. Welch, H. Oliver, 1935– II. Title.
 HG179.5.B73 2008
 332.6′2–dc22

2008001412

Printed in the United States of America

10 9 8 7 6 5 4 3 2 1

This book is dedicated to the Certified Financial Planner Board of Standards, Inc., the Financial Planning Association, and the National Endowment for Financial Education, which inspired us to write it, and to the more than 120,000 Certified Financial Planner™ certificants in 20 nations who are committed to bringing the values of financial planning to consumers.

Contents

Foreword

I t's not every day a profession is born.

If you have picked up this book, you most likely are involved in financial services, an industry comprising academics; product providers; financial planners; practitioners of specialized disciplines such as tax planning, accounting, or investment management; and organizations that provide oversight, education, and benefits to the industry's constituents. The focus here is on financial planning and the people and events that helped transform a concept of service into a profession of service. This is the history of financial planning.

You could say it started with one man, Loren Dunton, a mutual fund salesman with a desire to do more than sell products; he wanted to offer services and advice that would help his clients. But he knew he couldn't breathe life into this notion single-handedly. One man became two, became 13, and on December 12, 1969, became the College for Financial Planning and the International Association for Financial Planners. Yet even then, financial planning's genesis was in its early stages. It took a growing community of men and women sharing a noble calling, and the passion to cultivate it, for the profession to take root.

This book follows financial planning's odyssey over four decades, surveying a varied landscape of revelations and revolutions, false starts, missteps, survival, defeat, separation and union, innovation, trials, and triumphs. It presents a chronology of the profession's development by way of internal and external events, with a substantial thread of humanity woven in, as we introduce some key contributors to financial planning's story. Indeed, we present only *some* events and names, for to include in these pages everyone and everything that has played a role would be impossible. When it gets down to it, though, while those who lead and explore in any field clearly deserve recognition, it's what they create and discover that should endure, more than their celebrity.

The board of directors and staff of the Financial Planning Association appreciate the opportunity to contribute to this significant effort championed by E. Denby Brandon, Jr., CFP, and H. Oliver Welch, CPA, CFP, veterans and leaders of the financial planning movement. They devoted extraordinary personal effort, time, and financial resources to collecting volumes of accounts, dates, statistics, and their colleagues' stories as the basis of this history. Without a doubt, it was a labor of love and took an unswerving dedication to tell a powerful story of 40 years that, until now, has never been brought together in one place. I cannot thank them enough.

To reflect on these first 40 years of the financial planning profession is exciting. I am impressed and humbled by all that has been accomplished in this journey toward legitimacy. I am encouraged by the increasing reach of financial planning into the world, be it through new member organizations and educational programs in other countries, or the growing ranks of financial planners here in the United States, or in serving a wider range of demographics. I watch the impact of the profession's voice on legislative activities and decisions, and the energy generated by prolific, progressive research. I am touched by the generosity and compassion that so many financial planners exhibit through pro bono and volunteer work. I am heartened by financial planners' ability to deftly guide anxious clients through economic challenges. At the time of this book's publication, planners and clients together are being tested to their cores like never before. When the next edition of this history is updated, I believe that the wisdom and power of professionals who employ the financial planning process will prove to be a saving grace for many individuals and families in desperate times. This is where the financial planning profession of today will come of age, living by the immutable code on which it was built and on which it will base its future.

I hope you will learn from this history of financial planning, regardless of what business you're in or whether you're new or a veteran in your career. I hope this book adequately conveys to you the heart, soul, and tireless commitment that have added to the depth and richness of this profession. If you're a financial planner, I hope this historical perspective will demonstrate the scope of the community to which you belong. I hope you'll understand the critical relationship of the varied elements that play a part in this profession's excellence, such as academic research, product development, and legislative advocacy. Finally, I hope this history of financial planning will inspire you to be clear in your mission, adhere to your truths, and help your fellow residents of this world thrive and prosper.

MARVIN W. TUTTLE, JR.
Executive Director/CEO,
Financial Planning Association

Preface

I t was noon on September 10, 2000, in the Top of the Hub restaurant. The
view of downtown Boston was spectacular. Amid throngs of people were
members of the global financial planning community attending the inaugural
Success Forum of the Financial Planning Association. The occasion was the
annual luncheon for past chairs of the Certified Financial Planner Board of
Standards. The group felt it was time to initiate a project to preserve the
history of our new profession. Prior efforts of the individual organizations
were related to turf battles as opposed to preserving the history. It was
time to record our past as we united to build a stronger profession. Patti
Houlihan, CFP Board chair, said, "Denby and Oliver, as past chairs of CFP
Board, will you assume responsibility for the project?" It was decided that a
project of this magnitude should be a collaborative effort of CFP Board, the
Financial Planning Association, and the National Endowment for Financial
Education. When contacted, each group felt it was a worthwhile endeavor
and pledged their support. We promised to fund the project and contribute
all royalties to the development of the financial planning profession and
later expanded the agreement to include the Archives of Financial Planning,
which was established at Texas Tech.

Our research consisted of the three main methods: literature review, survey instruments, and personal interviews. Our literature research included
reviewing past minutes of the board of directors' meetings of the International Association for Financial Planning, the Institute of Certified Financial
Planners, and the Financial Planning Association, along with committee reports of these organizations. We reviewed numerous financial publications.
We mailed surveys to those who had been involved in the IAFP and ICFP,
to leaders of FPA (formed in 2000 by the union of the IAFP and ICFP), College for Financial Planning, NEFE, and CFP Board. Personal interviews were
conducted over the phone, in individual meetings, and with the assistance
of the faculty of Texas Tech University at several FPA annual conferences.
These interviews have been recorded and archived at Texas Tech.

The foundation of professional financial planning involves the way
financial decisions are made. The pioneers of the movement knew instinc-
tively that financial services consumers needed an objective professional

involved in improving their financial decision-making processes. Financial planning was born in the midst of a market break and recession in the United States in 1969 and is celebrating its fortieth anniversary in the midst of a market break and recession in 2009. It is during challenging economic times that the services of financial planners are tested.

There are at least five areas where financial planning has made significant contributions toward improving people's lives in both good and bad economic times during these 40 years:

1. Professional education programs for financial planning practitioners
2. Professional management of clients' financial assets
3. Financial literacy and maturity programs for consumers
4. Individual and family financial habits programs
5. Programs to help people's careers and investments be more profitable and to achieve more equitable ownership societies

In Chapter 1, we give you a picture of the environment out of which the financial planning movement emerged. We take you inside the watershed December 1969 meeting in Chicago that launched the movement. We begin introducing you to the cast of characters, including Loren Dunton, James R. Johnston, and Lewis Kearns. This cast included visionary, courageous, and talented people. A majority of them put the movement ahead of their personal goals. It also included others who were long on ego and short on performance. They were in the mix that laid the foundation for the most important new profession created in the last half of the twentieth century. This caused our interest in understanding them to rise to a new level. In Chapter 2, we take you through the formative years from the early 1970s through 1985. These years marked the near demise and the early glory years of the College for Financial Planning. Anthony Sorge and William Anthes were new factors in this drama. It included the phasing out of Loren Dunton and the emergence of J. Chandler Peterson. The membership organization, IAFP, found a profit center. The CFP professional group, ICFP, entered the scene. Kemp Fain and David King were early ICFP forces.

In Chapter 3, we focus on the last half of the 1980s. This was dominated by the lawsuit drama that ended in the formation of the International Board of Standards and Practices for Certified Financial Planners. The early story of what the IBCFP did with its ownership of the marks included decisions that vastly expanded the horizons of the financial planning movement and profession.

In Chapter 4, essentially the 1990s, we tell the story of the landmark event of the merger of the ICFP and the IAFP into the FPA at the end of the decade. The decade also marked a turning point for the College for Financial Planning. In 1992, the college created the National Endowment for Financial Education as a holding company. In 1997, NEFE sold the college to the Apollo Group, a for-profit firm. This changed NEFE's role permanently. NEFE became primarily a financial public education program to serve all Americans. This was also a decade in which the CFP grass-roots community spoke out against CFP Board's proposed Associate CFP designation. In Chapter 5, we focus on the new era begun with the birth of the 30,000-member Financial Planning Association in 2000. The momentum of a united membership organization was contagious. The unity was a big factor in financial planning's creative response to the dot-com market bust that began in 2000. Among the many accomplishments of FPA was the first National Financial Planning Week in 2002. The creation of the Financial Planning Standards Board in 2004 and the development of financial planning practice standards in the United States were both noteworthy.

In Chapter 6, we view the global expansion saga of the financial planning movement. It is the story of how the movement grew from only 42 CFP certificants in 1973, all from the United States, to over 120,000 CFP certificants in 20 nations in 2009.

In Chapter 7, we address the interaction of financial planning research, growth, and the world of technology. The incredible growth of technology during this 40-year period is detailed.

In Chapter 8, we trace the emerging growth of financial planning as a profession: education, examination, experience, ethics, method of compensation, government regulation, and social purpose.

In Chapter 9, we outline possible challenges and opportunities as the financial planning movement and profession face the future.

In its first 40 years, the financial planning profession has discovered and developed a dazzling treasure of potential, which is the heart of our story. Today there is even greater potential for the future. However, a clear view and a short distance are not necessarily the same thing. Also, the percentage of potential realized varies greatly. Within the ferment of the current turbulence and change it will be fascinating to determine how much of the short-term potential is realized and how solid a foundation is laid for the development of the long-term potential.

We are continuing our research program and encourage you to forward any comments to us at P.O. Box 770870, Memphis, TN, 38177-0870.

E. DENBY BRANDON, JR.
H. OLIVER WELCH

Acknowledgments

This project encompassed the 40-year history of the center of our major life work, took eight-and-a-half years, included encounters and transactions with hundreds of persons worldwide, and included dozens of people who partnered with us in understanding scores of documents, minutes, and periodicals. This makes it difficult to do justice to acknowledgments.

First, we thank CFP Board, the FPA board, and the NEFE board, and those individual members who selected us for this project in September 2000 and also those who supported us from beginning to end. This group included Patricia Houlihan, Elaine Bedel, Fredrick E. "Rick" Adkins, III, Tom Potts, Janet McCallen, Tim Kochis, Gwen Fletcher, G. Joseph Votava, Sr., Bill Carter, Roy Diliberto, William L. Anthes, Brent Neiser, Nan Mead, Ben Coombs, Graydon Calder, Robert Goss, and Elissa Buie.

Second, there were many other financial planning leaders who made numerous special contributions. These included Donald Pitti, Lewis Kearns, James R. Johnston, Eileen Sharkey, Dick Wagner, Lewis Wallensky, Noel Maye, John Carpenter, Alexandra Armstrong, Suze Sato, Harold Evensky, Deena Katz, Dan Parks, Guy Cumbie, James Barnash, Dave Yeske, William Hoilman, Henry Montgomery, Lewis J. Walker, Jack Blankinship, Robert J. Oberst, and scores of others.

Third, we could not have done the work without our home base at Brandon Financial Planning, Inc. in Memphis, Tennessee, and the use of the corporation's technology facilities. The support of the corporate management staff, Ray Brandon, Denby Brandon III, and Gary Kieffner, and the corporate administrative leaders, Lori Clark and Judy Pierce, was constant. Members of the Brandon Research Organization staff, including Thelma F. Scott, coordinator, Betty Potts, Melissa Danielson, and William Brandon, worked competently and diligently during both the workweek and weekends over the whole period.

Fourth, we are most grateful for the talent and dedicated work of all of our professional partners. Authors Michael Leslie and John Harkins made valuable suggestions during our research. Marvin Tuttle, Mary Corbin, Maureen Peck, Nancy Friedman, Catherine Newton, and Shelley Lee were invaluable in editing our work. We are most appreciative of the unique contributions of Bill Falloon and the development editing staff of John Wiley and Sons, Inc., including Meg Freeborn, Emilie Herman, and Laura Walsh. Their high ethical standards, objectivity, and availability were of great value to us in our integrity goal of accuracy, completeness, and balance, and in many other ways.

Fifth, we wish to express our appreciation to our wives, Helen Brandon and Pat Welch. They continued to support our efforts even when we seemed to let this project consume our every waking hour 24/7.

E. D. B.
H. O. W.

CHAPTER 1

A New Profession Emerges

To call it an unlikely revolution would be an understatement.

One of its principal architects was a onetime vacuum-cleaner salesman who had transformed himself into a marketing consultant and motivational writer. The other was a former insurance salesman turned school-supplies salesman who had a master's degree in psychology. Both were living in Colorado, far from Wall Street or any other financial capital.

The first planning session of the new endeavor, intended as a historic summit meeting, managed to attract just 13 attendees. Its timing—at the onset of one of the worst bear markets in U.S. history—was inauspicious.

Most discouraging of all, the fledgling movement had only the vaguest of action plans. And throughout its early existence, it was starved for capital.

There's no small irony in that last point. The revolution that began in December 1969 was intended to help ordinary Americans gain control over their financial destinies. How could that goal be achieved if the organizations created to realize it were barely solvent themselves?

And yet, despite huge odds, financial planning—the first new profession in the last four centuries—did succeed beyond the most fervent hopes of the revolution's founders, not just in the United States but around the world. Forty years after the profession's inauspicious birth, there are more than 120,000 CFP professionals around the world, educated in scores of colleges and universities.

This is the story of that astonishing success, of the people who built the movement, and of the seminal concepts that contributed to a robust and dynamic—and continuously growing—body of knowledge.

Before the Revolution

Worldwide, 1969 was a year of dramatic milestones. In July, Neil Armstrong became the first person to set foot on the moon. *Midnight Cowboy, Butch*

Cassidy and the Sundance Kid, and *The Wild Bunch* shook up the movie industry. Overseas, the war in Southeast Asia continued to escalate: More than 600,000 U.S. and allied troops were fighting in Vietnam, and the United States secretly bombed Communist bases in Cambodia—a harbinger of a more general attack that would take place the following year. But it was hard to see a reflection of those cultural changes in the financial services industry.

For decades, financial services had meant primarily one thing: sales. Mutual funds had been introduced in 1924, making it easier for small investors to enter the stock market. A decade later, the Roosevelt Administration successfully pushed for legislation to protect investors from a recurrence of the 1929 crash: The Securities Act of 1933, the Securities Exchange Act of 1934 (which created the Securities and Exchange Commission), and the Investment Advisers Act of 1940 established guidelines for regulating the investment industry and provided for disclosure and investor education.

And then, over the next 30 years, little changed. As the years rolled by, the same few large securities firms—whose salesmen were paid on commission—sold equities to wealthy clients. Banks provided trust services, also to wealthy individuals. For average Americans, an "investment" meant a life insurance policy, usually traditional whole life with a guaranteed death benefit and a guaranteed cash value; insurance salesmen also worked on commission. Lawyers drafted wills, created trusts, and sometimes gave tax advice; certified public accountants filed tax returns. The term *financial planner* was rarely used, and when it was, it often identified an insurance agent who offered estate planning and annuities in addition to life insurance. Or a "planner" might have a dual license in insurance and mutual funds. The financial planning process as it is known today was then only a loosely defined idea.

Rich White, an early chronicler of the financial planning profession, wrote about those early years:

> *As late as 1960, life insurance was the substance of financial planning. . . . By definition, a financial planner was an insurance man who offered the public more than money-if-you-die. Financial planners . . . estimated estate tax payments for wealthy customers and sold insurance to fund those payments. They formed clinics in which they analyzed financial goals and sold packages of life insurance, disability insurance and annuities.*[1]

But even though the surface remained placid, there were stirrings of innovation. Servicemen returning from World War II and the Korean

War created new markets for financial products, and a booming economy meant there was cash to invest. The traditional American way of retirement—supported by a company pension and Social Security checks—while still dominant, was being challenged: In 1962, when Congress passed the Self-Employed Individuals Retirement Act (better known by the name of its sponsor, Representative Eugene J. Keogh of New York), it gave partnerships and unincorporated businesses the same tax advantages only corporations had previously enjoyed.

Meanwhile, creative thinkers in academia, government, and business were beginning to reexamine the old financial services models and tinkering with new ones. Their ideas would have far-reaching consequences for the entire industry—including the handful of men who conceived of an entirely new approach to delivering financial services.

A Meeting of the Minds

Financial planning's official birth took place on December 12, 1969, in a hotel meeting room near Chicago's O'Hare Airport. Although the gathering's organizers, Loren Dunton and James R. Johnston, had contacted everyone they knew in financial services, only 11 men showed up, paying their own expenses to travel from Florida, New York, Ohio, and Pennsylvania. They included insurance salesmen and salesmen of mutual funds and securities. One was a financial consultant. One was a publicist. Many were members of the insurance industry's prestigious Million Dollar Round Table, which since 1927 has represented the most successful insurance and financial products sales professionals in the United States and the world.

These men came out of curiosity and a sense of shared mission: to raise the level of professionalism in retail financial services and to make "financial consulting," rather than salesmanship, the driving force of their industry.

Dunton and Johnston had been planning the meeting for months. They had first met the previous summer in Colorado, where both men lived. Johnston, a 35-year-old former life-insurance salesman who was selling school supplies, had come to Dunton's home in Littleton to get a copy of one of Dunton's books, *How to Sell Mutual Funds to Women*. But both men quickly found they had something bigger in common: a desire to improve the way financial services were provided. They also agreed that ongoing professional education would provide the route to that improvement.

Johnston had long been fascinated with motivational speakers. "I listened to them every chance I got," he reflected, decades after his first meeting with Dunton. "I was always impressed with their ability to motivate me. The trouble was, I'd stumble back to earth when I walked outside." Johnston thought the answer lay in "a follow-up educational program for new concepts and motivational speakers." He saw in Dunton a conceptual thinker and motivator, and regarded himself as the educator who would follow up after Dunton introduced his new concepts at motivational events.

At first, Dunton lacked Johnston's keen interest in education. However, he did recognize Johnston's talent for sales and promotion, and saw mutual benefit in an ongoing association. The two men continued to meet over the next 12 months, and on June 19, 1969, Loren Dunton registered a nonprofit 501(c)(3) corporation in Colorado to further the goals they'd been discussing. He called it the Society for Financial Counselling Ethics. (The name was later changed to the Society for Financial Counseling.)

The society's charter identified two purposes for the organization:

1. To supply recognition to those who meet not only the legal but also the ethical standards of financial counseling and conscientiously share their wealth of knowledge with the public
2. To establish an educational institute providing a certification program outside of either the mutual fund or insurance industry, to indicate the ability and desire in specific individuals, and to provide objective guidance and assistance to the public in the form of financial counseling

In addition to Dunton, the SFCE's trustees were Robert Leary of Denver, retired director of sales of Westamerica Securities; and Dr. Daniel Kedzie of Chicago, former director of education of the Chartered Life Underwriter (CLU) program. Dunton persuaded six additional men to serve on the board: Lewis Kearns, from Wellington Management; Jack Glassford, from International Securities; D. Russell Burwell, of Myerson & Co., a New York Stock Exchange member and a customer for Dunton's training films; Ben Cascio of *Mutual Fund Magazine*; Dr. Arthur Mason, dean of the University of Denver; and Walter Fischer, vice president of the Mutual Funds Council.

Despite this impressive roster, the SFCE floundered, raising only $3100 in its first nine months. (Dues had been set at $500 a year.) Although its stated goals were lofty, it offered no clear benefits to participants. For its mission to be realized the SFCE would need to be supplanted by a more effective organization.

Nevertheless, when he greeted his 11 invitees in Chicago on December 12, 1969, Dunton still felt bullish about his plan and his organization. And he refused to be discouraged by the small turnout. He believed his consulting firm, Loren Dunton Associates, could guide and finance the two new organizations that emerged from the two days of meetings in Chicago: a membership organization, the International Association of Financial Counselors;[2] and an educational institution, the International College for Financial Counseling, which would become the College for Financial Planning in mid-1970. Dunton also believed that the group's collective talents would attract additional capital.

Dunton turned out to be wrong about the capital, but his assessment of the attendees' talents was accurate. Though small, the group was skilled, experienced, and committed.

Lewis G. Kearns was director of financial planning for the Wellington Management Company, near Philadelphia, manager of the $1.5 billion Wellington Fund; he had strong convictions about the way mutual fund salesmen would be trained, and would eventually serve as the first chairman of the board of regents of the College for Financial Planning.

Robert Leshner of Cincinnati was already practicing diversified financial counseling with his firm, W.D. Gradison & Co. Like Kearns, he was passionate about professional education and a promoter of early workshops held by the fledgling IAFC.

Herman W. (Hy) Yurman was vice president of the Planning Corporation of America in St. Petersburg, Florida. He proposed that the educational program lead to a professional designation to be called Certified Financial Counselor.

Hank Mildner, a mutual fund salesman from Pompano Beach, Florida, brought his deep concerns about ethics to the meeting. He shared with the group a story about a widow who had lost more than $10,000 in a mutual fund; she had told the salesman, "All I want is safety of my principal"— instructions the salesman blithely disregarded.

Kearns, Leshner, Yurman, Mildner, and the other attendees returned the following day, December 13, to meet with representatives of Dunton's Society for Financial Counselling Ethics. After agreeing that the new membership organization and college would be managed by Dunton's company, LDA, they returned to their homes, ready to begin the crucial committee work that would build the foundations of the new institutions.

Two weeks later, on December 30, President Richard Nixon signed the Tax Reform Act of 1969, the most sweeping tax bill since the income tax was introduced in 1913. The act closed loopholes and dramatically altered tax rates, and had important consequences for investors and their advisers. But it could not stop the advent of the 11-year bear market that began in 1970—a downturn that created a new national anxiety that financial planners were poised to alleviate.

The Chicago 13

The 13 men who attended the December 1969 planning session in Chicago were:

1. **Herbert Abelow:** Queens County, New York. Vice president of sales for one of the largest offices of Dreyfus, a respected name in the mutual fund industry.
2. **Loren Dunton:** Littleton, Colorado. Meeting organizer; founder of Society for Financial Counselling Ethics; organizer of the December 1969 planning session.
3. **Walter Fischer:** Million-dollar mutual-fund salesman for Baxter, Blydern, Selheimer & Co.; vice president of the Mutual Funds Council.
4. **Jerrold Glass:** St. Petersburg, Florida. Regional vice president of Supervised Investors Services. Served on the first education committee (1970–1972) and on the College for Financial Planning's first board of regents.
5. **John Hawkins:** Pompano Beach, Florida. Owner of John Hawkins & Co., Inc., a securities firm. Served on the IAFC's original board.
6. **James R. Johnston:** Denver, Colorado. Co-organizer of planning session; became College for Financial Planning's first employee.
7. **Lewis G. Kearns:** Philadelphia. Director of financial planning, Wellington Management Company, which managed the $1.5 billion Wellington Fund. Chaired the planning session; served as interim chair of the education committee; served two years as College for Financial Planning's first board of regents chairman and later returned for a third term.
8. **Lyle Kennedy:** New York City. Principal in a broker membership.
9. **Robert Leshner:** Cincinnati. Salesman for W.D. Gradison & Co.; early promoter of IAFC sales workshops and memberships.
10. **Hank Mildner:** Pompano Beach, Florida. Veteran mutual fund salesman for Consolidated Securities.
11. **Charles Weitzberg:** A friend of Loren Dunton's.
12. **Herman W. (Hy) Yurman:** St. Petersburg, Florida. Vice president of Planning Corporation of America, a life insurance subsidiary of Raymond James and Associates. Served on first education committee; assisted in writing CFP curriculum.
13. **Gerald Zipper:** New York. Publicist and publisher of a financial newsletter.

Profile: Loren Dunton

By the time he met James R. Johnston in 1968, Loren Dunton was 50 years old and had already had several lifetimes' worth of experience. Born in the small mining town of Trail, British Columbia, he led "an exciting bachelor life in Seattle, Alaska, and San Francisco" before marrying at age 29, according to a biographical note. He sold vacuum cleaners and encyclopedias, then moved to Colorado, where he reinvented himself as a financial consultant and mutual-fund salesman. When Dunton was 45, he learned to parachute and published his first book, *Self Discipline*. It was followed by 12 more books with titles like *How to Sell Mutual Funds to Women, Your Book of Financial Planning,* and *Prime Time: How to Enjoy the Best Years of Your Life.* He made enough money from *How to Sell Mutual Funds to Women* to be able to take his wife and two daughters on a year-long trip around the world. Upon his return, he visited Donald Pitti—who would later assume a leading role in the financial planning movement—at Pitti's office at New York investment firm Arthur Wiesenberger & Co. "He told me that everywhere he went in Europe, people asked him why, if the United States was such a great country, its citizens had to rely on Social Security for their retirement," Pitti later recalled. "He thought we had to improve the way financial products were sold and delivered in this country."

Back in Colorado, Dunton started a consulting firm whose clients were mutual funds and insurance companies. In June 1969, observing a need for greater professionalism, he formed the Society for Financial Counselling Ethics (later called the Society for Financial Counseling), "an educational nonprofit trade organization of companies within the financial services industry that offer financial products, programs, and services."

After the December 1969 planning meeting in Chicago, Dunton took the reins of the Society for Financial Counselling Ethics and the International Association of newly formed Financial Counselors, with Lewis Kearns and James R. Johnston focusing on the International College for Financial Counseling (a product of the December meeting). But he proved to be more successful as a motivator than as an administrator, and both organizations struggled financially under his leadership. Dunton stepped down in 1974 and moved to San Francisco, where he wrote books, gave speeches, and founded several nonprofit groups, including the Institute for Consumer Financial Education. Loren Dunton died in 1997 at age 79.

> *"Financial education is the learning part. Financial planning is the doing part."*
>
> —Loren Dunton

The First Challenges

Before financial planners could help the public, they had to help themselves create a credible profession. They faced substantial hurdles.

Although the Chicago group had decided to launch a membership organization and a college, they were short on resources. They were not men of great wealth, nor did they have enough influence to reach into the deep pockets of wealthy financial services companies. They were not educators, nor did they represent educational institutions. Their working capital was inadequate. (The initial IAFP membership fee was just $10, low even for 1970.) Indeed, it's difficult to imagine a major movement getting under way with the odds stacked so heavily against its success.

Nevertheless, the 13 men were, in their different ways, exceptional people. They were sociable, energetic, knowledgeable, and respected by their peers. Perhaps most important, they represented an idea whose time had come.

To propel that idea, the early leaders of the IAFP decided to hold sales workshops. Robert Leshner helped promote the first one, held in Cincinnati on January 20, 1970. It drew about 40 attendees, most of whom signed up as new IAFP members. One of them was P. Kemp Fain, Jr., of Knoxville, Tennessee, an independent salesman for Financial Services Corporation, a national company with a reputation for innovation; its founders, John Keeble and Richard Felder, had created their first financial plan in 1963. By 1968, they were creating about 300 plans a month. When he returned home, Fain immediately organized the first IAFP chapter. (See the profile of P. Kemp Fain, pp. 162–163.)

The second IAFP sales workshop took place two weeks later in Winter Park, Florida, and attracted more than 60 people. Loren Dunton flew in to be the keynote speaker, and announced to the audience that IAFP membership was approaching 2,000. Whether or not this number was entirely accurate, it was true that by mid-1970 the IAFP had at least one member in every state except Mississippi, and checks were beginning to come in from all over the world.

Market Milestone: Money Market Mutual Funds

Originally called *investment trusts*, mutual funds had been around since the late nineteenth century. Little about them except their name changed until 1971, when two Wall Street financial consultants, Bruce Bent and Henry Brown, invented the money market mutual fund, which allowed smaller investors—who until then had been accustomed to putting their cash into low-earning bank accounts—to pool their money and reap the returns of the money market. Their creation, The Reserve Fund, limped along for almost two years until the *New York Times* published an article about it in January 1973. Other institutions soon launched their own money market mutual funds, creating new opportunities for financial planners to provide counsel on asset allocation.

A College Takes Shape

Lewis Kearns, who had attended the December 1969 Chicago meeting, was tapped to guide the creation of an educational institution that would train and certify financial planners. (Its original name, the International College for Financial Counseling, was changed in mid-1970 to the College for Financial Planning—another step toward solidifying support for the *planner* designation over rival terms such as *counselor* or *representative*.) Kearns formed a committee that met frequently between 1970 and 1972; its members included David Allard; P. Kemp Fain, Jr.; Jerrold Glass; Jim Johnston; J. Chandler Peterson; Shannon Pratt; Thomas Ritt; Larry Wills; and Hy Yurman. Their meetings took them to California; Georgia; Washington, D.C.; and Pennsylvania. It was decided that the college would be located in Denver, largely because Dunton and Johnston lived in the area.

"I had a compulsion to upgrade the profession for the sake of both the practitioner and the public, and I thought that education was the key."

—Lewis Kearns

Profile: Lewis G. Kearns

In 1969, Lew Kearns was 55 years old, held a law degree from the University of Michigan, and was a successful executive, educator, speaker, and writer. He was acquainted with financial planning, too. More than a decade earlier, Kearns had formed a new financial planning department at Wellington Management Company, near Philadelphia. Its purpose was to help investment representatives, primarily stockbrokers, serve customers by shifting from a product-centered approach to a client-directed one. To get the new training under way, Kearns wrote materials, conducted classes for brokers, and spoke to investment and insurance groups across the country. He also served on the adjunct faculty of Temple University's Graduate School of Business in Philadelphia. It was during that time that he met Loren Dunton and James Johnston, and committed himself to their endeavor.

"I had a compulsion to upgrade the profession for the sake of both the practitioner and the public," Kearns said in a 2008 interview, "and I thought that education was the key." After the 1969 Chicago meeting, Kearns became chair of the educational committee, and was charged with developing a curriculum for the fledgling College for Financial Planning.

Later, as chair of the College's board of regents, Kearns presided over the inaugural CFP commencement ceremony. "We knew we were breaking ground, but we didn't know what to call these graduates," Kearns recalled. "The word 'confirmand' was suggested." One of the graduates told Kearns it was an odd word choice—*confirmand*, he said, meant a religious pilgrim.

Kearns was not one of those confirmands. "I remember a board member asking me when I was going to take the CFP exam. I said that I guess I'd take it when someone else wrote it." The next year, the board awarded Kearns an honorary CFP designation.

Following his second term as chair, Kearns stepped aside, believing the "ship was starting to sail on its own," only to return at the board's request after Ferdinand Nauheim's tenure. "I agreed to come back for one more year and be the whipping boy—to stand by 'Certified Financial Planner,' not 'representative,' no matter what Washington said. I felt strongly that 'planner' was a much more meaningful word. It suggested an independent practitioner, not an employee-representative."

In 1973, Kearns removed himself from the national financial planning movement. After retiring from Wellington, he was a consultant for insurance and mutual fund companies and an active volunteer for causes as diverse as the Philadelphia Bible Society's Outreach to Prisons and the Wallingsford Swim and Tennis Club.

Kearns "put his reputation on the line for this profession," James Johnston later commented. Kearns himself, although he always believed the CFP designation would attract practitioners, "never expected the numbers to grow at the rate they have." His vitae, written in 2008 at age 94, states his personal goal: "To share the continued growth in professionalism of the financial planning movement."

Even before the college had an educational program, some individuals were eager to enroll. In early 1970, P. Kemp Fain stopped in Denver to check on the program's process and became its first enrollee—the only enrollee that year. Fain was already working in financial services; he said he saw the college's courses as an important step toward professionalism:

The tests weren't easy, even then. They were all essay questions, and you really had to know the materials and write good, representative answers. The designation wasn't popular; no one understood what it was. It wasn't until around 1978 or 1979 that you saw recognition in people's eyes when you said, "I'm a CFP."

Fain and other prospective students—more than 150 signed up in 1971—had to wait to take those tests. There was still no curriculum.

Lewis Kearns stepped in to fill the gap. He developed a syllabus for the first Certified Financial Planner program, a self-study guide divided into six sections that covered fundamentals, money management, reviewing financial media, the investment model, "considerations in effective financial planning," and "counseling and consumer behavior." According to Rich White, who chronicled the early years of financial planning in a series of 1979 articles for *The Financial Planner*, Loren Dunton had hoped to hire "a distinguished academician" to write the curriculum Kearns had outlined. "However," White wrote, "finances did not permit this, and Dunton turned to Jim Johnston, who had some background in the field. Johnston labored through the course material, adapting it to fit the best texts he could find."

Lesson Two succinctly explained the financial planner's five services:

1. Collecting and evaluating financial and personal information
2. Counseling on financial objectives and alternatives
3. Installing the financial program
4. Coordinating the elements of the financial plan that involved others
5. Keeping the long-range financial plan current in light of internal and/or external changes

Profile: James R. Johnston

In its early years, the financial planning movement needed a dedicated parent to keep the fledgling in the incubator. It found that caretaker in Jim Johnston, who had no fear of hard work or of taking a chance on something new. As a young man, he spent summers shoveling coal on iron ore ships as they crossed the Great Lakes. After college and a stint in the Navy (he eventually earned the rank of captain after 27 years in the reserves), Johnston worked for four insurance companies, sold educational equipment to colleges and school districts, and earned a master's degree in psychology—all before he turned 36.

Johnston had read one of Loren Dunton's books and was inspired to look the author up. But the "firecracker" that set off his interest in financial planning, Johnston recalled in a 2008 interview, was a course he took in personal finance as an undergraduate at the University of Colorado. "I'll never forget my adviser telling me the class would not count toward my major in finance and economics," Johnston said. "It wasn't important enough, I guess. But I disagreed. I was much more interested in an individual's situation than in the economy of some foreign country or how Ford Motors financed itself."

Johnston took a chance on Loren Dunton's "very nebulous" ideas, participated in the December 1969 Chicago meeting, and found himself as the first—and only—employee of the new College for Financial Planning. Later he became its first president and dean.

"At first, I had a room in Loren's office, and I was lucky to pay myself a small salary when students sent in their enrollment fees three times a year," Johnston said. "For extra income, I drilled on weekends with the Navy Reserves, sold health insurance, and delivered telephone books, among other odd jobs."

Why make the sacrifice?

I dreamed of a new financial professional who would provide better service to the consumer, and I thought that there was tremendous potential in the idea. I was interested in how we could offer education through long-distance learning, which I had seen used very effectively in the Navy. I thought that we could revolutionize the industry by teaching people to sit down with clients, talk about their goals, and look at the whole picture—not just recite a rote sales pitch, make a sale, and walk away. I was determined to make the college work, and I thought that I would eventually make some money doing it.

The financial rewards never materialized, however. During Johnston's tenure at the college, the school was always on the edge of financial collapse, and Johnston recalled not being paid for weeks at a time. In 1974, he even took out a $7,500 second mortgage on his house to pay some of the school's debts. (The mortgage was repaid a year later.) "It was such a lonely job at times," he said.

In 1975, the board of regents asked Johnston to step down as president and concentrate full time on course development as dean. "I agreed, but I was terribly hurt," he said. In 1977, he quit.

Johnston never returned to financial planning. He and his wife, Inge, eventually opened a health-food store, founded the National Institute of Nutritional Education, and developed the certified nutritionist credentialing program.

"Would I do it again?" he asked rhetorically in 2008. "Knowing what I do now, the answer is 'Hell, no!' The price I paid was too high. But as one of the pioneers of the financial planning movement, I am glad it has helped so many people and has such an excellent future."

Viewed from a twenty-first-century perspective, that first curriculum seems brief, even superficial. For its time, though, it was a groundbreaking achievement. First, it was created virtually from scratch—there were few relevant financial texts from which Kearns and Johnston could draw. (Kearns relied chiefly on training materials he had developed at Wellington and on a 1971 text by Hy Yurman and Jerrold Glass, *A Financial Planner's Guide*, which is considered the first book about financial planning *per se*, as distinguished from insurance planning.) It was consumer-oriented, stressing the need for a professional financial counselor to focus on the client's situation, needs, and objectives. It outlined a specific advice service that could be compensated by fees rather than commissions. It outlined the core of what came to be known as the financial planning process. And it emphasized using appropriate financial products to build the client's portfolio.

Throughout 1971, Johnston and others on the education committee—Hy Yurman, Jerrold Glass, Larry Wills, and Kemp Fain—continued to write other course materials in sequence, staying just one step ahead of the students. The first examination, consisting of 150 essay questions, was prepared at a Howard Johnson restaurant in Denver. Exam-preparation courses were held around the country, taught by financial planning practitioners and people with relevant graduate degrees; Lew Kearns himself taught one at Villanova University.

"We were always flying by the seat of our pants, struggling to meet great challenges with no money. But people kept enrolling, making it clear to us that the education and profession had great merit."
— James R. Johnston

In 1972, 137 people enrolled in the new CFP program. They were a diverse group that included certified public accountants, bank trust officers, real estate brokers, mutual fund salespeople, stockbrokers, and insurance agents. And they included Diane Blakeslee, the first CFP student to pay for the full course up front. At the time, Blakeslee was a homemaker and mother of small children. She graduated in the second CFP class, in 1974, and later became a member of the college's board of regents. "The CFP designation has opened doors that might otherwise have been closed to me as a female practitioner," Blakeslee observed 25 years later.

Encouraging as the early response was, the college faced serious financial problems. In 1971, it collected $16,145 and showed a deficit of $1,469. On August 18, 1972, recognizing that it couldn't depend on Loren Dunton's original organization, the Society for Financial Counseling, for funding, the college became a separate entity. Its books showed a debt of $30,000—a figure that would haunt the institution for much of the next decade.

CHAPTER 2

Building a Profession

By the end of 1972, just three years after its official birth, the financial planning movement had achieved remarkable results. The International Association of Financial Planners, its membership organization, had 3,000 members in 37 U.S. chapters and representation in 22 other countries. The College for Financial Planning had enrolled 137 students and had become an independent entity.

The successes were bright spots in an otherwise gloomy landscape—the profession's and the country's. Financial planning's impressive growth in membership and enrollment was not matched by a corresponding growth in funds: Throughout the 1970s, the IAFP and the College for Financial Planning struggled to stay afloat. Donald R. Pitti, who in the 1970s was president of the financial publisher Arthur Weisenberger—and who had advised Loren Dunton on the agenda for the December 1969 Chicago meeting—recalled that the early years were

> . . . *exciting and difficult. The existing powerful financial companies wouldn't return our phone calls, much less see us, and money was always scarce. We'd frequently hold board meetings at Arthur Weisenberger—one for each of the entities, IAFP, college, and publishers, consecutively over a box lunch. Then we'd ask Loren how much he needed and pass the hat.*

The larger economic context was dispiriting, too. As an unpopular war in Southeast Asia dragged on, the United States became mired in a deepening recession. The bear market of 1973–1974 drove stock prices down by 40 percent; mutual funds, which had been the darlings of the go-go 1960s, performed especially poorly. Meanwhile, the inflation rate steadily climbed—from 5.6 percent in 1969 (based on changes in the Consumer Price Index) to 12.3 percent in 1974. Making matters worse, in early 1973, the Organization of Petroleum Exporting Countries (OPEC) sharply raised oil prices; in October, responding to U.S. support of Israel in the

15

Yom Kippur War, OPEC imposed an oil embargo. Virtually overnight, gasoline prices quadrupled, and drivers lined up for hours at gas stations for limited supplies.

With these grim developments in the foreground, the pioneers of financial planning made several moves that would determine the course of the profession over the next quarter-century.

Defending a Designation

To a number of these financial planning pioneers, the "planner" part of "Certified Financial Planner" clearly communicated that they were more than salespeople. But there was considerable debate and resistance from outside organizations, and even within the ranks, over the best title for these new professionals.

Among the organizations keeping a watchful eye was the National Association of Securities Dealers (NASD), which had been created in 1939 in response to amendments to the 1934 Securities Exchange Act. (NASD created Nasdaq, the first computerized stock-trading market, in 1971; in 2007 it was folded into the newly created Financial Industry Regulatory Authority—FINRA.) On October 1, 1972, NASD president Gordon S. Macklin issued a notice to its member firms, warning them not to use *financial planning* or *financial planner* to describe the work of broker-dealer representatives. The notice cited a Securities and Exchange Commission (SEC) action in which a broker-dealer represented himself as a "financial planning expert" when he in fact was not; the broker-dealer had been found in violation of antifraud rules. A proposed alternative to *Certified Financial Planner* was *Certified Financial Representative* (CFR). At one point, Ferdinand Nauheim, chairman of the board of trustees of the College for Financial Planning, persuaded the college's trustees to change the CFP mark to CFR. But he wasn't prepared for the explosion of negative feedback from financial planners. Although the mark was new and the profession still small, planners had become attached to the CFP mark and everything it stood for.

Within months, Nauheim was out as chairman of the college's board of trustees, replaced by Lewis G. Kearns, who had been the board of regents' chair for its first two years of existence and was asked to come back for a third term. Soon afterward, Nauheim resigned from the board in protest. Kearns saw an opportunity to reverse the earlier decision.

"It was clear that practitioners favored CFP," Kearns said. "Once the first CFP class was certified, the designation was fixed." Indeed, by the end of 1974, the New York Stock Exchange authorized its members who had received College for Financial Planning certification to place the CFP mark on their business cards.

> *"The emergence of the CFP designation began to chip away at the public perception that all financial representatives were salespeople interested chiefly in the accumulation of sales commissions in a product-oriented industry. . . ."*
>
> —Gale Quint, College for Financial Planning historian

Breaking Away

Almost from the beginning, Loren Dunton's Society for Financial Counseling was a drain on the IAFP, which had to send $7.50 out of every $25 in IAFP dues to Dunton's magazine, *The Financial Planner*. To some people within the movement, it was becoming clear that disassociating from the Society—and from Dunton himself—was becoming necessary.

In April 1973, IAFP chairman Hy Yurman took the first step toward independence: He announced that George W. Ratterman, a former college and professional football quarterback and member of the CFP's first graduating class, would replace Loren Dunton as the IAFP's executive director. Ratterman had other impressive credentials: He'd served from 1961 to 1965 as the anti-vice sheriff of Newport, Kentucky; and he'd been an attorney, a real estate broker, vice president of a trust company, an officer in an investment holding company, and president of a mutual fund. Ratterman's new role with the IAFP sent a clear message that the organization would be welcoming fresh ideas and leadership. The enthusiasm turned out to be short-lived—and not well founded—but it did provide a much-needed buoying effect.

Then, in September 1973, the IAFP formally separated from the financially struggling Society for Financial Counseling and adopted an "open forum" philosophy, in which members from all financial disciplines were welcome, whether or not they had the CFP designation. The sole criterion for membership was a willingness to serve clients by using the financial planning process and putting their clients' interests first. Without a firm financial base, the Society for Financial Counseling dissolved in September 1975.

One additional significant break occurred in 1973, although it didn't appear at the time to represent a schism. On October 13, 1973, the College for Financial Planning confirmed its first class of 42 Certified Financial Planner designees on the campus of the University of Denver.[1] Out of that group, 36 gathered in a small basement conference room just hours after the confirmation ceremony to determine how they could promote the new profession they had just launched. The minutes of that first meeting—two typewritten pages—noted that the graduates wished to organize themselves "to obtain additional benefits from having the CFP designation." With Hy Yurman

> *"We knew we were blazing a trail that evening, but I don't think any of us were fully aware of the implications."*
>
> —Colin B. Coombs

acting as chair, the graduates elected a president—W. Robert Hightower of Raleigh, North Carolina—along with two vice presidents, a secretary-treasurer, and three directors. Annual dues were set at $10; most attendees paid on the spot. In addition, each member pledged $25 in support of the college. After much discussion, the graduates chose "Institute of Certified Financial Planners" as the name of the new alumni organization.

"We knew we were blazing a trail that evening, but I don't think any of us were fully aware of the implications," said Colin B. (Ben) Coombs, CFP, of Longview, Washington. Coombs was among the first class of graduates who founded the ICFP:

I came to the college's first conferment ceremony and the meeting that followed to find out what I was—what did it mean to be a "CFP designee." The founding of the institute wasn't so much of a plan as a welling up among the graduates to band together.

Graydon Calder, CFP, a San Diego planner, was elected western vice president that first evening and later served as the ICFP's president. He observed that one reason for the ICFP's momentum "was that the first graduates of the college came from all over the country. We went back home excited to promote the CFP designation in our area, and small pockets of us got active on the local level."

According to the minutes of that initial meeting, taken by Jordan Kokjer, the College for Financial Planning's dean, James Johnston, "expressed appreciation for the twenty-five-dollar-per-member pledge and in addition, pointed out that if each of the new confirmands were to produce ten new candidates, the college's financial problems would be solved." It would take several years for Johnston's brave optimism to be matched by reality.

For the next 25 years, the ICFP and the IAFP developed along parallel tracks, sometimes cooperating, often conflicting, as they struggled toward a shared goal: to move financial planning from a vague concept to a recognized profession.

Coming Together, Growing Apart

During those early days, many financial planners belonged to both the IAFP and the ICFP. Graydon Calder, for example, served simultaneously on the national boards of the ICFP and IAFP in the 1970s—and in that he was not unusual. Calder, like many of his colleagues, saw the IAFP as his trade association for financial planning and the ICFP as his professional association for CFP designees. When he volunteered to write and design the ICFP's first brochure, he persuaded the San Diego chapter of the IAFP to front the $500 needed to print 50,000 copies. The brochures were sold to ICFP members, and the profits—about $500—were split between the two organizations.

Not everyone was clear on the differences between the IAFP and ICFP. Some planners thought of the ICFP as an alumni association of the College for Financial Planning, over the strong objections of ICFP leaders. The confusion was understandable: The ICFP's early annual meetings were held in conjunction with the college's conferment ceremonies or during the IAFP's annual conferences. The ICFP simply did not have enough members—or dollars—to hold separate meetings.

For its part, the IAFP was experiencing its own growing pains. In May 1974, with the financial planning movement not quite five-and-a-half years old, the IAFP board met with the board of Loren Dunton's Society for Financial Counseling in King of Prussia, Pennsylvania, to discuss the challenges of the future. Both organizations were saddled with debt, mostly because of Dunton's complicated vision. By the end of the meeting, after much debate, a new course was charted. The society would be folded into the IAFP, and the IAFP would buy out Society Publishers, which put out *The Financial Planner*; it would clear Society Publishers' debts and pay a portion of Dunton's back-salary claims. George Ratterman, the executive director of the IAFP, would take on the added roles of editor and publisher of *The Financial Planner*, in the hope that he could find financial support—or even a buyer—for the magazine.

Most significant of all, Loren Dunton would no longer be involved in the leadership of the organizations he had created. The combined boards thanked him for his efforts, but the message was clear: They would be moving on without him.

Was Dunton forced out? That's what some IAFP members suspected. In California, Dunton loyalists threatened secession from the organization. But there had been no coup. As Rich White tells it in a 10-year-anniversary article published in the September 1979 *Financial Planner*, "In fact, Dunton had not been forced out. He had done himself in. The complex, intermingled

---

> *"If the movement was to grow, the promoter had to go."*
> —Rich White

finances and debts of his multitiered concept had become too unbearable. If the movement was to grow, the promoter had to go."

Six months later, a reorganized and reenergized IAFP held its first convention. The event, to be titled "Expanding Horizons," was held November 7 through 9, 1974, at the San Francisco Hilton. More than 500 IAFP members heard broadcast star Jack Linkletter (son of Art) deliver the opening address. IAFP members J. Chandler Peterson, Gus Hansch, George Hugg, Venita Van Caspel, and Donald Kanaly were featured speakers.

The convention turned out to be a unifying, uplifting experience for leaders and members alike. Out of crisis had come an opportunity to reaffirm their original motives in creating the movement—a short, intensive period of inspiration, education, and networking. Over the next turbulent year, the example of the first convention provided encouragement for a determined group of IAFP leaders.

Financial Crisis and Upheaval at the IAFP

Despite the high hopes pinned to him, George Ratterman proved unable to prevail over the huge financial challenges he faced as IAFP executive director. By the first quarter of 1975, the organization had members in 61 U.S. chapters, but its income averaged only $6,000 a month—against fixed expenses, including salaries and overhead for the Denver office, of about $10,000 a month. Worse, the IAFP still owed money to Loren Dunton's moribund Society for Financial Counseling, and had taken out $20,000 in loans from Denver banks.

To keep the IAFP afloat, Ratterman decided to sell *The Financial Planner* to Olympic Savings and Loan Association of Chicago. But the move failed to turn the tide. In fact, the terms of the sale meant the IAFP would owe Olympic $15 per member, per year, for magazine subscriptions.

Led by J. Chandler Peterson, the IAFP's executive committee decided a major change was required. Between March and April 1975, they dismissed George Ratterman and the rest of the IAFP executive staff. Ratterman never held an IAFP office again.

Next, Peterson moved all official operations and records from Denver to Atlanta, where he worked; at first, the IAFP office was a corner of Peterson's own office. The IAFP's executive committee appointed Fred S. Harris, an associate of Peterson's, as temporary executive director, a position made permanent in July.

On July 10, 1975, the IAFP executive committee called for a board meeting at a Marriott Hotel in Chicago. The large turnout—13 board members, the most to participate in a board meeting until then—attested to the meeting's importance. Peterson chaired; besides him, four additional future IAFP presidents were in the room: Richard Venezia, C. Robert Strader, C. William Hoilman, and Robert W. Spencer.

Peterson had given the meeting a theme: "Positive Mental Concepts." The first item on his agenda was a balanced budget. To achieve that goal, the board voted to keep using Peterson's office until the income picture improved. But in other matters Peterson urged the board to think big. Looking ahead to October, he recommended putting the full resources of the IAFP into planning the 1975 Expanding Horizons convention, scheduled for October 29 at Atlanta's Fairmont Hotel. For the movement to continue growing and for the IAFP to prosper, Peterson said, a professionally planned annual convention—with educational programs, exhibitor booths, and plenty of networking—was essential.

The IAFP had already retained the services of a convention consultant, Jay Lurye of Chicago. Peterson and his Georgia friends had contacted members of the Georgia IAFP chapter who pledged to work night and day toward the convention's success. Now Peterson outlined four important objectives for the convention:

1. Strengthening the connection of current members to the organization and the financial planning movement
2. Inspiring new members to catch the movement's vision
3. Serving as a recruiting tool
4. Generating income

Peterson's enthusiasm was infectious. Each IAFP board member agreed to sell at least one convention booth and register 25 attendees.

The effort paid off. More than 1,000 people attended the 1975 Expanding Horizons convention—double the previous year's attendance. Income from registrations and exhibitor sales produced a profit. The convention was the IAFP's first commercial success in its six years of existence.

Buoyed by this triumph, IAFP executive director Fred Harris began building a headquarters staff. His first hires were Judy L. Harris, who later would become the organization's director of meetings and conventions, and Lillian Correa, director of training. The IAFP had struggled to its feet and was now preparing to stride into a promising future.

"Those were exciting and pioneering times. Board members not only sacrificed their time, they also contributed by paying their travel and lodging expenses. I was impressed with their high ideals and their vision to help Americans become financially independent."

—Ronald A. Melanson, IAFP president and
chairman of the board, 1980 and 1981

Market Milestones: ERISA and IRAs

The collapse in 1964 of automotive company Studebaker Corp. left many longtime employees without pension coverage—even though the company had met its funding obligations every year, and no malfeasance was involved. The crisis was a wakeup call to all companies offering defined-benefit pensions—at the time, the most common form of pension offered to employees—but it took a decade for the federal government's response to be formulated. On Labor Day, 1974, President Gerald Ford signed the Employee Retirement Income Security Act (ERISA), which tightened restrictions on defined-benefit plans and required disclosure of plan details to employees. The act also introduced the individual retirement account (IRA), which allowed individuals who didn't participate in employer retirement plans to set aside tax-deferred money each year until they reached retirement age. In 1981, IRAs were extended to everyone. The new options meant new questions for taxpayers—and new business for financial planners.

Financial Crisis at the College

While the IAFP was achieving its first financial success and the ICFP was beginning to shape an independent identity, the College for Financial Planning was facing challenges of its own. Loren Dunton had resigned as formal head of the school shortly after it was incorporated; he gradually moved away from the educational effort and eventually concentrated on his own consulting practice and writing career. That left Jim Johnston to manage the executive, sales, and administrative affairs of the college singlehandedly. In later years he said of the early and mid-1970s:

> *We were always flying by the seat of our pants, struggling to meet great challenges with no money—the largest problem. There was a lot of skepticism on the part of outsiders who said it couldn't be done. But people kept enrolling, and others who lost faith or didn't have the time dropped out, only to return a few years later. It validated us, making it clear that the education and profession had great merit.*

Johnston recognized early that corporate support would be necessary if the college were to succeed. To that end, he negotiated scholarship arrangements with several large securities firms, including A.G. Edwards & Co., which sent 66 students; IDS Corporation, with 51 students; Financial

Service Corporation, with 46 students; Waddell & Reed, with 44 students; and Janney Montgomery Scott, with 30 students. Yet despite these efforts, the college met its November 1974 payroll only after taking up a collection at its board of regents meeting in San Francisco.

By Christmas Eve 1974, Johnston later admitted, he was despondent:

> *Loren Dunton, who had been my main inspiration, was gone from the movement.* The Financial Planner *magazine had been sold to a Chicago savings and loan. The Society [for Financial Counseling] was about to fold. The college had no money in the bank and no prospects until April, when the next batch of tuition checks would arrive. Unless the college could somehow find a few thousand dollars to meet expenses and payroll, it appeared to be a goner, too. I was sitting at my desk thinking, "What a terrible way for this to end."*

In desperation, Johnston called Bob Strader at Waddell & Reed in Shawnee Mission, Kansas, and told him, "It's all over. We need $12,000 and we don't have it."

"You can't let it go now," Strader said. "We'll get a check off to you for $1,500. Why don't you call Jay Hines at IDS and see whether he can help with the rest?"

"But it's five o'clock on Christmas Eve," Johnston replied. "Hines won't be there."

"What else can you do?" asked Strader.

Johnston made the call. As luck would have it, Hines was still in his office; he picked up the phone himself and immediately offered to prepay several thousand dollars' worth of scholarships for IDS students.

The crisis was over. "After that," Johnston later recalled, "I knew it all had to work out." Nevertheless, it would take a full decade before most financial services practitioners were willing to concede that the college was a viable institution and that education, certification, continuing education, and advanced studies were necessary elements in their profession.

Market Milestones: Recession and Inflation

The early CFP designees hung out their shingles during challenging times. Economic statistics from the 1970s tell the story:

- The United States was buffeted by two recessions, in 1970 and again in 1974–1975.

(*continued*)

> ## Market Milestones: Recession and Inflation (*Continued*)
>
> - After hitting 1,000 for the first time in 1972, the Dow Jones Industrial Average rarely ventured above 1,000 during the rest of the decade.
> - Marginal rate taxation was up to 70 percent. Interest in tax shelters intensified.
> - Gold's fixed price of $35 an ounce was abandoned in 1971; the price rose to $180 an ounce by 1974.
> - Government wage and price controls went into effect between 1971 and 1974.
> - Inflation rose to 7.4 percent in 1974–1975 and above 10 percent by the end of the decade.
> - The prime interest rate hovered around 15 percent in late 1979.
> - The minimum wage was $2 an hour. The average yearly wage was $10,020.

A Creed and a Curriculum

Besides finances, the most vexing problem for college officials was the "correspondence school" label outsiders often attached to their institution. It was true that courses were not presented in a traditional campus setting; instead, students across the nation participated either through self-study or in study groups under the supervision of well-qualified planners. But in every other sense the college was a true institution of higher learning.

To underscore that fact to both internal and external critics, in 1975 the college developed its first creed. Its wording was largely the work of Larry Wills, who had been in the college's first graduating class, in 1973, and who in 1975 served as chairman of the board of regents. The creed identified five objectives:

1. To pronounce, define, maintain, and promote ethical standards of professional conduct
2. To provide learning materials and instruction in the field of financial counseling
3. To test the knowledge, ability, self-discipline, and motivation of individual counselors
4. To enrich the careers of financial counselors through continuing education and information
5. To confer appropriate professional designations upon proof of satisfactory completion of prescribed examinations

Jim Johnston later said that "developing a tangible creed that we could refer to during tough times" was one of the early college's most important achievements. Among the others: obtaining nonprofit status, staying clear of government funding, and "creating a quality program that planners could use on a day-to-day basis."

At last, Johnston was getting much-needed support on program and curriculum development. A committee consisting of Larry Wills; Dave Allard; John Gray, CFP; William McMurry, CFP, CLU; and Dick Venezia, CFP, was assigned the task of beefing up the CFP courses by incorporating study guides into each of the five parts of the curriculum. Courses on "investments" and "professionally managed investments" were combined. Courses on tax planning, tax shelters, pensions, and profit sharing followed. Texts and supplementary readings were critically analyzed, and teaching methods were repeatedly evaluated.

When Wills's successor as chairman of the board of regents, Bill McMurry, reported in 1977 on the effectiveness of self-study, he said the performance of self-study students was comparable in most respects to that of students who learned in study groups. However, they trailed somewhat when tests moved from the theoretical to practical applications. In response, new CFP study guides included more case studies.

Not satisfied with curriculum alone, the college sought educational credibility as well. Courses offered a comprehensive, objective view of financial planning that has remained intact. For example, the program dared to propose that a person really could have "enough" life insurance, or that retirement and estate planning might need to weigh heavily in the creation of the optimum mix of investments and savings for a particular client.

One of the most important tests of the college's standard of professionalism came in 1975, when the regents denied certification to a CFP graduate because of legal and ethical problems. Although the planner had completed the course requirements for the designation, he had earlier pleaded no contest to a misdemeanor charge in connection with a 1970–1971 securities scandal. Only after he completed restitution requirements imposed by a California court and served his probation did the regents reconsider his application. "The CFP designation is a permissive thing, within the board's discretionary powers," said Lewis Kearns, who had been chairman of the board of regents at the time of the scandal. It is not, he said, "a matter of right that arbitrarily accrues to any candidate successfully completing the college courses."

Change and Growth at the College

After four years of intense work on all aspects of the College for Financial Planning, Jim Johnston stepped down as president in 1975 and became dean of the college, concentrating on curriculum management. Johnston's move was not entirely voluntary: A board of regents member, Jim Wasem, and the college's business manager, Anthony R. (Tony) Sorge, planned and executed a power play that elevated Sorge to president. Their reasoning: Sorge would be more effective at fundraising, and Johnston would be free to focus on his strength—academic affairs.

But the change satisfied no one. Johnston continued to write curricula, but by the time Congress rewrote the tax laws in the mid-1970s—necessitating further updates and corrections to CFP courses—he was approaching burnout. He left the college altogether in 1977.

For his part, Sorge brought a credible budgeting process and strong internal checks and balances to the school. But he had an autocratic leadership style that led to conflicts with personnel. He also provoked criticism by buying a tract of land for the college without first obtaining board approval. In late 1978, five members of the board of regents challenged Wasem and Sorge and proposed a more open, participatory style of management. Given the choice between working under the new system and resigning, Sorge chose to leave the college in May 1979. He was replaced by Graham Holloway, who served on a pro bono basis for a year while working full time at American Funds.

With 1979 came another significant change: the college's move to its first true headquarters. It had started its existence in a small suite in a southeast Denver office building and had moved to "the little house on the prairie," a two-story house in a Denver suburb. In mid-summer 1979, the regents moved the organization to an office building on Hampden Avenue in southeast Denver. The move involved not only staff but also technology. The college had successfully computerized several years earlier, and by 1978 it had three computer systems, including one to schedule and grade the CFP examinations. Accounting systems had also been brought online.

The Anthes Years

With new offices, 800 CFP graduates, and reserves of about $1 million, the college was ready for a new leader—an educator—to guide it through the next decade and beyond. While the board of regents undertook a nationwide search to find strong candidates for the new college president, board members served as interim college heads.

The process was challenging, as Graham Holloway later recalled, but in the end the College for Financial Planning had a solid leader: William Anthes, PhD, a young college educator from Kansas City. Holloway reflected,

We were looking for an individual who was both an educator as well as an administrator—and who could lead a nontraditional college. Although we received information on many promising candidates, William Anthes fit the bill perfectly. The college was going through growing pains, and it needed strong leadership. It was an opportunity for the college, for the program, and for Anthes.

Anthes's arrival marked the beginning of the college's years of stability, success, and influence in the financial services world. But in the beginning, he had his work cut out for him. In October 1979, he attended the IAFP annual convention in Chicago, not far from where the financial planning movement had been born. With him was Dale Johnson, then dean of the college. "I don't think I'll ever forget it," Anthes later said. "Dale took a thick yellow legal pad with him to write down the complaints of people he met. We heard some good things, and there was certainly a lot of interest in the college. But I remember Dale coming back with two or three pages, and maybe 35 to 40 complaints, from people not too happy about their experiences with the college. I wondered if this was an indication of what I would be encountering when I got back to Denver and officially began my duties as president."

Anthes acted swiftly and aggressively, contacting other educational institutions that wanted to provide financial education to professionals. Jim Johnston had attempted similar outreach as early as 1973, but had not succeeded. In January 1981, Anthes signed Golden Gate University in San Francisco as the college's first affiliate, offering CFP classes for academic credit outside the college's direct administration. By mid-1981, the college had a national affiliation network that included William Rainey Harper College in Palatine, Illinois, and Roosevelt University in Chicago. In addition, Anthes refined a nationwide network of independent adjunct faculty members—75 of them by 1981—who were authorized to provide CFP training on a class-by-class basis.

Anthes also strengthened internal academic resources. In 1980, he assembled a team that included a new director of academic programs and four distinguished academic associates. Together they held a brainstorming retreat in the Colorado Rockies to plan the first major revision of the CFP program. Ultimately, this process positioned the college as the leader in curricula for the professional financial planning industry.

Against a backdrop of recession, double-digit inflation, and heightened interest in financial news, the college achieved unprecedented gains. During Anthes's first year, enrollments in the CFP program nearly doubled, to 2,270, over the previous year. The numbers were 10 percent above projections. Two-thirds of the new enrollees completed the program. Throughout the first half of the decade, the college continued to log record numbers.

Profile: William L. Anthes

Bill Anthes was just 35 in 1979, when he was asked to assume the leadership of the College for Financial Planning. He'd had a solid education—an MBA from the University of Missouri, a Ph.D. in economics from the University of Arkansas—but only modest leadership experience: He had taught economics at the University of Nebraska in Omaha, and since 1976 had been serving as director of the evening division of Rockhurst College, where he'd received his undergraduate degree. Anthes had first heard of the College for Financial Planning when someone from the college asked whether he could move a class to Rockwell from its previous "campus," a local U-Smile Motel. Graham Holloway, chairman of the College for Financial Planning's board of regents, had a long list of promising candidates for the presidency, but Anthes topped the list. For his part, Anthes recognized the opportunity to help build a new and promising institution. "I'd been impressed by the college and its CFP certification education program," he recalled more than 20 years later. "It was fascinating to observe how dedicated the students were, how much they wanted to get the education. Their enthusiasm persisted despite administrative difficulties, poor service, late materials, outdated study guides, and tardy exams." His interest in the presidency, Anthes said, grew from "thinking of the students and their dedication to the college and financial planning, and the chance to bring increased organization and quality to the college's operations."

Anthes rose to the challenge. During his 18-year tenure as president, he improved the quality of the college's courses, created a master of science program in financial planning, and got the college accredited. In 1985, he led the creation of the International Board of Standards and Practices for Certified Financial Planners (IBCFP—now the Certified Financial Planner Board of Standards), which transferred ownership of the CFP marks from the college to the board.

Anthes was head of the National Endowment for Financial Education, its mission to focus on consumer financial literacy, when the holding company was started in 1992. He then ran NEFE as a private foundation from 1997 to 2005. After stepping down, he served on the board of directors of the Financial Planning Standards Board, the nonprofit association that owns and manages the CFP certification program outside the United States.

In 2002, Bill Anthes received the Financial Planning Association's P. Kemp Fain, Jr., Award, which recognizes individuals who have made outstanding contributions to the financial planning profession in the areas of service to society, academia, government, and professional activities. He is also the recipient of the 2003 William Odom Visionary Leadership Award, from the JumpStart Coalition for Personal Financial Literacy, and the 2005 EBRI Lillywhite Award, given by the Employee Benefit Research Institute.

The ICFP Forges a Separate Identity

While the college was making its impressive gains, the ICFP and IAFP were still struggling—against external forces and with each other. From their inceptions, the two organizations shared a commitment to the financial planning process and a desire to promote the importance of financial planning to the public. But while these common goals united them, by the late 1970s other forces began to pull them in different directions.

At first it appeared that the relationship would be collaborative. The minutes of an April 28, 1977, ICFP meeting noted that the institute was working in conjunction with the IAFP to draft legislation for regulating financial planners modeled after legislation licensing architects, attorneys, CPAs, and other professionals. "The biggest problem area," noted the minutes, "is defining 'financial planning' and the duties of a financial planner."

But the cracks were starting to form in the organizations' mutual foundation. One area of controversy was the donations regularly made by the institute to the college. For example, some rank-and-file members protested when, in July 1977, a $5,000 donation was given to the college for its building fund. There were also frequent $1,000 gifts. In its defense, the institute said the donations were a courtesy payment in exchange for free housing at the college and administrative and secretarial support. But after Tony Sorge resigned as president of the college in 1979, the ICFP was asked to set up an office of its own. Robert Loeffler, CFP, of Denver, offered to store the institute's records in the basement of his house; he brought them to every meeting.

Cut off from the college, with scarce resources, no headquarters or paid staff, and only about 500 members, the institute postponed hiring an executive director and grappled with defining its identity. A 1978 survey revealed that CFP members ranked three objectives as most important: promoting the CFP designation and the CFP practitioner, establishing and enforcing a strong code of ethics, and promoting continuing education. The goals were worthy, but the means to achieve them were limited.

At that point, two men stepped forward to provide leadership in the ICFP. Under the presidency of David M. King, CFP (1977–1979), work began on a strong, enforceable code of ethics. (King would later help form the IBCFP.) And the institute's board of directors began functioning more effectively, thanks largely to the energy and determination of Henry I. Montgomery, CFP. "Henry wouldn't take 'no' for an answer," financial planning pioneer P. Kemp Fain later recalled. "He demanded a real commitment."

Profile: Henry Montgomery

By the time Henry Montgomery developed an interest in financial planning, he was 48 years old and already had a noteworthy résumé. A decorated World War II veteran, he had been a field agent for the OSS and CIA in Europe, the owner of a soft-drink bottling company, and a franchise sales representative.

Then, in 1971, he heard Loren Dunton speak. "I knew nothing about money except how to borrow it and use it to pay bills," Montgomery later said. "But plenty of self-interested people wanted to help me with any money that I had left over. That brought me to the financial planning movement." In 1972, Montgomery formed Planners Financial Services in Minneapolis; he earned his CFP designation in 1976 and quickly rose to prominence in both the IAFP and ICFP, serving on the national boards of both and as 1980–1981 ICFP president.

Headstrong and opinionated, Montgomery insisted that ICFP board members pay their own way to meetings and commit to work on committees. "Some called me tough, mean, and even evil-spirited, but I always felt that you had to have some skin in the game," he said. (Fellow board member P. Kemp Fain, Jr., poked some well-meaning fun at Montgomery's presidency in verse. "The Reign of King Henry the 9th ... who steppeth upon toes of peasants and nobles alike," the poem went.)

In the early years of his practice, Montgomery freely admitted that he personally invested in too many tax shelters—"Was it survival or greed?" he later asked—and sold a lot of them to clients as well. His experiences eventually made him wary of product vendors and insist that the ICFP stay free of their influence, even if it meant the organization being "poor as church mice," as he described it.

In 1981, the ICFP was in particularly dire straits financially—$19,084 in the red, despite an increase in dues to $100 a year. One night, Montgomery had dinner with Bill Anthes, president of the College for Financial Planning. Anthes suggested including a one-year provisional membership in the ICFP as part of the college's tuition. "I almost kissed him," Montgomery recalled. "As I remember it, we negotiated $40 per student, which gave the institute much-needed cash to survive until we were strong enough to cut the umbilical cord."

In the summer of 2008, Montgomery, then 83, spoke at the annual Retreat of the Financial Planning Association, which was created out of the merger of the ICFP and IAFP in 2000. He reported that he continued to work with clients and still felt the same passion for financial planning. And, true to form, he shared a few opinions:

> *Financial planning has been called by some the greatest product delivery system in the world. That still makes the hair stand up on the back of my neck.... If I can't get clients out of a product tomorrow, I don't want to get them in. I worship liquidity and so should you.... Get off of your "you-know-what" and get active in your professional association because you are fighting for your professional life....*

Three months after giving that speech, Henry Montgomery died. In a tribute, FPA's executive director Marv Tuttle said Montgomery

> *...was a leader in the right place at the right time.... When the profession was hanging on by a thread in its quest for recognition and legitimacy, he stood for an unyielding commitment to the values and standards now embraced today by thousands of planning professionals throughout the world. His philosophy can be summarized in a few words: "Take care of your clients' interest first and before your own."*

It was during this period of identity-building, in 1979, that the IAFP first approached the ICFP about bringing it under the IAFP's significantly larger tent. ICFP president David M. King and other ICFP leaders considered the offer but turned it down, saying that the ICFP wanted to maintain a close relationship with the IAFP while remaining independent. The primary reason was the ICFP's focus on the CFP mark. This *CFP-centricity*, as it was later termed, was at the heart of the ICFP and, at the time, seemingly in conflict with the IAFP's commitment to an open-forum philosophy.

Henry Montgomery served on the boards of both organizations and as president of the institute 1980–1981. In his view, the institute was helping financial planning become a legitimate profession. He later recalled,

> *I'll never forget a meeting I attended when several IAFP leaders asked me which organization I would choose if I couldn't afford to belong to both. I laughed and told them that if I was ever so hard up that I couldn't afford to belong to both my trade organization and my professional association that I should get out of the business. If I was that broke, I told them, I would be a menace to my clients.*

Robert A. Hewitt, Jr., CFP, ChFC, CLU, was an IAFP board member and officer from Monterey, California. He watched in dismay as the competition between the organizations grew. "Early on, I felt that the missions of the two organizations were synonymous: to promote financial planners and the use of the financial planning process to the American public," said Hewitt.

Then the ICFP began to say that the CFP designation was the only one that held any credence, while the IAFP was not credential conscious. The two organizations began to get very competitive at that point to become the premier financial planning organization. It got crazy.

Another IAFP leader from that time, Larry W. Carroll, CFP, of Charlotte, North Carolina, summed up the primary point of conflict:

It boiled down to two issues. The ICFP had difficulty with the IAFP's open form concept because of allegiance to the CFP mark, and the IAFP had difficulty with the concept that the only way to be a financial planner was to be a CFP designee.

Charles G. Hughes, Jr., CFP, of Bay Shore, New York, served as president of the ICFP in 1987. He pointed to a different problem. "My first experience with the IAFP was in the 1970s when I attended their annual conferences as a mutual fund company representative," Hughes said.

The IAFP was very skillful in putting on these conferences, and they underwrote many of the organization's other activities. The problem was that a lot of these products were not good ones, and they went bust in the 1980s. In addition, a great deal of reward was given to product sales. Some of us felt that this could impinge on the objectivity of the practitioner. That's why the ICFP made the decision to avoid product sponsorship.

When the ICFP held its first Retreat in 1981, there was no commercial sponsorship or "product presence," as Hughes put it. "Being 'pure' got to be almost a religion with us," he added.

Newmark at the Wheel

By then, the ICFP had taken an important step to distance itself from the IAFP. In 1979, under the leadership of new executive director Bernice Newmark, the ICFP moved to West Palm Beach, Florida, where Newmark had her financial planning practice. Newmark, a founding member of the ICFP, had put together the first membership directory; she had big goals for the ICFP and the energy to realize them. She later recalled how she was hired for the top position:

> *I saw Henry [Montgomery] in the hallway after one of our meetings and I asked him what the institute was doing for my $35 [dues]. Henry answered me with his own question, 'What should we be doing?' So I went home and wrote him a 28-page letter with my proposal for moving the institute forward.*

Montgomery was impressed. He recommended hiring Newmark as executive director, noting that "she has the drive and the background to take on the job of making the institute well known to the public."

Although Newmark's position was described as part time—and her salary was just $250 a month—she dove into the job. She wrote the institute's first newsletter for members, *Newsworthy*, fielded inquiries from consumers looking for financial planners, and encouraged members to take on speaking engagements that would raise the profile of the ICFP. She revised its brochure and bylaws, hired an art school to develop a logo and stationery, and promoted the sale of the CFP-designee directory. In 1979, she published the first issue of the *Journal of the Institute of Certified Financial Planners*, known today as the *Journal of Financial Planning*. The table of contents in that first issue reveals the important topics of the day: "Seven Keys to Keogh," "Tax Shelters: The Real Rates of Return," and "ESOP's New Look Under the Final Regulation." Annual subscriptions cost $24 for ICFP members, $30 for nonmembers.

Newmark also took the show on the road. She bought an 18-foot motor home and traveled from Florida to California, meeting ICFP members at every stop along the way and working tirelessly to recruit new institute members. She gave public speeches to spread the word about financial planning. In an interview for the ICFP's twenty-fifth-anniversary publication, *A Look Back, A Look Ahead*, published in December 1998, she said,

> *I remember going to a department store in Omaha to give a luncheon seminar for women about money and planning for the future. I called the seminar "How to Survive Single Bliss." The idea was to get people to start seeking out the services of a CFP planner.*

Newmark's efforts paid off: The ICFP was receiving 300 to 400 calls a month from people seeking financial planning advice, according to the minutes of a November 1979 meeting.

Return to Denver

The following year, ICFP leaders decided to move their headquarters back to Denver to be closer to the college. The move marked the end of Newmark's tenure—a difficult break on both sides. Later in the year, the institute presented her with an Award of Special Merit for "her considerable contributions to the ICFP."

In Denver, the ICFP assumed a new role: monitoring and awarding post-certification continuing education (CE) credit on behalf of the College for Financial Planning. Previously, although the college had supported a modest CE effort, it had no system for tracking CE activity. The ICFP's policy was much more specific: 30 hours of CE annually, enforced on the honor system. Failure to comply could cause a member's status to drop from "regular" to "associate," and the ICFP reserved the right to randomly check documentation. Lack of documentation could be considered a violation of the ICFP's code of ethics.

Affiliation with the college brought financial gain to the ICFP, too, and not a moment too soon. In 1981, it hired its first full-time executive director, Dianna Rampy; by midyear the treasurer forecast a $46,000 deficit. Then, in October, the ICFP signed an agreement with the college to award automatic provisional membership for first-year college enrollees in exchange for a portion of each enrollee's registration fee. The college benefited as well: It had been suffering from attrition, and ICFP membership encouraged students to stay in the program and become credentialed.

Almost overnight, the ICFP blossomed into a full-service professional association. Within two years, membership swelled from 2,100 to 16,000, and the staff grew to 10. Most of those members were provisional; the number of "regular" ICFP members never rose above 3,000.

In 1981, the ICFP held its first Retreat at St. John's University in Collegeville, Minnesota. The college provided a quiet setting—not coincidentally, near the home of Retreat organizer Henry Montgomery—where practitioners could receive top-quality instruction on subjects such as "management by computer" and "what the CFP [practitioner] should know about taxes."

The Retreat proved so successful that in 1982, for the first time, the ICFP chose to hold its annual meeting during the Retreat instead of during the IAFP's national conference.

An additional reason for the move may have been the ICFP leaders' concerns over the IAFP's new registry. Some ICFP leaders had wanted the ICFP to distinguish CFP designees in public practice from those who had the designation but were not practicing. When the ICFP decided not to pursue the idea, the IAFP formed a committee to study the registry concept, and even suggested a new designation, *Registered Financial Planner*.

The ICFP responded quickly and heatedly. William B. Shearer, Jr., JD, who was president of the IAFP in 1981–1982, agreed to a compromise. There would be no new designation, but the IAFP would establish the Registry of Financial Planning Practitioners. A practitioner's designation would not be a criterion for inclusion or exclusion. However, practitioners were required to submit a financial plan for peer review, pass a Practice Knowledge Examination, and subscribe to certain other standards of practice, continuing education, and ethics.

The IAFP had seen the registry as a way to focus on the quality of planners and the planning process, rather than on a designation. The ICFP saw it differently. "We felt that the registry was nothing more than another designation, even if it was not presented in those terms," Hughes said.

The registry was never large—about 1,100 members at its height—but it remained a source of friction for the next 10 years. "The trust between the two organizations almost evaporated in the mid-1980s," recalled Dallas financial planner Bill E. Carter, CFP, ChFC, CLU. Carter served on the national boards of both organizations in the early 1980s and was president of the IAFP in 1983. The IAFP continued to pursue a merger, and approached the ICFP several times in late 1983 and early 1984. The ICFP did not respond. It would be a full 15 years before the two organizations would come together to form a unified Financial Planning Association.

CHAPTER 3

Growing Pains

A s financial planning entered its second decade, the image of the financial planning profession began to come into focus. Unfortunately, the picture that emerged wasn't a wholly flattering one.

The era of stagflation was finally drawing to a close, to be replaced by the long bull market that began in 1982. One of the principal causes of the upturn was the anti-inflationary policies of Paul Volcker, who had been appointed chairman of the Federal Reserve Bank by President Jimmy Carter in 1979, and who held the job through 1987.

A second contributing factor was deregulation, a hallmark of the economic philosophy of President Ronald Reagan, who took the oath of office in January 1981. For better or for worse, many industries were affected—financial services among them. With the loosening of restraints came a spate of new "opportunities," particularly limited-partnership tax shelters that took advantage of loopholes in existing laws. Some self-described financial planners who jumped on the tax-shelter bandwagon could be more accurately described as salespeople rather than planners. The profession as a whole was tarred by association: Planners as a group were attacked in the media as hucksters and scam artists who made hefty fees peddling questionable products. The financial media took disapproving note: During the mid-1980s the influential columnist Jane Bryant Quinn wrote a negative article about planners for *Newsweek*, and *Forbes* portrayed a financial planner as a monkey in a three-piece suit. "These days," *Forbes* told its readers, "everyone is a financial planner."

Changing the Message, Changing Attitudes

Hoping to promote a more positive message about the profession, the IAFP and the ICFP embarked independently on their first concerted public relations efforts. In 1981, the IAFP created the Foundation for Financial Planning, a 501(c)(3) charitable organization whose goals included providing the public with the tools for making intelligent financial decisions. The foundation's first project was developing a series of television programs to educate the public about financial planning.

For its part, the ICFP sent its 1983 president, P. Kemp Fain, Jr., CFP, on a media tour with its executive director, Dianna Rampy. They talked with newspaper, radio, and television journalists in New York, Boston, Houston, and Washington, D.C. The following year, the institute hired a public relations firm. It also produced public service brochures on financial planning and began a cooperative national advertising campaign with members.

"We spent a lot of time responding to media questions about why the CFP professional was head and shoulders above the crowd," recalled Marv Tuttle, who joined the ICFP in 1983 as its director of communications and became the Financial Planning Association's executive director and CEO in January 2004. "Public awareness was always a top priority: How could we get positive visibility for what financial planning is and what financial planners do?"

The most successful public relations effort of the mid-1980s, undertaken jointly by the IAFP, ICFP, and the College for Financial Planning, was the first nationwide Financial Independence Week in September 1986, aimed at teaching consumers that, through sound and thoughtful planning, they could achieve financial security. The program lasted several years; it was revived as Financial Planning Week in 2001 after the IAFP and ICFP merged in 2000 to form the Financial Planning Association.

These PR efforts slowly bore fruit. In October 1987, *Money* magazine, which covered personal finance, introduced a list of the 200 "best financial planners" with this subhead: "They're Masters of Budgeting, Investment, Taxes, and Retirement." It was one of the first times a major national publication had put financial planning in the spotlight. That was the good news. But the article began with a caveat:

> *In 1972, a few lonely souls called themselves financial planners; now more than 100,000 people do. But perhaps only one in three rightfully deserves the title, and unfortunately it is hard to know which ones they are. Alas, financial planning is an almost instant profession, with no government agency or professional association empowered to bar the door to the unqualified.*

The IAFP and ICFP worked together and independently to influence governmental relations. As early as 1977, they had collaboratively drafted legislation for regulating financial planners, following the model of licensing laws in other professions. "The biggest problem area," noted the minutes of an ICFP meeting in the late 1970s, "is defining 'financial planning' and the duties of a financial planner." In 1984, the IAFP established a Political

Action Committee (PAC) dedicated to preservation of free enterprise and promotion of capital formation. Two years later, the IAFP and ICFP joined forces to participate in the first Congressional hearings on financial planning. Participants from both organizations affirmed the need for members to provide full written disclosure to clients in advance of starting a business relationship.

The SRO Debate and the "Real Thing"

Nevertheless, the 1980s were marked more frequently by discord between the organizations than by harmony. One of the flashpoints during that period involved something that may have seemed inconsequential to the average observer but which aroused strong passions among those close to the issue: the question of a self-regulatory organization (SRO).

On one side was the IAFP, which proposed a self-regulatory organization in the mid-1980s so that regulation would be consistent across state lines. Among those favoring the SRO was Alexandra Armstrong, CFP, in Washington, D.C., the IAFP's president in 1985. "We thought that the best defense was to take the offense," she said. "But we may have been ahead of our time."

Profile: Alexandra Armstrong

During the SRO debate of the mid-1980s, few financial planners were as well positioned to tackle the issue of regulation as Alexandra Armstrong, who became the IAFP's first woman president in 1985. A native of Washington, D.C., whose family members had worked in government—one cousin was chairman of the Securities and Exchange Commission during the Eisenhower administration—Armstrong "was more wired into the Washington world than most financial planners" of the era, she recalled. The SEC, she said, "didn't know what financial planners did—they assumed we were all insurance people."

Armstrong was definitely not an "insurance person." After graduating from college, where she'd discovered an aptitude for mathematics, she spent the first 16 years of her career at a New York Stock Exchange member firm, Ferris & Co. (later Ferris Baker Walsh). Her mentor was Julia Walsh, the first woman in Washington to make it big in the brokerage business. Armstrong started as a secretary but soon became a

(continued)

Profile: Alexandra Armstrong (*Continued*)

registered broker; when Walsh left Ferris in 1977 to start her own firm, Armstrong joined her.

This was also the year Armstrong became a CFP licensee—the first in Washington, D.C. She had discovered financial planning the previous year, when *Money* magazine made its debut. "My clients were asking about estate planning," she recalled, "and I thought it would be helpful to know more about it." She established the financial planning department at Walsh's firm; six years later, when the firm was sold, Armstrong launched her own firm, now called Armstrong, Fleming & Moore, Inc., and took the financial planning practice with her. From the beginning, about half of the firm's clients were women, many of them widows—not intentionally, Armstrong said, but not surprisingly, either: Armstrong's mother was widowed young and bilked of her small trust fund by the unscrupulous trustee; Julia Walsh, Armstrong's early mentor, was a young widow supporting four children. In 1993, Armstrong co-wrote *On Your Own: A Widow's Passage to Emotional & Financial Well-Being*; by 2006, the book was in its fourth edition.

Armstrong's volunteer work has likewise reflected her commitment to community service. She was the first woman president of the Washington, D.C., council of the Boy Scouts of America and, with Don Pitti, helped revive and reshape the Foundation for Financial Planning. Its mission: to connect financial planners with people in need and help them take control of their financial lives. "Our big breakthrough was when American Express gave us $1 million," she said. "That gave us credibility." At first, the foundation mostly gave academic grants. Then, after 9/11, it funded New York City planners who assisted survivors of the disaster. The foundation also stepped in after Hurricane Katrina devastated the Gulf Coast in 2005. "No amount of money can cure all the problems we face," Armstrong observed, "but at least we've been able to help where we can."

The ICFP took the opposing view. The ICFP had sharpened its focus on regulatory matters in 1984, when the first formal hearings on financial planning were held by the North American Securities Administrators Association (NASAA). Institute leaders went on record as looking forward to sharing their input, especially about an entry-level examination for investment advisers or financial planners. (The Series 65 exam, an entry-level exam on investment adviser laws, was introduced in 1989.) Also in 1984, the ICFP wrote a position paper on financial planning regulation; in it, the institute emphasized CFP designees' "identity with our clients, because that is a distinguishing mark of the CFP [designee] rather than some other financial planners or individuals such as investment advisers."

The ICFP's regulatory committee, headed by Charles G. Hughes, Jr., CFP, also examined the issue of self-regulation. (Hughes served as the institute's 1987–1988 president.) According to the minutes of the April 1984 board of directors' meeting,

The feeling was that the Certified Financial Planner is only a segment of the financial planning profession, and...in our principal role as representing Certified Financial Planners, it may not be proper for us to serve as a self-regulating organization for the entire profession.

Daniel S. Parks, JD, CFP, who served as the ICFP's 1984–1985 president, said at the time that a federally legislated SRO was "an infringement on the client-adviser relationship and a move away from the eventual acceptance of financial planning as a profession, rather than a trade or a business." Instead, the ICFP advocated for wider registration and full disclosure under existing investment adviser laws, in particular the Investment Adviser Act of 1940 on the federal level and uniform securities laws using the NASAA model on the state level. "We felt that this approach allowed the CFP designation to grow in prestige and effectiveness over time," said Brent Neiser, a former state legislative analyst who joined the ICFP staff in 1985 and served in various roles, including director of government affairs and executive director. "We felt that the existing investment adviser law had an excellent disclosure requirement that would benefit both our profession and the consumers we served," Neiser said.

In a July 1985 message to ICFP members, President Parks summarized his objections to an SRO by evoking a classic battle of the brands:

My concern is the likelihood of creating an organization of financial planners based on their method of practice, rather than the rendering of professional advice to clients. This proposal towards what I would term the "real financial planner" reminds me of the battle presently being waged by Coca-Cola and Pepsi over whose product is the "real thing," and I ask, "compared to what, under whose standards and by what measurement?" Isn't it a question of public choice? Coca-Cola and Pepsi are both the "real thing" to those individuals that make that choice. Isn't financial planning much the same way?

Just about everyone who has rendered financial services and/or sold financial products has claimed that he or she is a "real financial planner."

Rather than debating that point, shouldn't the emphasis be more on a matching of the consumer's financial needs with the financial service or product? Look at the professions of law and accounting. You do not see the competition which exists in financial planning. There is no such thing as a "real attorney" or a "real accountant." There are, however, differences in expertise based on education and experience. Why can't financial planning be the same? . . .

The key is certification, full disclosure, and the public's right to select the client-service package that is appropriate to them.

The ICFP did, however, develop an official position in its regulatory liaison efforts. The position comprised four proposals:

1. A recommendation that CFP practitioner's firms register with the Securities and Exchange Commission as investment advisers
2. A recommendation that the ICFP's code of ethics continue to be enforced
3. Strong encouragement of uniform model legislation among states
4. A favorable stance toward self-regulation in the absence of licensing

The IAFP and ICFP found common ground only when the National Association of Securities Dealers (NASD) proposed that *it* serve as the SRO for financial planners. Both organizations quickly realized that, as Armstrong put it, "federal regulators did not understand what we were trying to do. They barely knew what financial planning was, let alone why two different groups were trying to represent financial planners."

As for the ICFP, "We already felt there was far too much industry influence in financial planning," said Mike Ryan, who served on the ICFP board in the 1980s. "Having the NASD as the SRO would be like asking the fox to guard the henhouse." The IAFP backed away from its SRO proposal, and both organizations acknowledged the need to present a united front to regulators.

"Coca-Cola and Pepsi are both the 'real thing' to those individuals that make that choice. Isn't financial planning much the same way?"
—Daniel S. Parks

Other Voices: NAPFA

The IAFP and ICFP weren't the only financial planning organizations on the scene in the 1980s, and Certified Financial Planner wasn't the only mark recognized among consumers—although it was the most widely known. By 1985, there were at least two competing designations: The American College's Chartered Financial Consultant (ChFC) designation and the Personal Financial Specialist (PFS) designation promoted by the American Institute of Certified Public Accountants.

In 1982, a group of fee-only practitioners attending an Atlanta meeting of the Society of Independent Financial Advisors began talking about the growing interest in fee-only financial planning—financial advice that doesn't depend on compensation from the sale of a financial product. The following year, they convened another meeting, inviting all interested fee-only planners. More than 125 people responded, and the National Association of Personal Financial Advisors (NAPFA) was born. The association today has a membership of about 1,300 NAPFA-registered financial advisers, as well as more than 800 fee-only practitioners, academics, and students in various other categories. It advocates professional standards, a comprehensive approach to financial planning, and a fiduciary relationship that places the client's interests above all others. Throughout NAPFA's existence, many of its members have also simultaneously belonged to IAFP or ICFP, or both, or to FPA after the 2000 merger of the IAFP and ICFP.

Unsettled Times at the IAFP

The 1980s brought mixed blessings to the IAFP. The association's membership grew steadily to a peak of just over 24,000 in 1986. But after the Tax Reform Act of 1986 put an end to the tax shelters that many IAFP members had been selling to clients, membership fell off steeply. (See "Market Milestone: The Tax Reform Act of 1986," p. 51.) By 1992, IAFP membership fell to just 10,975, a 55 percent decline from the peak.

Despite this declining trend, the association was in fact becoming stronger. It clarified its mission as an open-forum organization: a big tent encompassing anyone who claimed to be affiliated with financial planning—planners, product vendors, and ancillary support services. Yet the IAFP also sharpened its definition of financial planning. Under the presidencies of Don Pitti (one of the movement's original leaders) and Hubert (Herky)

Harris in the mid-1980s, the IAFP by then renamed the International Association for Financial Planning began focusing on true financial planners rather than salespeople. Pitti advocated better educational programs for members, more cooperation among mainstream financial planning organizations, and promotion of the Registry of Financial Planning Practitioners. In a September 1984 speech to the IAFP in Atlanta, Pitti noted, "The tide is rising for financial planning, for what it can do to improve the lives of every American family and for you and our association."

That "rising tide" washed over non-American shores as well. Financial planning made inroads in Australia around 1985; in 1990, Australia became the first member of the International CFP Council. Expanding Horizons, the annual IAFP convention, really *was* expanding its horizons: Financial planners from outside the United States were attending in increasing numbers. In addition, between 1985 and 1989 the IAFP sponsored world congresses in Japan, Hong Kong, Australia, Switzerland, and the United Kingdom. The global programs encouraged the spread of the financial planning profession and also enhanced the global perspective of U.S. planners—an advantage that would prove itself as investing became an increasingly global activity. (See Chapter 6 for an in-depth discussion of financial planning's international expansion.)

Internally, the expansion was perceived as a sign of healthy growth. But outsiders continued to criticize the IAFP, and financial planners in general, for being little more than a conduit for the sale of limited partnerships, mutual funds, and life-insurance policies. To counter the criticism, the IAFP had begun as early as 1983 to clarify its client-centered approach through what came to be known as "the six-step process." As articulated in a brochure promoting the IAFP's Registry of Financial Planning Practitioners, the six steps guided clients and their financial planners toward a successful financial plan.

For clients, these were the key steps:

1. Clarify your present situation by collecting and assessing all relevant personal and financial data.
2. Decide where you want to go by identifying financial and personal goals and objectives.
3. Identify financial problems that create barriers to achieving your goals.

The planner's role comprised three subsequent steps:

4. Provide a written financial plan that meets specific standards.
5. Implement or coordinate the implementation of the right strategy to ensure that the client reaches his or her goals and objectives.
6. Provide periodic review and revision of the plan to ensure that the client stays on track.

Over the years that followed, the language of the six-step process would evolve. But the underlying principles continued to serve as the framework for successful and ethical client–planner relationships.

Education and Ethics at the ICFP

While never as large as the IAFP—its regular (nonstudent) membership never rose above 3,000—the ICFP made important contributions to the profession throughout the 1980s. It reaffirmed its commitment to continuing education, increasing the requirement from 30 to 45 hours per year and establishing, in 1986, a residency program for less-experienced planners. Using a case study format, students were paired with CFP mentors during a week-long event on the campus of the University of Colorado in Boulder. After several years, the program was discontinued because of low interest and high cost; it was revived in 1998 under the direction of Kyra Morris and continues under the aegis of the Financial Planning Association.

In addition, the institute began formally chartering local study groups, which had sprung up in the 1970s as grassroots efforts. In 1982, ICFP officer Ben Coombs reported that a study group of about 60 CFP designees was meeting in the Los Angeles area; by 1983 there were 20 such groups either under way or being formed, including those in San Diego, Sacramento, Boston, Philadelphia, Atlanta, Phoenix, and Minneapolis/St. Paul, and in Arkansas, Michigan, and Kentucky. Designees who participated in the study groups were eligible for continuing education credit. Many of the study groups developed into local "societies" that were the equivalent of the IAFP's chapters; their development eventually contributed greatly to the ICFP's cohesion and focus.

The ICFP also applied itself to the task of strengthening its code of ethics, which had been part of its original constitution and bylaws and which was reworked several times during the 1970s. A key element of the code was its emphasis on what a 1985 position paper would call "the interest and well-being of the client and the public above all else." Nevertheless, the code lacked teeth: Compliance was voluntary, and the ICFP's only enforcement power was the ability to censure or expel members who did not abide by it. The first expulsion occurred in 1978, when it came to the ICFP's attention that a member had lost his insurance license, been enjoined for violating various state securities laws, and was facing possible criminal charges. A 1982 report to the institute's board of directors, "Concepts of Professional Ethics," reinforced the significance of the ethics code. In 1984, the ethics committee reviewed some 20 potential violations of the code of ethics, from inappropriate advertising to investment scams. In 1986, 60 cases came before the committee. Clearly, a new approach to internal housecleaning was needed to prevent the resource-strapped institute from going under.

One measure supported by the institute was the Financial Products Standards Board, established in 1984 as an independent organization but funded by the institute as a public service. Henry Montgomery, CFP, became its chair; Government Affairs Director Brent Neiser spent half of his time as the FPSB's managing director. Working with volunteers from the real estate industry, the FPSB drafted guidelines and standards for structuring real estate limited-partnership investments. Other task forces drafted benchmarks for the mutual-fund and oil-and-gas industries. But the financial burden of supporting the FPSB eventually became too great for the institute; the program was terminated for lack of funding.

In the face of these budget concerns, some organizations might have sought a direct route to financial salvation. Instead, the ICFP chose a contrarian path—one that, in the short term, actually diminished its cash flow but in the long run proved to be both wise and provident: It separated itself from the College for Financial Planning and from the income that association had guaranteed.

Profile: Ben Coombs

"Mavericks, misfits, and renegades" is how Colin B. (Ben) Coombs described the founders of the Institute of Certified Financial Planners in an article he wrote for the ICFP's twenty-fifth anniversary, in 1998. He included himself among them: An Oakland, California, native, he had left UCLA's graduate business school in 1961 without an MBA or a clear sense of direction, floundered during his early career as a life insurance salesman, and failed at his first attempt at financial planning. As a member of the College for Financial Planning's first graduating class in 1973, he was entering, in his words, "a new profession at a time when the economy was in trouble." One early financial planner served a prison sentence for problems associated with land fraud; another was shot in his condo.

Yet, as Coombs noted later, his timing proved to be good. "Everyone had a financial toothache," he said, "and they were looking for someone to relieve their pain." He set up his financial planning practice in California's Central Valley and stepped up his involvement in the ICFP. In 1985, he assumed the institute's presidency and adopted the theme of "Building Bridges," announcing his intention to repair the ICFP's relationship with the IAFP. Fifteen years later, the organizations would finally merge.

Coombs also made education a top priority: Under his leadership, the board of directors increased the ICFP's continuing education requirement from 30 to 45 hours per year, and established the ICFP's residency program, in which less-experienced planners were paired with CFP mentors. In addition, the ICFP adopted its first code of ethics; in 1986 alone, the Ethics Committee reviewed 60 cases. Still, Coombs warned members that it was just the beginning: Things would get tougher under the new IBCFP's jurisdiction. "In the future," he said, "the penalty for violations…will involve not only a loss of member status, but the possible loss of the CFP designation as well." The one-time "maverick and misfit" had come a long way—as had many of his pioneering colleagues.

Getting Off the Gravy Train

Almost from its inception, the ICFP had had a disproportionate number of student (provisional) members compared with regular members. In 1985, the ratio was five to one. "We wanted to distinguish the institute as an organization of practicing financial planners," said Charles Hughes, Jr., head of the regulatory committee, "but when we looked at the membership rolls, we saw that they were dominated by students." First-year College for Financial Planning students contributed a large share of the institute's income. As one leader said at the time, the imbalance "restricts the institute in pursuing its goal of achieving professional recognition through its membership, although we would not have been able to promote the CFP designation without the college's help."

In the end, the ICFP leadership made the tough but necessary decision. Beginning in 1985, the institute would gradually, over a four-year period, wean itself from dependence on income generated by first-year college enrollees.

"We made the decision to give up the gravy train," Hughes said. "It was a difficult time—trying to face the financial reality of what was basically a philosophical decision" to become a professional rather than a student organization.

Despite budget concerns, the institute made two key hires: the first full-time director of local societies (there were 51 in 1985) and Brent Neiser as its director of government affairs. Almost immediately, regulatory activities picked up. Under the leadership of institute president Daniel Parks and regulatory affairs committee chairman Charles Hughes, the institute adopted a statement of policy toward self-regulation and government regulation. In explaining the institute's opposition to an SRO, Parks used the Coca-Cola/Pepsi analogy of the "real thing." He wrote,

> *More and more, the public will come to see the difference, the "real" difference among financial planners because of preference. [T]he institute*

*is willing to let consumers decide who their financial planner should be
based on full public disclosure and a matching of service and products
to the consumer's needs.*

Neiser believed the institute had a "strong base" from which to speak—a
base that included the "toughest code of ethics in the profession; no product
influence or affiliation; and a committed board and staff." He continued, "We
can do and say things many others can't. Because of that freedom we can
also afford to alter a position when it is in the best long-term interests of
the qualified planner and the public."

A Board of Standards Emerges

Meanwhile, the College for Financial Planning was facing its own growth
challenges. The burgeoning ranks of CFP designees—by the mid-1980s,
there were more than 10,000 in all, with 2,000 to 5,000 being added each
year—seemed to demand a different type of attention, service, and monitoring than what the college had been providing.

William Anthes, the college's president, began receiving complaints
from the public about perceived misconduct on the part of a few CFP
designees. "I had a box on my desk with complaints concerning ten or
fifteen former students," he later recalled. "To my knowledge, the college
had never revoked the CFP marks from any graduate of the college, but we
knew the time was coming when we would have to address the issue."

As the college's board debated how to investigate these complaints and
discipline unethical behavior—and even whether it was a proper role for
an educational institution to do so—it also began considering a dramatic
new undertaking: the establishment of a separate organization to oversee
the CFP marks.

The impetus for that new direction was a lawsuit regarding the ownership of the CFP mark. In 1980, the college had sued Adelphi University
of Long Island City, New York, for attempting to bestow the CFP mark on
graduates of Adelphi's financial planning certificate program without authorization from the College for Financial Planning, which claimed ownership
rights to the marks. The suit dragged on for several years until an out-of-
court settlement was finally hammered out in 1985. Anthes reflected in 2008
on the development:

*I don't remember who first suggested that a solution to the lawsuit would
be to establish a new organization, but the college's board saw it as a
way to address both the Adelphi situation and our internal debate about
how to oversee the use of the marks. We could have gone to trial with the*

Adelphi lawsuit, and some on our board were confident that we would win because the college owned the CFP marks. But we decided to take a long-term view and voluntarily transfer the CFP marks to a new organization that would be structured to monitor the marks and discipline CFP designees who engaged in unethical professional behavior. In addition, we agreed that the new organization would have the authority to allow other appropriate educational programs to award the CFP designation, which satisfied Adelphi's demands.

What emerged on July 17, 1985, was an independent nonprofit organization called the International Board of Standards and Practices for Certified Financial Planners, Inc., or IBCFP (later renamed the Certified Financial Planner Board of Standards, Inc.). The IBCFP, not the college, would own and manage the CFP marks; it would also establish standards for the activities of CFP registrants and oversee the administration of the CFP certification examination process. Moreover, because the IBCFP owned the marks, it could revoke the right of financial planners to use them. This power strongly differentiated the CFP marks from an educational credential.

It was a bold and risky move. The college would become one of many curriculum providers in a new, openly competitive environment. Giving up control of the CFP marks signified a commitment to the financial services industry as a whole. In announcing the decision in 1985, Anthes said:

We have heard from regulators, educators, members of the press, and industry leaders that the public interest demands that persons who hold themselves out as financial planners should meet minimum educational and experience requirements and practice in accordance with recognized professional standards of conduct. The [college's] CFP designation has become a nationally recognized symbol of excellence in financial planning, but it would not be proper or useful for the college, as an academic institution, to undertake the broad responsibilities in areas affecting the professional lives of Certified Financial Planners, such as professional standard setting, discipline, and industry and government relations, which appear necessary to further the growth and acceptance of the CFP designation.

"By . . . giving up control of the [CFP] marks and by leading in the formation of the IBCFP, the college has taken the single most important step our industry has seen since its formation. . . ."

—P. Kemp Fain, Jr.

The inaugural IBCFP was funded by $2.5 million from the college, which also helped the IBCFP find its first office space. The initial 11-member IBCFP board was chaired by David King, who had served as the ICFP's president from 1977 to 1979 and had also chaired the college's board of regents. The original board's members, who served from 1985 to 1987, were William Anthes; E. Denby Brandon, Jr.; Colin "Ben" Coombs; P. Kemp Fain, Jr.; Tahira K. Hira; Charles G. Hughes; Raymond A. Parkins; Daniel S. Parks; Gilman Robinson; and H. Oliver Welch. The original IBCFP board soon formed three subsidiary boards: the board of examiners, the trial board, and the appeals board.

King called the creation of the IBCFP "a timely opportunity for CFPs to shoulder the responsibility for the future of our profession . . . a move that will further elevate CFPs to the level of respected professionals in the business and financial community." P. Kemp Fain, Jr., who served as the institute's president in 1983–1984, later wrote:

> By the unselfish act of giving up control of the [CFP] marks and by leading in the formation of the IBCFP, the college has taken the single most important step our industry has seen since its formation. Now the CFP designation can be promulgated everywhere as the standard of excellence in financial planning. We will soon have the strength of both quality and numbers.

Ethics and education would be the primary focus of the IBCFP in its early years. By June 1986, the IBCFP adopted a code of ethics and standards of practice as well as a set of disciplinary rules and procedures. Other elements of the certification process quickly followed: the registration of financial planning educational programs of institutions other than the college in 1987; opening examinations to candidates from those institutions (also in 1987); continuing education requirements in 1988; and the delineation of experience requirements and annual licensing procedures by 1989. The College for Financial Planning, Anthes said, would continue to maintain the quality and integrity of its own program, but it would add to the breadth and depth of the educational alternatives open to planners by offering a diverse selection of courses.

In the early years of the IBCFP, the ICFP board had "intense discussions about the prerequisites for a profession," recalled Mike Ryan.

> Many of the early leaders of the IBCFP participated in those ICFP board discussions. We recognized that there were three determinants: a high minimum education requirement, rigorously enforced ethical standards, and standards of practice. The CFP mark met the education requirement. The ICFP was setting and enforcing ethics, and this duty was transferred to the new [IBCFP].

Market Milestone: The Tax Reform Act of 1986

Initiated by the Reagan Administration and enacted by a Democratic House of Representatives and a Republican Senate, the 1986 Tax Reform Act dramatically cut tax rates and simplified tax laws. The top marginal tax rate on the country's wealthiest individuals was reduced from 50 percent to 28 percent, while the tax base was broadened to prevent individuals and businesses from escaping taxation. The new law also subjected a larger number of taxpayers to the alternative minimum tax—a change that would have enduring consequences. Perhaps most significant for the financial planning profession, the law introduced "passive loss" rules that effectively prevented individual investors from taking deductions from the tax shelters that had become increasingly popular in an era of stagflation—most notably, limited partnerships that owned hard assets such as real estate or oil and gas. The new rules not only put the tax-shelter industry out of business; they also canceled the livelihoods of many self-described financial planners who had depended on large commissions from sales of tax-shelter partnerships.

As for practice standards, they would develop gradually, mostly in the decades ahead.

There were at least six key IBCFP achievements during those early years. In ethics, it created a legally enforceable professional code of ethics and practice standards. In education, it created a structure for the proliferation of institutions that teach the CFP curriculum and—by severing ties with the College for Financial Planning at the end of the five-year joint-ownership agreement—it leveled the playing field for all institutions interested in educating candidates for CFP certification. It also laid the groundwork for globalizing the CFP marks: first, by signing agreements with Australia and Japan, in 1990 and 1992, respectively, and second, by creating in 1991 the Board of Affiliated Associations, the forerunner of today's Financial Planning Standards Board, which controls the licensing of CFP certificants outside the United States.

Finally, by creating an ongoing certification fee, the IBCFP laid the foundation for its financial independence.

Although the college and the ICFP, and many practicing financial planners, viewed the IBCFP's existence as essential for continued growth, the new organization wasn't universally welcomed. The IAFP rejected the IBCFP's offer to reserve two seats for IAFP members. In a letter to IAFP members, then-president Alexandra Armstrong said that "our participation on the board of the IBCFP would indicate to our members we were endorsing one designation for financial planners over others. This would be in direct conflict with our basic philosophy of an Open Forum organization which accepts all professionals in the financial planner community."

The American College in Bryn Mawr, Pennsylvania, was an even more vocal critic of the IBCFP. The American College, founded in 1927, had been offering a diploma and the Chartered Financial Consultant designation to students who completed its course in financial planning. Its vice president for public affairs, David Bruhin, publicly called the IBCFP

> ... the most self-serving of any regulatory scheme yet proposed for financial planning. ... At a time when The American College and other educational and industry organizations have been discussing approaches to achieving common standards for financial planners, we consider a unilateral action by one of the institutions involved to be disruptive.[1]

Eventually, both the IAFP and The American College reversed their positions and worked cooperatively with the IBCFP. The American College today is one of the leading institutions that prepares students for CFP certification.

The IBCFP, in the meantime, set itself the task of enforcing its code of ethics—a potentially risky stance, given the fact that it still lacked professional liability insurance to protect it from charges of false complaints. In 1987, the IBCFP had its first high-profile case: Tony Sorge, who had been the College for Financial Planning's second president, later was an official of a corrupt California equities firm; he served a four-year prison sentence for mail fraud. In 1987, the IBCFP permanently revoked Sorge's right to use the CFP marks.

The College Hits Its Stride

During the 1980s, while the IAFP and ICFP struggled to define themselves, the College for Financial Planning was enjoying unprecedented success. In the fiscal year that ended in September 1985, the college experienced its largest enrollment ever: 10,103 students.[2] At industry conferences and meetings, potential students lined up to enroll in the curriculum. Nan Mead, the head of the college's communications department at the time, remembered attending IAFP conventions in 1985 and 1986 at which she and five other staff members fielded questions about the college and the CFP program at an exhibit booth. "There weren't enough of us to talk to each new participant who approached the booth," Mead said. "What was most surprising was that some of the crowd were enrollees or graduates who wanted to express their enthusiasm or discuss what they had learned from the curriculum."

Many new enrollees were responding to significant enhancements in the college's programs. The curriculum was revised twice, in 1982 and again in 1984, to reflect growing interest in tax planning, retirement and estate planning, and other specialties. As the number of enrollees steadily grew, monitoring compliance with continuing-education requirements became increasingly challenging. William Anthes later recalled that a single staff member was responsible for tracking attendance at external seminars and workshops.[3] The college's first coordinator of continuing education arrived in mid-1981, and in 1983 a continuing education department was formed specifically to serve graduates. New products and programs proliferated: taped and printed materials, workshops and seminars, a management institute, summer sabbatical programs, and a national conference. These changes were reflected in the department's name change, in 1986, from Continuing Education to Professional Development.

The college also began examining ways to expand its service. In 1983, the Financial Paraplanner Program—designed for people who assist financial planning practitioners—was created to provide basic education about the process of personal financial planning, financial products, and basic planning techniques. A pilot course attracted 62 students, each sponsored by a CFP candidate or graduate. The course opened to general enrollment in September 1984.

Encouraged by that success, the college created the High School Financial Planning Program to address an area rarely covered in American schools. Over a three-year period beginning in 1984, the curriculum was developed, tested, and refined, then introduced in Denver schools as a public service at no charge to students or schools. Financial planners Rich Miller, CFP, CLU, and Sally Button, CFP, took the lead. Miller later recalled that early experience:

I taught in the inner city. Some kids didn't care and didn't relate. The first year we tried to teach percentages, but many [high school seniors] weren't getting it because they hadn't learned the concept in math. We went back to the basic concepts of paychecks and insurance and let them read and inquire further on their own if they were interested.

Rocky start notwithstanding, within its first five years the high school program spread nationwide (and continues to be implemented 25 years after its inception). In 1988, the program was recognized with the National C-Flag Award from the President's Citation Program for Private Sector Initiatives. And in 1991, the program expanded its educational network through a three-year partnership with the U.S. Department of Agriculture's Cooperative Extension Service, a national educational network.

The college also turned its attention to a growing community of CFP Program graduates eager to expand their expertise. Many wanted more than mere continuing education credits: They sought innovative, practical course-work designed for the real world. In response, the college consulted with advisory groups, academics, and professional practitioners and developed four specialty areas: wealth management, tax planning, retirement planning, and estate planning. These tracks became the foundation for the 16-course Advanced Studies curriculum, introduced in 1987, the year of the college's fifteenth anniversary. A year later, the college was authorized by the state of Colorado to grant a Master of Science degree.

One of the advanced tracks, tax planning, proved to be especially pop-ular. The increasing complexity of tax law—despite the intent of the Tax Reform Act of 1986 to simplify it (see "Market Milestone: The Tax Reform Act of 1986," p. 51)—set the stage for the college's Tax Preparer Program,

Market Milestone: Black Monday

The single-largest one-day percentage decline in U.S. stock market his-tory occurred on October 19, 1987—Black Monday—when the Dow Jones Industrial Average tumbled 508 points, or more than 22 percent. The U.S. crash was part of a worldwide market phenomenon that be-gan in Hong Kong and worked its way west through Europe; markets in Australia and New Zealand were especially hard hit. Analyses of the crash have not identified a single cause. One popular theory ascribes Black Monday to program trading, then a recent innovation, in which computers perform rapid stock executions. Another theory points to a dispute over monetary policy among the G7 industrialized nations. When the United States tightened policy more quickly than the other countries, the dollar-backed Hong Kong market collapsed, sending rip-ples throughout the world. Although the cause of the crash remains a mystery, its resolution is well documented. Markets around the world were put on restricted trading to give them time to sort out incom-ing orders. (Computer technology was not yet sophisticated enough to handle the challenge.) In the interim, the Federal Reserve and other central banks were able to pump liquidity into their respective systems. Nevertheless, it would be nearly two years before the Dow regained its August 25, 1987, closing high of 2,722.

introduced in 1988. That program in turn led to the 1990 founding of the college's Institute for Tax Studies.

Interest in financial planning education was proving to be an international phenomenon: The college was fielding inquiries from Australia, England, France, Germany, Indonesia, Italy, and Japan about developing programs similar to the CFP program in their respective countries. In 1987, the college responded by co-creating the College for Financial Planning in the United Kingdom. Three years later, though, as legislative efforts to mandate testing of financial-services professionals lagged in the U.K., the college's William Anthes reluctantly passed responsibility for maintaining and administering the program to the London-based Chartered Insurance Institute. But Anthes noted that the venture had been worthwhile:

We take great pride in the fact that we have been able to take our domestic program and convert it to the nomenclature, laws, tax system, and client scenarios found in the United Kingdom. The U.K. presented an ideal opportunity for us to take our message abroad, and I am pleased that an organization of CII's quality and widespread influence will carry forth our effort.

As it turned out, the international expansion wasn't misguided—just premature. Within a decade, financial planning and the CFP marks would be well rooted in 10 countries around the world.

CHAPTER 4

One Profession, One Designation

As the 1980s drew to a close, significant forces were reshaping the geopolitical and economic landscape. The fall of the Berlin Wall in November 1989 and the dissolution of the Soviet Union in February 1990 signaled the end of Eastern European Communism and the old Cold War alignments. Iraq's 1990 invasion of Kuwait shifted international focus to the Middle East and precipitated the U.S.-led Desert Storm operation in early 1991.

There was domestic upheaval as well, especially in the world of financial services. The Tax Reform Act of 1986 (described in Chapter 3) wiped out the market for tax shelters and limited partnerships, which had been tainted by fraud. The stock market volatility of 1987 and 1989 served as a sobering reminder that markets go down as well as up. Then, during the late 1980s, more than 1,000 U.S. savings and loan institutions, with assets totaling more than $500 billion, went into bankruptcy. The complex causes of the failure included a web of public policy decisions, some with roots in New Deal era reforms, as well as the wave of deregulation that began during the Reagan Administration. The crisis peaked in 1989; the cost to taxpayers of bailing out the National Savings and Loan Insurance Corporation, which insured S&L deposits, eventually exceeded $153 billion.[1] One immediate consequence of the S&L crisis was a slowdown in the housing market, which contributed to a recession in 1990 and 1991. A more lasting effect was the breakdown of barriers between commercial banks and deposit banks.

The turbulence at home and abroad made many Americans more aware than ever of the need for sound financial advice and careful planning. And the financial planning profession was finally becoming mature enough—and respected enough—to provide that support. Throughout the 1990s, the profession added members to its ranks, increased its global reach, enhanced its practice standards, and gradually moved toward unity between its two primary membership organizations.

The Challenge to "Unify and Professionalize"

The seeds for that development had been sown in 1987 with the publication of a white paper with the somewhat unwieldy title, "Unifying and Professionalizing the Financial Planning Segments of the Financial Services Industry." The paper's author was P. Kemp Fain, Jr., CFP, then the chair of the International Board of Standards and Practices for Certified Financial Planners (IBCFP), the body that had been created in 1985 to own and manage the CFP marks and to bring professional education to college and university programs other than the College for Financial Planning. In the paper, Fain outlined why the financial planning profession should coalesce around a single designation, the CFP mark. "One profession, one designation" was the way Fain summed up his argument, and the short phrase soon became a rallying cry among financial planners. Fain himself used the language of faith to explain his reasoning: "We need CFP practitioners to preach the gospel of CFP," he said.

Why so much fervor? Because it was by no means clear at the time that any single professional designation would predominate in financial planning. The International Association for Financial Planning (IAFP), after all, still advocated the concept of the *open forum*. Fain, however, wrote in his whitepaper that unifying the profession under a single designation was "a worthwhile goal" requiring "equal and enthusiastic participation of all industry organizations." The need, Fain said, was urgent:

> *Time is of the essence in order to avoid the continued proliferation of competing certifications and to eliminate public confusion regarding the validity of financial planning credentials. The reasons for using the IBCFP and the CFP mark as unifying elements are several and convincing. First, the CFP mark is a true indicator to consumers of a professional because the IBCFP grants use of the mark only to those candidates who have fulfilled significant educational and experience requirements and have passed rigorous examinations. Second, the CFP mark is widely recognized by the public as the "mainstream" certification of financial planning professionals. Third, and perhaps most important, the CFP mark is the only financial planning certification that has legal trademark protection. As a result, the IBCFP, which owns the marks, can strongly regulate CFP professionals by granting or withholding use of the marks. The IBCFP is in an effective position to address the four essential components of professionalism: education, examination, experience, and ethics.*

> *"The IBCFP is in an effective position to address the four essential components of professionalism: education, examination, experience, and ethics."*
>
> —P. Kemp Fain, Jr.

The remainder of the paper laid out a three-phase plan for bringing all financial planners into the Certified Financial Planner tent. The first two phases covered the years 1987 through 1992, and established educational and experience qualifications for receiving the CFP marks. After 1992, "the experience requirement would become very 'tight' and would concentrate on experience directly relevant to the financial planner's job. . . . [A]ll examinations would be administered at one time over a three-day period, and all candidates for CFP certification would take a practice exam." By 1993, Fain wrote, "the Certified Financial Planner professional" would be "the recognized professional, in the public practice of financial planning, to the exclusion of all other designations."

Fain lobbied hard for "one profession, one designation." At a national meeting of financial planners in 1988, he exhorted his audience to rally around the CFP designation, arguing that the financial planning profession, beleaguered by bad press and consumer confusion, was at a crossroads. Among his supporters was Charles G. Hughes, Jr., president of the Institute of Certified Financial Planners in 1987–1988. Hughes advocated bringing the IAFP and ICFP together, but not under the terms proffered by the IAFP in 1987, when it proposed a merger of the two organizations. The IAFP's proposal, according to the minutes of the ICFP's September 1987 board meeting, was "unacceptable as presented, but was a basis for discussions to move towards one organization, one designation."

Central to the conflict was the ICFP's insistence that the IAFP was an "industry" association rather than a "professional" one. (That dispute over identity would persist for many years, even after the two organizations merged.) Writing in the July 1988 issue of *Institute Today*, Hughes offered his perspective on the issue:

At the heart of the matter is the significant and far-reaching involvement, financial and otherwise, of product manufacturing and distribution in the purposes and structure of the IAFP, an entirely appropriate strategy for an industry association, but questionable in a professional association. . . .

A suspicion exists among the public: "Is financial planning for some practitioners a forum for giving advice or for distributing products?" The conflict-of-interest issue, whether real or perceived, is a serious matter for both financial planners and the associations representing them. . . . To suggest or force a merger for what may be short-term and, principally, economic expediencies could be a serious error at this stage in the development of financial planning as a profession.[2]

Years later, Hughes described the mood of that time. "There was a groundswell, a cry, from membership in both organizations that there was too much duplication of services, that there were two different voices in the regulatory area," he said. "Members asked how we expected to achieve results when we were talking against one another."[3]

From the ICFP's perspective, there was another incentive to join forces with the IAFP: money. Madeline Noveck, CFP, who served as the institute's 1991–1992 president, remembers joining the board of directors in 1987, when the organization was "struggling with several reduced financial circumstances and changing industry conditions." Some longtime institute members, she said, "felt the ICFP could not survive as an independent organization supported only by CFP member dues.

"Then-president Charlie Hughes sent a letter outlining the problems and various solutions," said Noveck.

I delayed responding and finally Charlie called on the phone. I said I was deeply troubled by the letter. More accurately, I said the letter made me sick to my stomach. There had to be an institute. There had to be a professional association. If we let it go now, it would take fifteen years to re-create.

The Joint Organization Committee

Despite their serious philosophical differences, the IAFP and ICFP forged ahead with discussions about unifying the profession and created a joint organization committee, chaired by Fain, to negotiate the realignment. The organizations had one thing in common: Both were experiencing membership decline, although for different reasons. From its peak of nearly 24,000 members in 1985, the IAFP's membership sank to 11,000 because of the loophole-closing restrictions of President Reagan's Tax Reform Act of 1986. The ICFP's membership dropped to 7,000 members, largely because it eliminated free memberships subsidized by the College for Financial Planning. There were other differences as well. The ICFP, which had a budget of $3 million, envisioned a new organization with a new name and a new location. The IAFP, with a $14 million budget, wanted to keep its name and remain in Atlanta; it suggested that the institute's promotion of the CFP designation be consolidated into a "practitioner division" that included a section for "other professional practitioners." IAFP chair Larry W. Carroll, CFP, explained in a November 1987 letter to the ICFP why *CFP* should coexist with other designations:

> *We recognize and appreciate the interest of the members of the ICFP for the "certified financial planner" or CFP to be acknowledged as the one and only professional designation in the field of financial planning. It does not appear practical at this time that stating such by the unified organization would be helpful. It would cause severe difficulties for the IAFP members who are not CFP certificants.*

The joint organization committee worked throughout much of 1987 and 1988. The IBCFP acted as mediator and facilitator, hoping for "one profession, one designation," as the outcome. All of the parties finally hammered out an agreement in principle under which two separate, distinct, yet closely linked organizations were to be created. According to observers, the agreement was signed "amid much fanfare" during a general session at the IAFP's annual convention in New York City in September 1988 by Eileen Sharkey, CFP, president of the ICFP, and Larry Carroll, chair of the IAFP. In December, the committee's members agreed unanimously to a five-point package that described a professional association and an industry association with restructured boards; the IAFP's Registry of Financial Planning Practitioners would be transferred to the professional association's board.

The package was adopted by the boards of the ICFP and the IBCFP in January 1989. But when it came before the IAFP's board in February, it was voted down. The IAFP gave as its reason a preference for a total organizational merger with economies of scale.

Charles Hughes later recalled, "The discussions took place at a time when the institute was going through an enormous identity crisis. There was a real sense of failure that the reorganization did not finally go forward. After that, we had to figure out who we were, who we represented, and what we wanted to do."

Bob Hewitt, who served as the IAFP's president in 1989–1990, offered his organization's perspective: "On the surface, the agreement looked fine, but there were issues below the surface that caused the deal to fall apart. People got cold feet."

Richard Wagner, who would serve as ICFP president for the 1992–1993 term, was more blunt in his assessment. He called it "betrayal" on the part of IAFP leadership: "They recanted their support. They stood for self-interest, not for the profession."

> *"There was a real sense of failure that the reorganization did not finally go forward."*
>
> —Charles Hughes

Rebuilding Separately

Disappointed yet determined to keep moving the profession forward, the two organizations looked toward the future. The IAFP applied itself to regaining the members it lost when thousands of practitioners left the industry after the 1986 Tax Reform Act and the stock market drops of 1987 and 1989. The ICFP, also struggling to attract new members, focused on strengthening the definition of a "practitioner"—that is, a CFP certificant in the public practice of financial planning. Eileen Sharkey and her successor, John T. (Jack) Blankinship, Jr., decided the institute would implement the five-point package on its own, and established a committee on practice standards to define "good standards of practice." Blankinship, who took over the institute's presidency in 1989, insisted that CFP practitioners develop a "professional culture" that centered on fiduciary duty to clients.

One of the ICFP's efforts in this area proved controversial. In 1989, it created its own Registry of Licensed Practitioners to identify those ICFP members who worked with the public and who agreed to abide by certain professional standards—for example, to provide full written disclosure to clients about the practitioner's experience, education, method of compensation, and potential conflicts of interest.

Blankinship explained the registry's rationale: "We wanted to identify those CFP certificants who were in the public practice of financial planning and agreed to abide by certain professional standards. We searched for a different word than 'registry,' because we knew the IAFP would be sensitive to that, but we couldn't find one." The explanation did not satisfy the IAFP's Bob Hewitt, who said in a December 1989 letter to Blankinship that the institute had "gone too far." The following month, Blankinship fired back: "The IAFP posturing has reached new heights. . . . We do not recognize you as the spokesman for the profession. For you to attempt to play such a role would be ethical bankruptcy. . . ." A meeting between the two leaders later in January lasted all of 18 minutes, during which Blankinship informed Hewitt that the institute had no intention of changing the name of its registry.

The registry wasn't an instant hit with ICFP members, either. They expressed confusion: Was the institute trying to indicate that some CFP professionals—there were 4,500 in the registry in 1990—were "better" than others because their names were in the registry? Was the ICFP registry simply a means of retaliating against the IAFP and that organization's registry? Even

> *"It won't be long when we shall look one another in the eye and know we have fought the good fight, that we held fast . . . that we are professionals practicing in a recognized profession."*
>
> —John T. Blankinship

the IBCFP expressed concern over the institute's use of the words *registry* and *licensed* in the name.

But Blankinship and other institute leaders held firm. They saw the response, positive or negative, as a good thing, one that was "getting people out in the field to look at what our mission is all about, what a profession means," according to the minutes of the institute's March 1990 meeting. In his last letter to members as president, Blankinship wrote in August 1990, "It won't be long when we shall look one another in the eye and know we have fought the good fight, that we held fast, that the public recognizes the Certified Financial Planner professional as the financial planning advisor of choice, that we are professionals practicing in a recognized profession."

Despite the rancor over the dual registries, the IAFP and the ICFP began the new decade in a spirit of tentative cooperation. Each organization offered the other complimentary registrations at their annual conferences. And both organizations participated in a new Financial Planning Organizations Forum, initiated by IAFP leaders with the goal of encouraging dialogue. Besides the IAFP and ICFP, other participants included the IBCFP, NAPFA, the College for Financial Planning, the American Society of CLU & ChFC (later known as the Society of Financial Services Professionals), and The American College. The group met at least yearly for almost 20 years.

Strengthening Professional Standards

While the IAFP and ICFP competed to attract members, the IBCFP moved on multiple fronts to pursue the goal of "one profession, one designation" first articulated by P. Kemp Fain in 1987. Despite the conflicts within and between the membership organizations, the IBCFP was single-minded in its commitment to higher standards, a strong educational program, and clear ethical guidelines.

"Many leaders of the fledgling financial planning movement realized that standards had to be put into place and they couldn't be lip-service, voluntary standards," observed Marv Tuttle, who held leadership roles in the ICFP in the 1990s and became the Financial Planning Association's CEO and executive director in 2004. "They knew that unless a new self-regulatory structure for the CFP community was created and enforced, financial planning didn't have a chance with the media, government, and the public." The IBCFP, Tuttle said, "went to great lengths to work with recognized third parties in academia, professional testing, accreditation, and allied international organizations to ensure that the IBCFP could assure the public it would be well served by those who have earned the CFP marks—to the point that those practitioners were willing to give up the marks if they did something to tarnish them."

Among the key developments of the decade was the creation in 1995 of CFP Board's Board of Practice Standards, charged with putting teeth into the professional code of ethics developed a decade earlier. The board, composed exclusively of Certified Financial Planner practitioners, solicited input from CFP certificants, consumers, regulators, and organizations; it also used the results of three financial planner job analyses conducted in 1987, 1994, and 1999 (the latter two by outside organizations). It then drafted and revised the standards, which CFP Board's board of governors adopted.

The standards were not intended to prescribe services or procedures, nor were they a basis for legal liability. Instead, they identified six elements of the financial planning process and paired them with "authoritative and directive" practice standards. They remain in force today.

The Financial Planning Process and Practice Standards

Financial Planning Process	Related Practice Standards
1. Establishing and defining the relationship with a client	100-1: Defining the Scope of the Engagement
2. Gathering client data	200-1: Determining a Client's Personal and Financial Goals, Needs and Priorities
	200-2: Obtaining Quantitative Information and Documents
3. Analyzing and evaluating the client's financial status	300-1: Analyzing and Evaluating the Client's Information
4. Developing and presenting financial planning recommendations	400-1: Identifying and Evaluating Financial Planning Alternative(s)
	400-2: Developing the Financial Planning Recommendation(s)
	400-3: Presenting the Financial Planning Recommendation(s)
5. Implementing the financial planning recommendations	500-1: Agreeing on Implementation Responsibilities
	500-2: Selecting Products and Services for Implementation
6. Monitoring	600-1: Defining Monitoring Responsibilities

For financial planning to be recognized as a true profession, it needed to be supported by a rigorous academic foundation. Accordingly, the IBCFP invited representatives from the Academy of Financial Services, representing U.S. business schools, and the Association for Financial Counseling and Planning Education, representing university economics programs, to help chart a course for the next decade. By the end of the 1990s, more than 100 colleges and universities were offering programs leading to CFP certification.

In 1991—right on schedule—the IBCFP fulfilled P. Kemp Fain's dream of a single certification examination. Work toward that goal had begun at least five years earlier with discussions by the CFP Board's Board of Governors, the ruling body of CFP Board. Tim Kochis, who was a new member of the CFP Board's Board of Examiners at the time, recalled the significance of the change:

> *I wasn't yet a CFP certificant, and most of the members of the board of governors were CFP certificants who had received their education through the College for Financial Planning and had taken the college's six-part serial exam. So imagine how some of them felt when I, a junior member, raised my hand at the back of the room and said that a serial exam was fine for an academic credential, but if we wanted CFP to be respected as a professional credential, the exam needed to be a single comprehensive exam that was not part of any one school. Some on the board of governors saw that as a totally left-field idea, and some felt that it somehow diminished what they had accomplished by taking a six-part exam. But, of course, the majority eventually supported the idea. Everyone who already had their CFP designation was grandfathered in—they didn't have to take the comprehensive exam.*

Bob Goss praised the development as "a tremendous milestone for the CFP designation," adding, "The process will now be similar to the bar exam and the CPA exam."[4]

The comparison to the legal and accounting professions was significant. As part of its campaign to heighten awareness and strengthen the perception of professionalism, the IBCFP had begun networking with the legal and accounting professions through their membership organizations, the American Bar Association and the AICPA, and on a one-to-one level. The board also worked directly with government agencies, including the National Association of State Securities Administrators (NASAA), the National Association of Insurance Commissioners (NAIC), and the National Association of State Boards of Accountancy (NASBA), to secure waivers for CFP certificants from state examinations and continuing education requirements, including the new NASAA Series 65 and 66 competency exams for investment adviser representatives. (For its part, the ICFP had hired a legislative lobbyist, Duane Thompson, in 1995 to work on regulatory issues, including the National Securities Market Improvements Act of 1996, which imposed uniform requirements on investment advisers.)

The IBCFP also reached out to consumers, directly and through consumer groups. It conducted surveys that revealed high awareness levels of the CFP marks and high levels of consumer satisfaction with CFP certificants. To build on this foundation, and to encourage consumers and leaders of financial services firms to share their opinions and to learn the value of certification, the IBCFP created a Consumer Advisory Council and a Financial Services Advisory Council.

As important as the IBCFP was in this decade of progress toward the goal of professionalism, it wasn't the only engine of change. Widespread adoption of desktop computers and the development of sophisticated financial planning software programs greatly streamlined the work of financial planning and allowed planners to increase the size of their practices. New theoretical insights, especially in economics, also advanced the profession. From within financial planning, the advent of *life planning* and *interior finance*—related terms for a holistic approach to money—broadened the scope of planners' offerings. For more on these developments, see Chapter 7.

College for Financial Planning Makes Key Moves

The struggles between the IAFP and ICFP left their sister institution, the College for Financial Planning, largely unscathed. With its twentieth anniversary approaching, the college was maturing into a respected—if nontraditional—provider of education for the entire financial services industry. In 1990, it had nearly 40,000 alumni and more than 25,000 enrolled students. It had a visible symbol of its success in the form of a new national headquarters building in a southeast Denver business park. College staff, which now numbered just over 100, had moved into the 86,000-square-foot, $7.3 million building on June 5, 1989. And the college would soon achieve an even more meaningful milestone when, in 1995, the college received accreditation status with the Distance Education and Training Council (DETC). The move sent a signal to educators, financial planners, and consumers that the CFP marks had intrinsic value.

In 1992, its twentieth-anniversary year, the college created the National Endowment for Financial Education (NEFE) to serve as its holding company and to allow the college to develop and perpetuate its educational programs for financial planning professionals. Under the leadership of Bill Anthes, who held dual titles at the college and NEFE during NEFE's first decade,

NEFE also greatly expanded its consumer financial education efforts. In 1995, Anthes created NEFE's Public Education Center, with Brent A. Neiser, CFP, as its executive director.

In 1997, NEFE became a private foundation after selling all of its professional education programs and related divisions—including the College for Financial Planning and more than 40 products offered through NEFE's professional development department—to Phoenix-based Apollo Group, Inc., a publicly owned corporation established in 1973 to offer higher education to working adults. The sale, for approximately $35 million (not including NEFE's headquarters building and reserves), enabled NEFE to further refine its mission to improve the financial well-being of all Americans. The Public Education Center was transformed into a new division, Collaborative Programs, directed by Neiser; the new NEFE also included the High School Financial Planning Program (HSFPP), originally created in 1984 with a partner organization, the Cooperative Extension Service of the U.S. Department of Agriculture, to increase the financial literacy of America's youth. By 1997, nearly 800,000 students had completed the NEFE High School Financial Planning Program. Over the next two years, NEFE undertook a dramatic expansion of the program, and in 2000 it began partnering with a national association, America's Credit Unions, which helped promote and team-teach the program. By the end of 2006, nearly five million HSFPP books had been sent into at least 50,000 classrooms.

In addition, Collaborative Programs began partnering actively with other organizations—including the American Red Cross, the American Indian College Fund, Habitat for Humanity, and the National Urban League—to identify, understand, and connect with different groups of consumers, especially those who are underserved by mainstream channels. By the end of the decade, the endowment had created more than 100 programs to benefit people in a variety of life circumstances.

The sale to the Apollo Group brought benefits to the college as well. It continued to strengthen and expand its educational offerings while maintaining the Financial Paraplanner Program. In 1995, the college received accreditation from the Commission on Institutions of Higher Education of the North Central Association of Colleges and Schools; during the same year the Master of Science degree program was accredited by the Distance Education and Training Council. The college also joined the Internet era: By the end of the decade it transitioned from paper-and-pencil exams offered three times a year to online testing and study review.

Meanwhile, instruction leading to Certified Financial Planner certification was increasingly offered in colleges and universities throughout the United States and in other countries. (For the international scope of Certified Financial Planner instruction, see Chapter 6.) In early 2000, one institution, Texas Tech, even began offering a Ph.D. program in financial planning.

The Personal Economic Summit

"It's the economy, stupid" had been the mantra of Bill Clinton's 1992 presidential campaign, and many of his stump speeches emphasized the personal economics of American citizens. In 1993, as Clinton assumed office, the ICFP determined to celebrate its twentieth year by bringing financial literacy to the forefront with a "Personal Economic Summit" in Washington, D.C. "I predict it will be an historical event for the country and the profession," wrote Richard Wagner, who was midway through his term as ICFP chair.

> *The institute is twenty years old this year, and with our "coming of age"*
> *we feel we are ready to embrace the responsibilities of a true profession.*
> *One of these responsibilities is to understand the economic forces that*
> *affect the lives of average Americans, help our clients deal with these*
> *forces, and communicate what we've learned with those who make policy*
> *decisions.*

ICFP president Terry Siman added, "We are a different voice than the securities, insurance, banking, or accounting industries. We are the voice of a new professional advisor that represents the clients' interests in all these areas."

Some 300 representatives from business, government, academia, the media, consumer groups, and financial planning attended the summit. Among them were former U.S. Senators Bob Dole (R-Kansas), Paul Tsongas (D-Massachusetts), and Warren Rudman (R-New Hampshire), and former Colorado governor Dick Lamm. In panel discussions, open forums, and a town hall meeting, the summit addressed the major issues of the day: savings and debt, retirement, investments, and health care. The summit was reported on CNN and carried live in part by C-SPAN. Siman termed the event a "huge public relations success."

But it was not a moneymaker. Even though the ICFP had said at the outset that profitability was not its first priority, the setback caused some ICFP leaders to question the wisdom of sponsoring similar events in the future. In fact, the 1993 Personal Economic Summit was the first and last of its kind.

New Directions

The 1990s represented the maturing of the financial planning profession, as the once-warring IAFP and ICFP moved gradually but inexorably toward unity. It was also a period of international expansion: The IBCFP authorized the granting of CFP marks by financial planning organizations in Australia,

> *"We entered the world of professional legitimacy on January 1, 1993."*
> —Richard Wagner

Japan, and the United Kingdom in the first half of the 1990s, and seven additional countries—Canada, New Zealand, France, Germany, Singapore, South Africa, and Switzerland—between 1996 and 2000. (The IBCFP became the Certified Financial Planner Board of Standards, or CFP Board, on February 1, 1994.) It was also a period of intensified focus on professionalism, ethics, and regulation. The media, which just 10 years earlier had been skeptical of the financial planning profession, began recognizing its achievements. In 1994, the respected *Worth* magazine began including CFP professionals in its "Best 200 Financial Advisers in America" roundup; by 1996, the list included 173 CFP certificants.

Worth and other publications could not have failed to notice that the profession had redoubled its commitment to cleaning house and enforcing standards. A code of ethics had been an integral part of the ICFP's original constitution; it was formally adopted by members in July 1974 and reworked several times over the next decade. In the early 1990s, the IBCFP embarked—with input from the ICFP—on a new revision of the Code of Ethics and Professional Responsibility. It became effective in January 1993 and was formally adopted by the institute, which agreed to follow all future ethics rules established by the IBCFP. (Certified Financial Planner certificants who were not members of the institute were also subject to the IBCFP's Code of Ethics.) "We entered the world of professional legitimacy on January 1, 1993," wrote ICFP president Richard Wagner. "On this date, every CFP designee became subject to the letter and spirit of this excellent document. . . . I suggest that we be both proud and thankful."

The new code met its first major test not long afterward. J. Chandler Peterson, who had played a leading role in the IAFP during the 1970s, ran afoul of the law in the early 1990s, when he was convicted of theft, subjected to National Association of Securities Dealers (NASD) sanctions and fines, and found culpable in several civil matters. In December 1994, CFP Board (formerly the IBCFP) formally revoked Peterson's right to use the CFP marks. Although embarrassing to the profession, CFP Board's action sent a clear signal that no practitioner, no matter how prominent, would be exempt from the code of ethics.

At the same time, the ICFP strengthened its commitment to its members. It dropped its affiliate membership category in January 1995, and stopped distinguishing between CFP licensees who declared themselves as practitioners and those who did not. One reason for this decision was CFP Board's acquisition, also in early 1995, of the Registry of Financial Planning Practitioners from the IAFP. The IAFP's registry had been a disappointment to some and a flashpoint for many since its inception in 1983; because it was "designation neutral," many CFP licensees opted not to join it, and it never had more than about 1,000 members. The registry's transfer to CFP Board represented the culmination of several years of top-level diplomacy between the organizations, mostly on the part of Bill Carter, a former IAFP president who was chairman of CFP Board in the early 1990s. "I totally supported the notion of 'One Profession, One Designation,'" Carter later recalled. "I believed that the financial planning profession needed to coalesce around one mark."[5]

Profile: Bill E. Carter

Bill Carter thought of the IAFP's Registry of Financial Planning Practitioners—launched during his tenure as chair of the organization in 1983–1984—as his "baby." But a decade later, it was Carter who led the transfer of the registry to CFP Board, spending countless hours and his own money to travel across the country convincing IAFP leaders that it was time to let the registry go.

"The registry had become a barrier to a more important goal: getting the IAFP and the ICFP together," Carter said. "I figured that if CFP Board owned the registry, the two organizations would not have anything more to argue about."

Tim Kochis, J.D., CFP, was president of CFP Board at the time. He wrote in 1995, "Bill was probably the only person in the industry who could have built the bridges between the organizations to make this happen."

That ability to see the larger picture, combined with political savvy and intrinsic optimism, put Carter in a unique position to move among IAFP, ICFP, and CFP Board leaders. "I could get along with all sides," he said, "but I always thought that it was a waste of money and talent to have two organizations. Neither the IAFP nor the ICFP had had much credibility in Washington—government regulators hesitated to take sides because they didn't know which organization would be left standing."

Raised on a farm near Decatur, Texas, Carter completed a stint in the Army and took a chance on an advertising franchise in Indiana, where he was defrauded of $15,000 in borrowed money. "I moved back to Texas at the ripe age of 26, broke and very humiliated," he recalled. There he met Kay Baird, a member of the first graduating class of CFP certificants, who introduced him to financial planning. Carter found his calling and soon became involved in financial planning organizations. He served simultaneously on the national boards of the IAFP and ICFP from 1980 through 1983, and was chair of the IAFP in 1983–1984. He also served as president of CFP Board in 1993, chair of CFP Board in 1994, and chair of the Foundation for Financial Planning in 2003.

Although the transfer of the registry to CFP Board helped pave the way for the eventual formation of the Financial Planning Association in 2000, it came at a price that Carter did not anticipate. In 1996, the year after Carter left CFP Board, the registry was retired. "I went ballistic," Carter later recalled. "I had sold the idea to IAFP leaders on the basis that the registry would be administered by CFP Board, not shut down. It put me in a terrible position because it looked like I had gone back on my word.

"I still think that there should be a registry," Carter added. "Consumers need a way to find CFP certificants who practice comprehensive financial planning."

In the years after stepping down from leadership positions at the IAFP and CFP Board, Carter devoted much of his time to the Foundation for Financial Planning, an organization he said "matched up with my values." The financial planning profession makes a living from the public, he observed; it's important to give back to the public as well. "My work for the foundation has truly been a labor of love," Carter said. "Fulfilling the foundation's purpose—educating the public about the value of the financial planning process—will continue in perpetuity."

Jack Blankinship was chairman of CFP Board in 1995. "I had some misgivings about spending the money to acquire the registry and the test questions from the IAFP's Practice Knowledge Exam," he said. "But we wanted to get the job done. The registry had been such a contentious thing over the years. We wanted the CFP mark to represent the highest standard in financial planning, and we felt that acquiring the registry was a step in that direction."

As part of the agreement, the ICFP agreed to end its own registry. And, after years of being "purer than thou," as one critic described it, the ICFP began accepting corporate product exhibits for ICFP events at its 1994 Retreat in Colorado Springs.

The Foundation for Financial Planning

For the IAFP, 1995 was significant for another reason. In January of that year, the association restructured its nonprofit IAFP Foundation as an independent entity and renamed it the Foundation for Financial Planning. The original foundation had been created in 1981 to assist the IAFP with public awareness activities. By 1988, however, the IAFP had too many financial challenges to do anything but maintain the foundation in a caretaker mode, where it remained for the next seven years.

The newly independent foundation had a revised mission: to develop resources and make grants rather than to implement programs. With the help of a consulting firm, the foundation surveyed financial planners and discovered enthusiastic support for this goal and for an endowment to fund it. With Don Pitti chairing the effort, the foundation embarked on its first endowment fund campaign, raising nearly $7 million from individuals and corporations.

In October 1998, the foundation awarded its first grants: a $10,000 challenge grant for a research project to identify the financial planning needs of college students and a $20,000 grant for the development of a community-based financial education center. In the decade that followed, it awarded 58 grants, totaling more than $200,000, to nonprofit organizations that connected people in need with the financial planning community. The foundation is incorporated in the state of Georgia and reaches out nationwide to individual financial planners and companies that provide products and support for the profession.

Legal Milestone: *Ibanez v. Florida*

When is it permissible to use the CFP marks in advertising? That was the First Amendment issue tested in the early 1990s—when advertising by professionals was newly sanctioned—by Silvia Ibanez, a lawyer in Winter Haven, Florida, who was also a certified public accountant and a CFP certificant. Primarily engaged in the practice of law, Ibanez used her CPA and CFP credentials to advertise her qualifications to the public. The Florida Board of Accountancy, however, wanted her to cease and desist from using those credentials, calling it false, deceptive, and misleading advertising.

Despite support from CFP Board, Ibanez lost her 1994 case before a state administrative tribunal; she appealed to the Florida Supreme Court, and lost there as well. Undaunted, Ibanez decided to take her case to the U.S. Supreme Court. CFP Board filed two amicus briefs: one requesting the appeal and a second on the merits of the case, citing data on the meaning and value of the federal marks. Ibanez argued the case herself, asserting her right to truthful information that could be useful to clients.

"I sat in the court and watched her," Bob Goss—executive director of CFP Board at the time—later recalled. "You talk about passion—she had a *lot* of passion. We won big time, and the justices quoted from the board's brief about the value of the CFP designation."[6] In its decision on June 13, 1994, the U.S. Supreme Court noted that more than 27,000 people nationwide had earned the CFP designation and that more than 50 accredited universities and colleges had established courses of study in financial planning registered with CFP Board. The Court also acknowledged that the CFP Board required rigorous examination of candidates before conferring the CFP designation.

Other legal victories followed, including a 1998 U.S. District Court ruling that the CFP marks were "distinctive and famous." These victories were a major confirmation of the value of the CFP mark and important acknowledgment that financial planning was, in fact, a profession on a par with others.

"I believe we truly are a new and vibrant profession, not merely a movement. Movements have a historical tendency to fade, while the profession of financial planning is the service profession for the future."

—John S. Longstaff

Storm over "CFP Lite"

In its initial decade, CFP Board was widely regarded as a politicized body torn between the conflicting philosophies of the IAFP and ICFP, many of whose leaders assumed key CFP Board roles. Larry Hayden, the body's first executive director, told a reporter for *Financial Planning* magazine that "an atmosphere of controversy has surrounded the board since its inception." That atmosphere reached a high-pressure point in 1999, when CFP Board's board of governors proposed licensing a second professional mark, Associate CFP, for entry-level practitioners.

The outcry from Certified Financial Planner licensees was swift and impassioned. Many practitioners disdainfully labeled the proposed mark "CFP Lite." At a meeting at the Adam's Mark Hotel in Dallas, Hayden's successor, Robert P. Goss, faced a crowd of licensees angered not only by the Associate CFP proposal but by the fact that they'd heard about it from a source other than CFP Board itself.

In the cover story for the September 1999 issue of *Financial Planning*, Eva Marer described the scene in Dallas:

"Was there a fire?" asked one man. "Why not give us some facts before you make a decision that directly affects our livelihoods?"

"CFP Lite is a hoax on the public!" asserted another licensee, to wild applause, "and a hoax on the CFP community!"

In measured tones, Goss pointed out that CFP Lite was not an officially recognized expression.

Despite his unemotional demeanor, and although as a nonvoting member of the board of governors he had not voted on the proposal, Goss in fact felt strongly about the Associate CFP mark. He hoped the new entry-level designation would give all Americans, regardless of income, access to a financial planner who had met at least a minimum industry standard. "We're engaged in a cause that's monumentally important to Americans of all backgrounds," Goss told *Financial Planning*.

In the end, Goss and other proponents were outnumbered. "Ninety-nine percent of the people in the room were enraged," recalled Richard Wagner, who attended the meeting. "Nobody supported CFP Lite except Goss and the CFP Board. It was a bad idea presented badly, not a good idea whose time hadn't come."

The grassroots protests prevailed. At the next CFP Board meeting, Goss recommended that the action be rescinded, and "Associate CFP" was withdrawn.

Profile: Robert P. Goss

When the IBCFP established a search committee in 1991 to find a successor to Larry Hayden, the organization's first executive director, the committee drew up a list of 21 characteristics it felt the chief staff person should have. Tom Potts, who led the search, told *Financial Planning* magazine in 1999 that Bob Goss "had nineteen of those characteristics."[7]

Goss moved from the ICFP, where he had served three years as executive director. (Before that, he had worked with elected officials in Washington, D.C., and many state capitals.) Between 1991 and 2000 he shepherded CFP Board through many major events, some lauded as advances for the financial planning profession, others criticized as heavy-handed decisions made in a vacuum. Goss's self-composure no doubt helped him ride the waves, but it was not the only quality attributed to him. His supporters and critics variously labeled him as visionary, enigmatic, strategic, secretive, and misunderstood.

And also modest. Asked in 2008 to name his top accomplishments at CFP Board, Goss said, "Some things occurred on my watch that I believe furthered the financial planning profession, but it wouldn't be fair to say that they occurred because of me. It was a team effort of CFP Board's many volunteers and the staff."

From his perspective, those team accomplishments included expanding the CFP certification program to colleges and universities across the United States; administering a new, comprehensive certification examination; beginning the process of developing practice standards for the profession; overseeing the revival of peer review and disciplinary process for ethics complaints; protecting the status of the CFP marks in the United States and overseas; developing strategic relationships with other professional and consumer groups, academia, and government regulators; promoting a global financial planning profession; and positioning CFP Board as the profession's self-regulatory organization.

Not every initiative met with success, and one produced a major upset: a proposal to establish an Associate CFP designation—"CFP Lite," as critics called it. Years later, Goss recalled the genesis of the idea. "We were concerned that financial planning had a standard of no standard," he said. "In other words, anyone could do financial planning, and we were seeing some evidence of a growing number of so-called financial planners who did not adhere to standards. We asked ourselves what we could do to encourage more people to adhere to at least some standard, as a way to protect the public, even if the standard was not as high as required for CFP certification." The concept met with so much resistance from CFP certificants that CFP Board rescinded the proposal upon Goss's recommendation. Still, Goss never changed his mind about an entry-level designation being "a worthwhile idea" in the absence of government-imposed entry-level standards.

The following year, Goss resigned from CFP Board, although he denies that his departure had anything to do with the Associate CFP controversy; he cited exhaustion and family obligations. Goss, whose credentials included a law degree and a Ph.D. in public administration, eventually moved to Provo, Utah, where he became a faculty member and assistant dean at Brigham Young University's College of Family, Home and Social Services.

Marv Tuttle, CEO and executive director of the Financial Planning Association, praised Goss in 2008. "The CFP certification marks would not be down the road this far today if we had not had Bob Goss in

(continued)

Profile: Robert P. Goss (*Continued*)

the 1990s," he said. Kevin Keller, CEO of CFP Board, added, "Bob's legacy endures today, as the rigor and structure of the CFP certification requirements receive increased recognition."

During a roundtable discussion in 2000, Goss reflected on what financial planning meant to him. "Financial planning may be a business, but it's not inherently a business," he said. "It's an act to serve in the best interests of others. That's the heart and soul of it for me."[8]

Unification Revisited

More than one leader of the financial planning profession credits an article that appeared in *Financial Planning* in September 1997 as the catalyst for a renewed attempt at unification between the IAFP and ICFP. The article, written by outgoing IAFP president Peggy Ruhlin, was titled "If I Ruled the World."

"It was my last article as president," Ruhlin later recalled, "and I decided to say what was on my mind." In one paragraph, she wrote that if she ruled the world, anyone who called himself or herself a financial planner would be a CFP licensee, and the IAFP and ICFP would merge. She showed a rough draft of the article to the IAFP board in August, and "it caused quite a stir," she said.

As Ruhlin explained it in her article, if the American public, the media, and regulators were to recognize financial planning as a true profession, they needed to be able to identify a single standard for minimum competence. "Here's how I looked at it," Ruhlin later said. "If I were giving advice to a young person who wanted to enter this profession, what would I say? I would advise that they get their CFP license, and I think most planners, even those with other credentials, would agree with me."

As it happened, the executive committees of the IAFP and ICFP boards had scheduled a joint meeting in August, at the same time that Ruhlin was circulating her draft. "Someone suggested that I share the article with the ICFP," Ruhlin said. "So we made copies of the manuscript and passed it around."

The results were stunning. Judy Lau, CFP, 1997 president of the ICFP and a longtime friend of Ruhlin's, stood up, pointed to the paragraph about merging, and said, "Where do I sign?"

After the meeting, Ruhlin and Lau talked privately. "Judy told me that it would be great if the two organizations could unite," Ruhlin later recalled, "but she didn't see how the two groups could begin to talk until the IAFP endorsed the CFP designation."

Ruhlin took that message back to the IAFP board, suggesting that it revisit the designation-neutral position. "Things began to move quickly," she said. "We knew it was a leap of faith to endorse the CFP mark in the hopes of getting merger talks going again, but it also wasn't reason enough to vote for it. I asked the board to vote yes only if they felt in their hearts and minds that it was the right thing to do."

The endorsement passed unanimously. In October 1997, IAFP executive director Janet G. McCallen said, "As the financial planning community grew and more consumers recognized the need for the financial assistance, the IAFP felt that the time was right to unite the profession behind one widely recognized designation and reduce consumer confusion."

For the ICFP, the endorsement was a watershed event. "We had been doing a lot of strategic thinking in the late 1990s," Judy Lau later said. "It was clear that we needed to expand our ranks if we were to have the clout necessary to move this profession forward. We also agreed that if the IAFP ever decided to back the CFP mark, it would change the world we lived in."

Now that the major barriers between the two organizations had disappeared, the IAFP and ICFP began cooperating in earnest. Each organization named seven members to a project team; two of them, Eileen Sharkey (a financial planner and past president of the ICFP) and M. Anthony Greene (president of a broker-dealer firm and past president of the IAFP), had been on opposite sides of the fence during the previous merger attempt, 10 years earlier. Their historical perspective proved valuable, Ruhlin noted.

The IAFP and ICFP split the costs of hiring a consultant to facilitate the project team's discussions. One of his first recommendations: The team should explore the creation of a new financial planning association rather than merging the two existing organizations.

"We agreed because it opened up our thinking to new possibilities," said Roy T. Diliberto, CLU, ChFC, CFP, an IAFP project team member who in 2000 became the first president of the newly formed Financial Planning Association. Peggy Ruhlin agreed. "The 'M' word, *merger*, was forbidden. We always talked about The New Organization, or TNO. It could become the organization of our dreams, not a power struggle of who would take over whom."

"The 'M' word, merger, *was forbidden. We always talked about The New Organization, or TNO."*

—Peggy Ruhlin

Meeting about every six weeks, usually in Chicago, the team eventually hammered out a "core ideology," which it presented to a joint meeting of the IAFP and ICFP boards in Philadelphia in October 1998. According to notes from that meeting, the purpose of The New Organization was to "be the community responsible for establishing the value of financial planning and the success of the financial planning profession." It would have one primary goal: *There will be universal acceptance of the value and necessity of professional financial planning.* And it would have these core values:

- Financial planning improves the quality of life.
- The highest level of competency and integrity is paramount.
- Success of members is key.
- Inclusiveness of an open forum must be maintained.
- The financial planning profession needs one common designation.
- Clients' interests should come first.

The boards approved the goals and gave the project team the green light to flesh them out. Meetings continued throughout 1998; by early 1999, the team had drafted a memorandum of intent, which was passionately debated for two months. It was finally approved in March. The name chosen for the new organization was the Financial Planning Association. Bylaws were drafted, and in May the ICFP board was ready to take the plan to a vote by its members. The IAFP did not hold a formal membership vote; instead, it gauged members' support through informal discussions and surveys.

In a letter to members, ICFP president Elissa Buie, CFP, made the case for the Financial Planning Association:

> *The strength of the ICFP has always been its focus on the CFP licensee. The strength of the IAFP has always been its focus on the value of including everyone who champions the financial planning process and the opportunity for those people to interact. We have found these two organizational values, which at one time might have appeared mutually exclusive, to be compatible and even synergistic. This new organization will become the community responsible for promoting the value of financial planning and the success of the financial planning profession.*

ICFP bylaws dictated that for the board's recommendation to pass, at least 10 percent of CFP members needed to vote and more than two-thirds of those voting had to approve the recommendation. In fact, 66 percent of eligible voters cast a ballot and 81 percent voted in favor.

The vote was a "fantastic mandate," according to the ICFP's 1998 president, Robert J. Klosterman, CLU, ChFC, CFP, who had been a member of

Market Milestone: The World Wide Web

There would be no Google, Amazon, Wikipedia, or Facebook, no on-line shopping or polling or test-taking—and certainly no FPAnet.org—without the contributions of Tim Berners-Lee. It was Berners-Lee, an English scientist working at the Swiss research facility CERN, who developed hypertext markup language and created the first Web server and Web site—all between 1989 and 1992. He was building on the Internet, which had been created more than two decades earlier as a way for university and military computers to exchange information. What Berners-Lee and other Web pioneers did was enable any computer user, on any platform, to transmit and receive not just data but images and multimedia files as well.

By 1994, two giants of the new technology, Netscape and Yahoo!, had emerged. Netscape's initial public offering, in August 1995, foreshadowed the dot-com fever that soon followed: In its first few minutes of trading, Netscape's share price rose from $28 to $54, valuing the company at $2 billion. The rush was on. In June 1998, a *Time* magazine reporter gushed that "[n]ot since Bill Gates took Microsoft public in 1986 has Wall Street witnessed anything like the wealth-creating power of today's Internet stocks." By March 10, 2000, Internet stocks led the Nasdaq Composite Index to its highest close yet, 5,048.62. Some market watchers predicted a "long boom" or an eventual Dow Jones peak of 36,000. But by mid-2000 the party was over, and by late September 2002, the bear market had resulted in the loss of $4.4 trillion in market value—at the time, the largest stock market collapse in world history.

the project team. "We had worked very hard to break through barriers and get to a better place, and I think we did that."

Throughout 1999, the two boards applied themselves to finalizing the details of the new organization. The stage was set for the long-awaited debut of the Financial Planning Association on New Year's Day, 2000.

CHAPTER 5

Responding to New Challenges

The Financial Planning Association came into being at a giddy global moment. Driven by the technology boom of the 1990s, stock market indexes had soared, and tales of overnight wealth were spread throughout the news media. On January 14, 2000, two weeks after FPA's official launch, the Dow Jones Industrial Average closed at a then-record 11,722.98; the Nasdaq Composite reached a never-before-seen 5,048.62 on March 10; and the broader Standard & Poor's 500 index closed at 1,533.11 on March 24. There was talk of the boom continuing forever, of the Dow eventually reaching 36,000.

That sense of optimism carried over to the first meeting of the FPA board in early January. The new millennium had begun; a sense of unity and purpose animated the participants. Roy T. Diliberto, CLU, ChFC, CFP, of Philadelphia won a coin toss with Guy Cumbie, the ICFP's president-elect, and became FPA's first president. (Diliberto had already been serving as the IAFP's president-elect.) The former presidents of the IAFP and ICFP—Joseph Votava, Jr., a lawyer and CFP certificant based in Rochester, New York, and Elissa Buie, CFP, of Falls Church, Virginia—served as co-chairs. Convening at Miami's Fontainebleau Hotel, the board formally ratified the merger and also approved the final mission statement, which said, in part,

> *The primary aim of the Financial Planning Association (FPA) is to be the community that fosters the value of financial planning and advances the financial planning profession. . . . FPA welcomes into membership all those who advance the financial planning process and promotes the CFP mark as the cornerstone of the financial planning profession. . . . FPA believes that everyone needs objective advice to make smart financial decisions and that when seeking the advice of a financial planner, the planner should be a CFP professional.*

"What is the Financial Planning Association?" the introductory statement continued. It answered the question:

The Financial Planning Association is the membership organization for the financial planning community. FPA has been built around four core values—competence, integrity, relationships, and stewardship. We want as members those who share our core values.

Those hopeful sentiments and high ideals would soon be put to the test.

Building a New Organization

The stock markets began their decline in the second quarter of 2000 as the dot-com boom turned to bust. But the year was a productive one for FPA, which now had 100 chapters and more than 30,000 members as a result of the merger—approximately 17,000 from each of the merged organizations, with about 4,000 members who had held dual memberships.

The mood was upbeat in September, when nearly 3,800 FPA members and guests gathered in Boston at Success Forum 2000, the new organization's first annual conference. (The first FPA Retreat, for advanced practitioners, had taken place in Phoenix the previous April.) "Things are going great," FPA president Roy Diliberto told the Boston audience. "The merger has significantly helped our stature and impact with respect to government and media relations," observed FPA co-chair Elissa Buie. The other co-chair, Joseph Votava, Jr., sounded only a mild note of caution: "Our chapters around the country are going through [a] process of recombining members and geography"—making sure chapter territories didn't overlap and underserved members were picked up. "In some cases, they have had to reincorporate and dissolve old legal entities. That's difficult, and it's taking time."

Some chapters were in cities where only one predecessor organization had existed, so there was no need for merger. In cities where the IAFP and ICFP had coexisted, members pitched in to speed up the restructuring. Volunteers "had to find time to write bylaws, file new incorporation documents, and sign affiliation agreements with the national FPA," said Wendy Todd, who was serving as director of chapter relations. FPA executive director Janet McCallen had high praise for the effort: "The chapters accomplished on a local level in nine to twelve months what had taken the national organization two and a half years to get done."

> *"The chapters accomplished on a local level in nine to twelve months what had taken the national organization two and a half years to get done."*
>
> —Janet McCallen

The process wasn't always seamless. In some places, database problems made it nearly impossible to reconcile local and national records. In May 2000, the national staff stepped in and offered to work with local chapters; 44 chapters accepted the help.

"FPA's chapters are the foundation on which this organization is built," Todd said at the time. "The board of directors made it a priority to support the chapters with time, dollars, and staff." Todd was supported in her job by a chapter advisory council made up of 16 former leaders of IAFP chapters and ICFP societies.

FPA gathered momentum on the national level as well. Its representatives met with CFP Board to begin developing a strategic partnership and participated in International CFP Council meetings in South Africa and Germany. (For more about international developments, see Chapter 6.) Two new departments, career development and research and community development, were created to help new and veteran planners alike. With FPA associate executive director Marv Tuttle as its editor and publisher, the *Journal of Financial Planning* increased its publishing schedule from 8 to 12 issues a year. And a new government relations office in Washington, D.C., headed by former lobbyist and FPA director of government relations Duane Thompson, established FPA as an authoritative voice for the financial planning community.

The new association also took stock of its accomplishments. In an article titled "To Feel...Like a CFP," published in the July 2000 issue of the *Journal of Financial Planning*, Elissa Buie, CFP, reflected on how far the profession had come since the publication of Dick Wagner's "To Think...Like a CFP," a decade earlier, and acknowledged that the journey was still in progress:

> *If we have come so far to fulfill Dick's vision, then why are financial planners leading "lives of quiet desperation"? Why is it so difficult to define financial planning and a financial planner?...*
>
> *The answer may be because as we have progressed with the thinking part of being planners, we've discovered we need a lot more progress in the feeling part. Our emphasis on thinking without commensurate attention being paid to feelings has led to uncertainty....*
>
> *When at our best, we combine our true understanding of finances with our understanding of and care for the client to provide recommendations that come from the heart and that provide opportunities for clients' lives that might otherwise go unconsidered. This is a unique ability of the financial planning profession. It is what makes this profession distinct from the purveyors of its component parts—and what makes it great.*

"When at our best, we combine our true understanding of finances with our understanding of and care for the client."

—Elissa Buie

Profile: Elissa Buie

In the early 1980s, Elissa Buie was working at Heritage Financial Group, a boutique brokerage firm in Falls Church, Virginia, doing "what then passed for financial planning—cash flow, tax analysis, observations and recommendations that were too often designed to encourage a transaction." At night, as part of her MBA studies at the University of Maryland, she took a course in financial planning. "The light bulb went on," she said. "I asked the brokerage firm if I could start a financial planning division where we would write real financial plans. They said yes, and I never looked back."

Buie joined the board of the Northern Virginia ICFP Society in 1989, shortly after she earned her CFP certification. She eventually became president of that local society and in 1994 joined the national ICFP board.

By the time merger talks with the IAFP began, in 1997, Buie was serving as the ICFP's president-elect. By February 1999, she was the institute's president, and negotiations over a memorandum of intent were still continuing. "We would send a version to one organization and they would say, 'Oh, no, this is horrible!' Then they would rewrite it and send it back, and the other group would say, 'Oh, no, this is horrible!'" Her role, she said, was to "help create the space for open, impactful dialogue that led to a new professional association with more potential for building the profession than either association had previously envisioned."

After the merger, Buie and Joseph Votava, Jr., became FPA's co-chairs, and Buie took responsibility for establishing FPA's brand in the marketplace, using the CFP credential as a platform. The CFP mark, she maintained, "represents a body of knowledge, a code of ethics, and practice standards. The letters 'CFP' become a way of discussing what they represent with the public." Her reflections on brand and image led her to write "To Feel . . . Like a CFP," which was published in the *Journal of Financial Planning* in July 2000.

Buie remained actively involved in the financial planning profession after she completed her term. She became dean of FPA's Residency program in 2007 and has served on several FPA committees and task forces, including the Leadership Development Subcommittee. She also served on the Foundation for Financial Planning's board of trustees.

CFP Board Fleshes Out Its Mission

After the debacle of the Associate CFP initiative, Bob Goss resigned as president of CFP Board. Dede Pahl became interim executive director until Lou Garday was hired to fill the position permanently; Patricia P. Houlihan, CFP, became chair.

Houlihan and Garday faced the tough task of rebuilding relationships with CFP certificants who had been angered by "CFP Lite" while designing a structure that would accommodate the profession's rapidly expanding international movement. "The 1999 meeting in Dallas was a watershed," Houlihan later said. "It forced the board to understand the importance of transparency—to acknowledge that it's never good to do everything in secrecy."

In the 2000 CFP Board annual report, Houlihan introduced four fundamental values intended to inform the public and provide direction for CFP Board's governing boards and staff:

1. ***Accountability to the public.*** *We believe that the primary reason for our existence is to promote the public welfare through standards in personal financial planning. We value client-centered relationships and the differentiation of personal financial planning professionals from other financial service providers and advisers.*
2. ***Trust derived from standards.*** *We believe that CFP Board's individual certification standards advance the systematic body of knowledge and enhance respect for the personal financial planning professional. We value the demonstration of the initial and ongoing competency required for a professional to obtain and retain the CFP marks.*
3. ***Commitment to excellence.*** *We believe that the CFP marks represent excellence in personal financial planning, not as an educational credential, but as a professional obligation to a higher standard of conduct. We value the seven principles of integrity,*

objectivity, competence, fairness, confidentiality, professionalism, and diligence that exemplify professional behavior.

4. **Respect for professionals.** *We believe that the public benefits from the existence of a growing pool of competent financial planning professionals who place the interests of the client first. We value the input and involvement from individuals, organizations, and firms who are committed to serving the public by strengthening the culture of professional financial planning.*

During 1999 and 2000, CFP Board also began discussions with the International Organization for Standardization (ISO) about global standards for financial planning. (For more on ISO, see Chapter 6.) It partnered with the Securities and Exchange Commission in an investor town meeting, collaborated with the Social Security Administration to do financial planning education in workplaces, and worked with the U.S. Department of Labor to produce a booklet highlighting the role financial planning can play in saving for retirement.

Despite these achievements, CFP Board was still experiencing turbulence. Between 2000 and 2004, four people occupied the CEO seat. Two of them—Bob Goss and Lou Garday—left their posts abruptly. The other two—Dede Pahl and Gary Diffendaffer—served on an interim basis while CFP Board conducted searches for permanent leadership.

Their efforts notwithstanding, by November 2004, when Sarah Teslik arrived in Denver to take the reins, CFP Board was facing a financial deficit and a number of operational snafus. "Seven million dollars on computers over three years and people couldn't always sign up for the exam online and use their credit card," was how Teslik described the situation in an interview with the *Journal of Financial Planning*.[1] Teslik, a lawyer and the founding executive director of the Council of Institutional Investors, made waves by reducing CFP Board's staff by more than half—from 80 to 30—in less than nine months. She eliminated the organization's financial deficit and also introduced ambitious plans for reaching the public through new vehicles. But her term was noteworthy mostly for tension and conflict with CFP certificants. She was replaced in November 2006 by yet another interim CEO, Don Tharpe.

Hopes for stability ran high with the hiring of Kevin R. Keller, CAE (Certified Association Executive), as CEO in April 2007. Keller came to the job after more than 20 years in association-management leadership, including 16 years at the Association for Financial Professionals. Keller accomplished the move of CFP Board from Denver to Washington, D.C., in late 2007 and began positioning it as a voice on public policy matters. He also rebuilt the organization's professional staff, severely reduced during Teslik's tenure.

Crisis and Catastrophe

Despite the continuing slide of the financial markets, 2001 looked to be a promising year for the financial planning profession. The biggest boost came from *The Jobs Rated Almanac 2001,* by Les Krantz, which rated financial planner as the number-one job in the United States. Of the six criteria—environment, income, outlook, physical demands, security, and stress—only the last received a poor score. Krantz wrote, "Facing the crises of market volatility and economic cycles can be stressful. Recommending the best financial decisions for clients can be stressful. When financial plans fail to perform up to expectations, there is stress."

But *stress* was too mild a word to describe the horror and panic of September 11, 2001, which struck at the very heart of American capitalism and shocked the financial services community. Enveloped by smoke and ash, the New York Stock Exchange remained closed for four business days—the first time since 1933 that it had shut down for so long.

"The 9/11 attacks were a wake-up call for FPA and the profession," said Guy Cumbie, who was serving as FPA president at the time. He and the rest of FPA's board of directors were in San Diego, preparing for the Success Forum. Marv Tuttle recalled the scene:

> *The board of directors was having breakfast while watching the events unfold. The only business we conducted on September 11 was to elect a new president-elect for the organization and to determine whether Success Forum should go on. The answer was obvious: the U.S. transportation system had been shut down, and members and exhibitors would not have been able to get to San Diego. We immediately began an intensive communications effort to members, attendees, exhibitors, sponsors, and vendors to minimize the impact on all those who would be affected. We returned registration fees, exhibit fees, and sponsorship fees. The board voted to cover all costs out of reserves if cancellation insurance did not come through.*

Fortunately, FPA's chief financial officer, Curt Niepoth, had secured an event-cancellation insurance policy just weeks before the event was to take place. "The cost was about $20,000, and I had to strongly encourage FPA to agree to it," Niepoth recalled. (In a twist of fate, the insurance agent for the policy was Aon, whose New York offices occupied nine floors of the World Trade Center's south tower.) From the nearly $2 million in insurance money, FPA was able to refund conference fees. But Success Forum was not forgotten: Between November 1 and December 4, FPA conducted a "virtual Success Forum," a phone and Web presentation of the education programs that had been planned for San Diego.

Next, FPA turned its attention to the after-effects of the September 11 terrorist attacks.

Clare Stenstrom, CFP, president of FPA's New York chapter, had been in San Diego in preparation for the Success Forum. Because planes still weren't flying, she drove back to New York, listening to the radio and thinking of ways she could help those in need. "I couldn't touch those who had been hurt," she said later. "But I felt I could do something unique to help. I found many other planners who felt the same way."[2] With the support of the national FPA board, Stenstrom began calling other chapter leaders and the Foundation for Financial Planning. Guy Cumbie, at FPA, and Don Pitti, the foundation's president, pledged their support. Help also came from Susan Bradley, CFP, founder of the life-transition resource center Sudden Money Institute; she made her training protocol available free of cost to all volunteers. Money Tree Software, makers of a popular financial planning program, donated software licenses. Word quickly got out, and 400 planners signed on to learn how to deal with grieving families' financial challenges. Eventually, more than 700 planners from across the country volunteered to work with 9/11 families.

As their efforts continued, it was clear that volunteerism and in-kind donations would not be sufficient to sustain them. Marv Tuttle at FPA wrote grant proposals to the Foundation for Financial Planning and Chase Manhattan Bank and negotiated final funding that totaled more than $330,000. With that money, and with office space donated by Chase, FPA established the National Financial Planning Support Center and hired a full-time paid staffer, banking and financial services veteran Clara Lipson, who began work in March 2002.

"Our volunteers provided basic financial planning to victims and their families," Lipson said. "Many widows had no clue about their husbands' finances." Indirect victims, such as limousine drivers who had abruptly lost their livelihood, also sought assistance. In addition, the center trained pro bono attorneys, most of them trial lawyers who volunteered to help families deal with lump-sum settlements, in the fundamentals of financial planning.

The outreach continued for several years following the attacks. The American Red Cross provided additional grant funds, and FPA volunteers established working relationships with the Salvation Army, FEMA, and other social-welfare and governmental agencies. In October 2003, FPA took out a full-page advertisement in the *New York Times* and *Washington Post,* offering every family directly affected by the 9/11 tragedy "immediate and long-term financial planning advice—without charge." The ad enumerated a host of available services, including consultation about medical, disability, and life insurance; help with bill paying, budgeting, and cash-flow management; and coordination with relief agencies to receive benefits.

The financial planning community's response to 9/11 marked the beginning of an ongoing movement to provide pro bono services in times of need. "Individual planners had been providing pro bono services for many years," noted Jonathan Sprague, who became FPA's director of pro bono services in 2006, succeeding Clara Lipson. "But it wasn't until 9/11 that an organization-wide effort was implemented." In 2005, a similar response was mobilized for the Gulf Coast victims of Hurricane Katrina—including members of FPA. More than 50 FPA chapters continue to manage active pro bono programs in their communities with grant support from the Foundation for Financial Planning.

Favorable Signs

The stock markets continued their slide throughout 2002 as the dot-com boom turned into the "dot-bomb" bust; by late September, the Nasdaq closed at 1,185, and investors had seen the loss of $4.4 trillion in market value[3]—at the time, the largest stock market decline in history. Yet despite the terrible economic news, the financial planning profession continued to grow in absolute numbers and in stature. The number of CFP certificants worldwide increased 11 percent in 2002, to 73,618, and grew another 9 percent in 2003, to 80,973. Growth outside the United States was especially impressive; between 2000 and 2002, financial planning organizations in Hong Kong, South Korea, Austria, Brazil, and Malaysia became authorized to certify CFP professionals. CFP Board chair Patricia Houlihan went on record predicting a time in the near future when the CFP marks would become truly global. (International growth is covered in greater detail in Chapter 6.) FPA's net assets climbed steadily as well, reaching nearly $4.5 million at the end of 2003. In 2004, the association finally closed its Atlanta office, a legacy of the IAFP era, and consolidated its headquarters in Denver. The move was both symbolic and practical: It communicated a unity of purpose to members and allowed FPA to save on operating expenses.

The old financial services establishment, at least in the United States, was not faring as well. Conflicts of interest and outright fraud in securities firms had caused thousands of investors to lose millions of dollars. In the spring of 2002, the New York Supreme Court ordered Merrill Lynch to reform its business practices;[4] the state's attorney general, Eliot Spitzer, fined Merrill Lynch $100 million. In subsequent months, 12 other Wall Street investment banks were assessed a total of about $1.4 billion in fines and penalties for conflicts of interest and other infractions. "This system was rotten, and no one seemed interested in fixing it, so I moved in," Spitzer said. Other corporate giants brought low that year included Enron (wire fraud, money laundering, conspiracy), Tyco (whose CEO was indicted on 31 felony counts), and ImClone (insider trading).

For the most part, though, the financial planning profession escaped being tarred with Wall Street's brush. It achieved a significant milestone in 2002, when the U.S. Patent and Trademark Office approved the trademark registration of *CFP*. The increased level of protection afforded by federal registration strengthened CFP Board's ability to distinguish the services and standards of CFP certificants on behalf of the public and the profession. As with other trademarks, *CFP* was to be used as an adjective only—as in "a CFP certificant," not "a CFP"; its use with the registration symbol ($^{®}$) was similarly authorized.

Financial planning brought its message of competence and impartiality to the public in the first National Financial Planning Week, held in October 2002. Aided by information from the national association, more than 80 state and regional FPA chapters partnered with schools, libraries, and other groups to offer clinics, seminars, telephone hotlines, and other services to groups of all ages, incomes, and interests. Heather Almand, who served as FPA's director of public relations from 2002 through early 2009, oversaw the rollout of the program, which continues to be held each October.

Financial Planning Standards Board

The rapid increase in the number of CFP professionals around the world—from 31,000 in 1996 to just over 120,000 in 2008—was cause for celebration; it was also a signal that a new model was needed for managing the expanding international program. It was becoming increasingly impractical for CFP Board to give the international side of its organization the attention it needed while also focusing on the U.S. agenda.

In 2002, CFP Board and the International CFP Council began laying the groundwork for the creation of Financial Planning Standards Board Ltd. (FPSB). This nonprofit association was launched in December 2004 to develop and manage certification, education, and related programs for financial planning organizations worldwide, with an objective of setting, upholding, and promoting global financial planning standards. In his formal announcement of FPSB's creation, made in London in 2004, CFP Board chair David H. Diesslin, CFP, noted that "the trajectory of the international CFP marks has been phenomenal since CFP Board signed a license and affiliation agreement with Financial Planning Association of Australia in 1990. The time is right to have the international CFP marks and certification program managed, developed, and operated by international staff, volunteers and consultants."

Founding members included financial planning associations and standards-setting bodies in 17 countries: Australia, Austria, Brazil, Canada, France, Germany, Hong Kong, India, Japan, the Republic of Korea, Malaysia, New Zealand, Singapore, South Africa, Switzerland, Taiwan (referred to as Chinese Taipei), and the United Kingdom. China and Indonesia joined the organization in 2006; in 2007 Ireland and Thailand joined as affiliate members and the Netherlands became an affiliate member in 2009.

As of April 2009, FPSB had members in 23 territories, including the United States. By the end of 2008, the majority (almost 120,000) of the global CFP professional community was doing business outside the United States.

Raising the Bar for Education and Ethics

As one of the "four Es" deemed essential to the profession's growth, education was a major theme of the post-merger period. In 2000, the first Ph.D. program in financial planning was created at Texas Tech; two years later that university added two related Ph.D. programs—in agricultural economics with a minor in personal financial planning, and in finance with a minor in personal financial planning. As of 2007, a bachelor's degree was required for CFP certification. And in 2008, Kansas State University registered its Ph.D. program in human ecology "with an emphasis in personal financial planning."

Ethics and practice standards, key cornerstones of the profession, also received ongoing attention. The first extensive revision in more than 12 years of CFP Board's code of ethics went into effect July 1, 2008; it comprised 46 pages of principles, rules of conduct, and practice standards as well as clear definitions of terms such as *compensation* ("any non-trivial economic benefit, whether monetary or non-monetary, that a certificant receives..."); *fiduciary* ("one who acts in utmost good faith, in a manner he or she believes to be in the best interest of the client"); and *fee-only* ("...client work comes exclusively from the clients in the form of fixed, flat, hourly, percentage, or performance-based fees"). The emphasis on fiduciary responsibility was both the motivation for the revision and the key differentiator between it and previous codes.

The Broker-Dealer Exemption

In 1999, the SEC had proposed an exemption for broker-dealers, allowing them to provide financial planning services without having to register under the Investment Advisers Act of 1940, which mandates a fiduciary duty. Dubbed the "Merrill Lynch Rule," after the brokerage firm, the proposal touched off several years of internal debate within FPA, culminating in the filing of separate lawsuits against the SEC, in 2004 and 2005, in federal appeals court in Washington.

"While we wanted to maintain a healthy relationship with the SEC, we felt the agency had made a significant mistake in granting the loophole," explained Duane Thompson, who set up FPA's legislative office in Washington, D.C., just before the 2000 merger. "The SEC felt that broker-dealers always offered comprehensive advice. We disagreed, and maintained the law said they couldn't receive special consideration." Meanwhile, said Thompson, "The other side—Wall Street, securities lawyers—regarded our response as nuisance lawsuits."

Dan Moisand, CFP who served on FPA's board beginning in 2003 and became the organization's president in 2006, was blunt in his assessment of the broker-dealer rule. In an interview published in the January 2006 issue of the *Journal of Financial Planning*, he said,

> *It's pretty simple: the rule stinks and we want it vacated. It was flawed from day one. The broker/dealer exemption has always been touted as a benefit to the consumer, but that supposition simply doesn't hold up to the most rudimentary logic. If it's so great, why does it need what amounts to a consumer warning label? The SEC added some disclosure when the first version was proposed in 1999 because it recognized that there was considerable room for consumer confusion. They were right—it is confusing. In fact, it is confusing even to the attorneys at many firms that supported the exemption. If the securities attorneys are confused, how does the average consumer stand any chance of understanding? We have the means, we have the resolve, we are the best positioned to take on the fight and, most importantly, we believe we are right. Without some significant consolation from the SEC, we have little choice but to continue. They have offered nothing. So we march on.*

"The SEC felt that broker-dealers always offered comprehensive advice. We . . . maintained the law said they couldn't receive special consideration."

—Duane Thompson

Profile: Dan Moisand

Already a successful practicing planner, prolific writer, a *Financial Advisor* magazine "Future Star," and one of *Financial Planning* magazine's "movers and shakers" in the profession, Dan Moisand was only 38 when he assumed the FPA presidency in 2006, at a critical moment in the association's short history: After more than five years of fruitless discussions, the broker-dealer lawsuit against the SEC was coming to a boil, and the coming fight would demand both Moisand's experience and his youthful energy.

The lawsuit was the most significant decision FPA faced during his tenure as board member and president, Moisand later said. "It was the first time that financial planners as a group said, 'We stand for certain things, and confusing the public is not among them. We put our clients' interests first.'" FPA's victory in 2007 was sweet, Moisand said, but standing up for principle was even more meaningful.

It was another crisis—the stock market crash of 1987—that had awakened Moisand's interest in finance. He was attending Florida State University at the time, "and it looked like the end of our financial system. I began to recognize that making good financial decisions was important for people." After receiving a degree in finance in 1989, he worked for an insurance company and IDS (later acquired by American Express). He also studied for the CFP exam, and received his CFP certification in 1994. "The comprehensive exam was still so new then," he recalled, "that there were only five people in the room—including the proctor." Financial planning itself was an unfamiliar concept for much of the public, Moisand said: "When I'd tell people I was a financial planner, they'd tell me they weren't interested in buying insurance." The striking change in that public attitude over the next 15 years has had much to do with the efforts of Moisand, who is widely regarded as one of the leading advocates for financial planning as a true profession.

While building his financial planning practice—first with an independent broker-dealer, and eventually with partners Charles Fitzgerald and Ronald Tamayo, Moisand joined the ICFP and quickly became involved in its activities. As president of his Central Florida chapter in 1998, he got to know national leaders and soon found himself working on practice standards with CFP Board. After the merger with the IAFP, he served on FPA's professional issues subcommittee and joined the

(continued)

Profile: Dan Moisand (*Continued*)

FPA board in 2003—another inflection point in recent financial history. "It was not that long after 9/11, and FPA was feeling the pinch," he said. "By the time I left"—after serving his term as president—"we had succeeded in turning FPA around."

That sunny picture turned cloudy in 2008, after the collapse of many national and global financial institutions. "In the long term, the economy and markets will recover," Moisand said, "but for most of us, planners and clients alike, this crisis feels very different from previous downturns. We could understand why the tech and real estate bubbles burst: prices were just going up too fast not to come down. We could understand the 9/11 effect. But the new crisis—with collateralized debt obligations, auction-rate securities, and so on—seems like a foreign language to our clients.

"I emphasize to my clients that no one knows what's going to happen, but everyone can benefit from tried-and-true principles. Don't spend more than you make. Balance risk. Manage credit wisely. Start with a goal and analyze your situation in light of that goal.

"As for my peers, I encourage them to think long-term. The demand for financial planning is going nowhere but up. And the passion financial planners feel for their work—for the positive impact it has on the lives of their clients—is growing stronger every day."

In the end, the three-judge panel sided with FPA, handing down a two-to-one decision in March 2007 that forced the SEC to vacate the entire rule. "We pretty much hit a home run," Thompson said. "The victory generated incredibly positive news coverage and helped put FPA on the map in Washington."

It wasn't the final chapter in the story, however. After the judgment, the SEC commissioned a study by the RAND Corporation on services offered by broker-dealers, financial advisers, and financial planners. The report, released in December 2007, gave no policy advice, but the SEC had planned to use it as the basis for its own recommendations. The financial crisis that descended in 2008 postponed that action. In the meantime, FPA entered into a coalition with CFP Board and NAPFA to consider how financial planning could best achieve regulatory recognition within an expected overhaul of financial services. The three groups announced their partnership in December 2008 and released a statement of understanding outlining how they would pursue regulatory reform.

Financial Services Institute

Before the merger that created FPA, independent broker-dealers who were not CFP certificants had long found a home in the IAFP, where they were able to network, share information, and benefit from the IAFP's advocacy efforts. Broker-dealers were excluded from the new organization's mission, but they weren't overlooked by the planning community. "In 2000, the same year FPA was created, things began getting tough for independent broker-dealers," said Dale Brown, who had joined the IAFP's staff in 1988 to work on governmental and corporate relations. A slew of corporate accounting scandals involving Enron, Tyco, and other corporations prompted the passage in 2002 of the federal Sarbanes-Oxley Act, which established new or stronger standards for all public companies and accounting firms. At the same time, "FPA felt it would send a confusing message to regulators—and be a potential conflict of interest—to represent both financial planners and broker-dealers who sold products," said Brown. He and other FPA staff members met with volunteers, FPA board members, and executives of broker-dealer companies to determine how to give broker-dealers the advocacy they deserved. By 2003, they had concluded that a new, separate association would best achieve that goal. FPA provided nearly $2 million to fund FSI's launch, in effect releasing broker-dealer membership fees and conference revenues to FSI.

The Financial Services Institute opened its office in Atlanta on January 1, 2004, with Brown as its director. Membership was open to NASD-registered broker-dealer firms only for the first year; in early 2005, it was extended to independent advisers who offer financial planning services. In its first five years, said Brown, FSI built a solid base of 116 member companies representing more than 142,000 independent registered representatives; together, member firms generated $13 billion in annual revenues.

"We have made great progress," said Brown. "We've gained credibility with federal and state regulators and weighed in on several important issues, especially those having to do with the impact of privacy rules on the broker-dealer business model."

"Independent broker-dealers have survived and thrived by adapting to the marketplace more quickly than the large institutional brokers," Brown added. "Like them, the Financial Services Institute leverages the power of technology to adapt to a changing economic environment." As the FSI's mission statement declares: "We are working to ensure that our voice is not just heard, but that it influences the outcome."

Global Financial Crisis

By 2007, the once-bubbling U.S. housing market had begun to show signs of boiling over. By early 2008, anyone who followed the headlines knew what "subprime mortgages" were and why they were having a disastrous ripple effect throughout the world economy. High-risk lending practices had depended on a nonstop rise in housing prices; when prices started to fall, mortgage defaults and foreclosures climbed. The crisis rippled from Main Street to Wall Street, where in June 2007 two Bear Stearns hedge funds with large holdings of mortgage-backed securities were forced to dump their assets. Other investment firms and banks in the United States and Europe also began reporting huge losses; in 2008 Bear Stearns and Lehman Brothers, two of Wall Street's most venerable firms, collapsed; Merrill Lynch barely survived, thanks only to a shotgun merger with Bank of America; mortgage giants Fannie Mae and Freddie Mac were placed in "conservatorship" by the U.S. Treasury, effectively nationalizing them; and AIG, the world's biggest insurer, had to be bailed out by the U.S. Federal Reserve. In the closing weeks of a tense U.S. presidential election, Congress rejected a $700 billion plan to bail out the financial system, then passed an amended version of the plan, which President George W. Bush signed into law.[5]

The picture was no more promising outside the United States. On a single day, October 10, 2008, the Japanese Nikkei stock index and the London FTSE each fell almost 10 percent; the Dow Jones index dropped 700 points; and the Icelandic bank Kaupthing was nationalized. The slide did not abate after the November presidential victory of Democrat Barack Obama: On November 20, the Dow fell below 8,000 for the first time since mid-2002.[6] (It would plummet even further in early 2009.)

The financial planning profession had faced many challenges in its nearly 40-year history, but this confluence of events was unprecedented. On November 3, 2008, the day before the U.S. election, FPA took out a full-page ad in *USA Today* that struck a tone of sobriety and reassurance. It said, in part,

> *The Financial Planning Association (FPA) represents more than 29,500 financial planning professionals who are dedicated to helping people come to terms with the crisis. We implore our next President and Congress to take this unprecedented opportunity to immediately correct inherent problems in America's antiquated financial system, with a sharp focus on protecting and serving the best interests of the consumer first in all financial advisory relationships.*

Many people have lost faith in various sectors of the financial services industry. A recent study indicates that those with a financial plan feel more on track and confident with the focus of their future goals and dreams, even during market turmoil. Our members' clients understand that objective and thorough professional financial planning serves as a road map through treacherous economic terrain.

Simply stated, we cannot invest our way out of the crisis, but we can plan our way through it.

Please consider the skills and knowledge of a competent and ethical financial planning professional who puts your best interests before their own. As your partner in financial planning for your family or your business, a financial planning professional can offer you objectivity and insight about all the financial decisions that affect your life goals.

Transformation and Opportunity

Many Americans had already endorsed the message in the *USA Today* ad. By 2008, financial planning had achieved what had been unimaginable a quarter-century earlier: It had become one of the most respected professions in the United States and around the world. When CareerBuilder.com, a recruitment and job-search site, published its list of the 30 most attractive jobs of 2008, "financial planner" was ranked sixth. The television network MSNBC included financial planning in its "Top Twenty Jobs of 2008" list.

In April 2009, Jeanne A. Robinson, CFP, and Charles G. Hughes, CFP, applauded that progress in an article they co-wrote for the *Journal of Financial Planning:* "We seem to have a convergence of forces at work, suggesting that this is the time we collectively move from, as Dick Wagner encouraged, 'thinking like a CFP' and as Elissa Buie advanced, 'feeling like a CFP' to finally—*finally*, acting like a CFP."

What does "acting like a CFP" mean, they asked? "Always putting the client's interests first. Period."

In 1990, Dick Wagner argued that for financial planning to be accepted as "real professionals," CFP practitioners must start thinking like professionals. Ten years later, Elissa Buie told readers it was time to balance "the skill of financial planning with the art of feeling."

As financial planning approached its fortieth anniversary, Robinson and Hughes challenged readers to transform thinking and feeling into action. Where at one time some planners' loyalty had been divided at best between vendors and clients, the new code of ethics made it clear that clients now stood in first place. They wrote,

> *To be a professional, to "profess," is to stand for something in a public context, to make a promise of service to the public. . . . Let's set aside "the profession" as our destination and, instead, make "professionalism" our ongoing journey. Let's focus on our role, not our place. Accept that planning is a function, but a client-centered advisor is who we are. Know that it's not what we do, but who we are that will make the lasting impression. And who we are is a professional. It's time to start acting that way . . . to start acting like a CFP.*[7]

CHAPTER 6

Global Expansion

As ambitious as they were, it's unlikely the 13 men who met in Chicago in 1969 to launch the financial planning movement could have predicted a gathering that took place halfway around the world nearly 40 years later.

The date was October 31, 2008. The place was Shanghai, China. The convener was Financial Planning Standards Board Ltd. (FPSB), which had been established in 2004 to oversee CFP certification around the world. The purpose of the meeting: to adopt common global standards for financial planning. In attendance were delegates of financial planning organizations from 23 countries and territories. Together, they represented nearly 120,000 CFP professionals whose clients numbered more than 20 million.

The significance of the event wasn't lost on those who attended. And neither was its urgency. "The need for standards that put clients' interest first has never been greater," announced Selwyn Feldman, CFP, of Cape Town, South Africa, FPSB's chair. He continued,

In this environment of market volatility and uncertainty, consumers have the right to advice from a qualified, competent, and ethical financial planner. We believe those who call themselves financial planners should meet rigorous professional standards, and we are pleased to have now defined these standards for the global community.

In retrospect, the journey from Chicago to Shanghai occurred at near lightning speed, but for those involved, the road was far from straight and the destination mostly unclear. "There really was no strategy early on for an international financial planning movement," said Noel Maye, FPSB's chief executive officer. Rather, the story of the global expansion of financial planning provides a glimpse into the evolution of a concept—and a profession—whose time had come.

First Forays

When Loren Dunton and others in the Chicago group formed the International Association of Financial Counselors (IAFC), the name was more wishful than descriptive. "We put 'international' in the name to make our start-up organization look bigger than it was," recalled James Johnston, who brainstormed the original concept with Dunton. Yet even before the IAFC was renamed the International Association of Financial planners, the organization was attracting international members. Early in 1970, the IAFC had 114 members in Canada, 24 in Germany, 6 in Spain, and 5 in Switzerland. Many of them were employed by Investors Overseas Services, a huge mutual fund conglomerate that toppled in scandal soon afterward. Applications and $10 membership checks also arrived from Argentina, Democratic Republic of the Congo, Guam, Hong Kong, and Thailand.[1]

The IAFP welcomed them all. Don Pitti, an early IAFP leader, recalled that people from Australia, England, France, Italy, and Japan attended some of the first conferences:

> We didn't consciously try to attract international attendees, but we were getting some publicity in the Wall Street Journal, the New York Times, and other publications, and people in other parts of the world started to hear about us. They came because they wanted to know more about this concept called financial planning.

> We embraced them with open arms. We did everything we could to help them take the financial planning movement back to their own countries.

In the mid-1980s, under the leadership of Executive Director Hubert (Herky) Harris, the IAFP sponsored a series of world congresses that carried the financial planning message abroad. Bill Carter, CFP, attended the first world congress in Monte Carlo and later remembered speakers from all over the world assembling to talk about investments, financial planning, and the economy. In subsequent years, the IAFP sponsored two additional world congresses. One took place in Australia, and the other was held in Japan, Hong Kong, and China.

"Everyone paid their own way," said Pitti, who went on the China trip. "It was a movement of people who believed in a good thing and wanted to spread the gospel of financial planning around the world."

The ICFP also turned its attention to the wider world. Beginning in 1984, the institute sponsored several international retreats. The first, held in London, was touted as a way for ICFP members to gain a global perspective from international financial experts and to make business contacts with overseas advisers and money managers. Said Lewis Walker, CFP, who organized the first international retreat: "The progressive planner cannot sit at home, run a domestic practice, and ignore the broader spectrum."

> *"The progressive planner cannot sit at home, run a domestic practice, and ignore the broader spectrum."*
>
> —Lewis Walker

International retreats were also held in Switzerland, Hong Kong, and Japan. The last retreat took place in 1987, the same year that the ICFP's *Journal of Financial Planning* published its first issue devoted to international topics, including "How and Why to Diversify Internationally."

But while these international forays were important activities for the two membership groups, there was no mechanism in place to export the CFP marks overseas. It would take a new organization, a determined Australian woman, and a gentleman from Tennessee to make that historic jump.

Financial Planning Comes to Australia

Gweneth Fletcher's interest in financial planning began in the early 1980s, when she traveled from Australia to the United States to speak about investment opportunities in her homeland on behalf of her employer, Dalserv. By 1982, Fletcher had become the second Australian to join the IAFP; the first had been Jeff Dalco, who headed Dalserv. (Dalserv was the first company in Australia to be granted a government license to give investment advice as financial planners.) In an article written by her biographer, Julie Bennett, and published in Australia's *IFA* magazine in 2007, Fletcher said she saw the IAFP as a group of professionals who earned a living helping ordinary people reach their financial goals. She added that while Australia had had a long history of financial advisers, they were typically stockbrokers, life insurance agents, bankers, and accountants. As far as she knew, no one had ever mentioned financial planning in Australia prior to the 1980s.[2]

"The IAFP presented a different way of thinking about investment advice," Fletcher was quoted as saying in the magazine. "It called for qualified advisers to provide quality, holistic financial planning advice to clients.... I thought it was a very forward-thinking, logical approach, and I became convinced that Australians, as much as Americans, really needed it."

Fletcher began attending IAFP conferences in the United States, often at her expense, to promote Australia as a land of investment opportunity. In the process, she made the acquaintance of Loren Dunton, Bill Anthes, Bill Hoilman, Vernon Gwynne, Denby Brandon, Don Pitti, and other financial planning movers and shakers. At a 1983 IAFP conference Fletcher declared, "I will have an IAFP in Australia by 1984."

She immediately set about meeting that goal, compiling a list of Australians who held investment licenses and inviting them to a meeting to discuss establishing an IAFP in Australia. Out of 600 letters, she received only a handful of responses. To her further disappointment, the small group that eventually met voted not to follow an American-designed IAFP model, but rather to establish an association made up of investment advisers only. Although Fletcher agreed to support the new Australian Society of Investment and Financial Advisers, she also persisted in forming IAFP Australia. (In 1992, the two organizations merged to form the Financial Planning Association of Australia.)

At the first meeting of the new Australian organization, Don Pitti was invited to make the keynote address. He recalled the group's enthusiasm. "The Australians had an insatiable thirst to know how financial planning was practiced in the United States," he said in 2009. "It was an exuberant meeting and fascinating to witness the enthusiasm that Aussies are famous for as they focused on how they could do more for their clients and fellow countrymen."

Still, Fletcher quickly realized that a financial planning industry would never transform itself into a profession until its members were properly educated. In the mid-1980s, with her business partner, John Green, she established the Investment Training College, Australia's first financial planning educational institution. To help Fletcher set up the school, William Anthes, president of the Denver-based College for Financial Planning, sent Fletcher course materials at no charge. She "Australianized" them, as she put it—adapting the coursework to Australia's laws while maintaining a high standard for the education of the country's future financial planners. "Bill [Anthes] not only encouraged and advised us, he generously provided coursework that we could not have afforded otherwise," Fletcher later said.

The only thing missing was a designation to signify what these new financial planners had achieved. Fletcher immediately thought of the CFP marks:

> There were some in Australia who did not want to copy the CFP marks or be obligated to pay sums to the States to use the marks. They didn't want to feel subservient to America in any way. But my feeling was that the United States had ten years of experience in developing standards for CFP certification and that we should take advantage of that experience. I didn't see any problem with being a copycat in those days.

There was one glitch, however. IAFP Australia soon discovered that the IBCFP (later named CFP Board) owned the CFP trademarks in Australia. Even though the organization had no defined plan to export the marks, it had been registering them in countries outside of the United States, including Australia, to protect its property rights. The IBCFP also was fielding inquiries about its certification program from Brazil, Canada, France, Germany, Great Britain, Greece, Italy, Japan, New Zealand, and Singapore.[3]

Despite the issue of the marks' ownership, Fletcher and IAFP Australia persisted. "I knew some of the IBCFP board of governors members, including Denby Brandon and Oliver Welch, and I told them that I would like to get the CFP marks for Australia," she said. For two years, from 1988 to 1990, the two organizations discussed how this might be accomplished.

In the fall of 1990, representatives from the IBCFP and IAFP Australia met at the Marriott Hotel in New Orleans, where the IAFP was holding its annual Success Forum. Fletcher, president of IAFP Australia, and Martin Kerr, the organization's CEO, had arrived for dinner that night expecting to seal the deal with a handshake. The IBCFP, however, had brought two "bloomin' lawyers," as she put it. With no legal counsel to represent IAFP Australia, Fletcher felt that she had no choice but to tell the group that she and Kerr would have to withdraw from the room while the IBCFP came to a decision. Fletcher later recalled: "While we waited, I told Martin that I may have blown the very thing I wanted—CFP for Australia."

Five minutes later, Fletcher and Kerr were invited back into the room. With the attorneys noticeably absent, IBCFP chair Denby Brandon, CFP—a planner from Memphis, Tennessee—extended his hand to Fletcher and said that a handshake sealed a deal in America, too. He told her that by a unanimous vote, the IBCFP had agreed to ratify a license and affiliation agreement that would make IAFP Australia the first organization outside of the United States authorized to grant CFP certification to qualified Australian candidates. "There were hugs all around," Fletcher said.

Years later, Brandon confided to Fletcher that when she left the room that night in 1990, he told his fellow board members that this was their chance to extend CFP certification beyond U.S. borders. "If you do it tonight," he told them, "you will have taken the first step toward internationalization of the CFP marks. And," he added, "you have five minutes to decide."

Attorneys later worked out the agreement's details, including how certification standards in Australia would be similar to those set by the IBCFP for the United States, and in December 1990, the license and affiliation agreement was signed between the two organizations. As part of the agreement, IAFP Australia agreed to pay the IBCFP a percentage of the annual license fees it received from CFP designees in Australia, and the IBCFP agreed to assume responsibility for the legal costs of registering and defending the authorized use of the CFP marks in Australia. (This fee arrangement continued for affiliates until 2000, when a sliding scale was established based on the number of CFP certificants in a country.) In 1991, IAFP Australia was renamed the Financial Planning Association of Australia, Ltd., and by 1993, 154 of that organization's 4,798 members had been granted the CFP designation.[4]

Profile: Gweneth E. Fletcher

Dubbed "Australia's First Lady of Financial Planning" in Australia's *IFA* magazine, Gwen Fletcher is credited with bringing the financial planning profession to her country. In 2007, her efforts were recognized by Australia when Fletcher was appointed a Member of the Order of Australia (AM) in the Queen's Birthday Honours list for her "contributions to the development of the financial planning profession." Also in 2007, she became the first recipient from outside the United States of FPA's Heart of Financial Planning Distinguished Service Award, given for contributions to the profession.

Born in Sydney to a Baptist minister and schoolteacher, Fletcher worked for the U.S. Army during World War II, and after the war for the United Nations, before beginning a career in Australia's male-dominated insurance and accounting industries at a time when it was considered unacceptable for women to have careers of any kind.

Fletcher soon began to see the limitations of accounting, however. "I realized I was only recording what people and companies were doing," she said in 2008. "By comparison, the new idea of financial planning was *personal*. It encouraged people to work out what to do with their money."

Fletcher played a pivotal role in establishing IAFP Australia, serving as the organization's first treasurer and going on to the positions of secretary, president, and chair—the only individual to hold all executive roles in the association.

After leaving active practice in 2003, Fletcher devoted her energies to improving the financial literacy of high schoolers in Australia through the Financial Planning Association of Australia's Education in Schools Project and mentored young women through Australia's Women in Finance Association.

In 2008, Fletcher reflected on the financial planning movement, which by that time included 5,430 CFP certificants in Australia. "The beauty of financial planning is that it can be applied to any country," she said. "Those in America who came up with the idea of financial planning were very forward-thinking individuals, and they were generous enough to share it with the rest of the world.

"Now we need to do more pro bono work and find ways to make financial planning advice more affordable for the average individual," she said. "I don't want financial planning to be seen as 'wealth management.' I want financial planning to help people learn how to save to get to the point where they have a chance of becoming wealthy in the first place."

Japan Joins the Movement

It wasn't long before the next country knocked on the IBCFP's doors. Japanese business leaders had heard about financial planning from their contacts in the United States as early as the 1970s. Among them was Shojo Kawashima, an executive at Nomura Securities Investment Trust and later at Kokusai Securities (a merger of Nomura and two other securities firms).

Kawashima had attended an Investment Company Institute conference in 1976 and was impressed by a session that talked about financial planning as a way to sell mutual funds. His interest eventually led to Kokusai Securities' sponsorship of an IAFP world congress held in Kyoto that was attended by several individuals who, two years later, founded the Japan Association of Financial Planners (JAFP).

JAFP soon began offering a designation, Affiliated Financial Planner (AFP), to its members. But after the organization's founders—including Satoshi Ihata, Atsushi Mihara, Misao Makiuchi, Tetsuo Akimoto, and CEO Kazuo Tanaka—learned about the CFP credential, they were no longer content solely with the AFP designation.

"They were interested in the CFP designation because they thought it offered an advanced level of financial planning certification, plus they felt that the CFP marks would be better recognized internationally," explained Suzue Sato. Sato, a Japanese-born U.S. citizen, was hired as an independent consultant by the JAFP in 1990 to negotiate with the IBCFP for authorization to grant the CFP marks in Japan. She later became director of the JAFP's U.S. office in Denver.

Negotiating the agreement proved a challenge on both sides, Sato recalled in 2008. The IBCFP's only experience drafting international agreements was the one it had recently finalized with Australia, so the Australian document became the template and was modified to reflect Japan's laws and culture. The IBCFP's continuing education requirement, for example, was not typical for professionals in Japan. "We did not change any of the basic CFP certification requirements, but we went back and forth several times on all the details," Sato said. "At the time, I was trying to save some money, so I hired an attorney to work with us in a limited capacity. He asked why we didn't simply create our own designation. I told him that the JAFP board believed that CFP was the future of global certification."

> *"Financial planning is essential for all families and citizens of the world in order for them to be able to feel the comforts of financial well-being. Financial planning is a global profession that does not recognize borders."*
>
> —Suzue Sato

Market Milestone: Japanese Market Crash

As CFP licensees gained a foothold in Japan, they found themselves helping their clients deal with challenging economic conditions. From 1975 through 1989, Japan had experienced a huge economic boom, fueled in part by rapid growth in high-tech industries and real estate values. Japanese citizens, traditionally very conservative with their money, began investing in the stock market. A popularly quoted statistic at the time claimed that 55 percent of the population—including babies—was invested in stocks. By the end of 1989, however, the Japanese economy began to falter. Property prices dropped almost 40 percent, and the Nikkei stock index plummeted from a high of 38,000 during the boom years to 7,000 in 2008. Japanese citizens, frightened to borrow or spend, retreated to traditional, guaranteed savings accounts available from the Japan Postal Agency. The government stepped in, spending billions of dollars to bail out banks and keep people working, but at the first signs of economic rebound, the stimulus programs were cut amid deficit concerns. The economy collapsed again and was still struggling to recover as the world ushered in a new century.

After two years of negotiations, the IBCFP and JAFP signed a license and affiliation agreement in 1992. In 1993, the first CFP certification examination in Japan produced 241 new CFP licensees from the ranks of the JAFP, which had approximately 6,800 members at the time. Bill Carter, president of the IBCFP that year, traveled to Japan for the ceremony and signed the first certificates. He was accompanied by Dick Wagner, chair of the ICFP, and Oliver Welch, former IBCFP chair.

JAFP continued to offer its original AFP designation to intermediate-level planners and positioned CFP certification as an advanced credential. The stringent CFP certification standards were reflected in Japan's pass rate for its six-part examination in 2008—about 10 percent when the six parts were taken at one sitting. By 2008, there were nearly 16,000 financial planners in Japan who held the CFP certification, compared with approximately 136,000 who had the intermediate-level AFP designation. The vast majority of Japanese CFP professionals (around 70 percent) worked for banks, insurance companies, and securities firms; only 10 to 12 percent classified themselves as independent practitioners.

IBCFP Takes Charge

With the growing international interest in CFP certification, the IBCFP realized it needed a better way to manage its activities in this area. In 1991, the organization established a subsidiary Board of Affiliated Associations. The board comprised two directors from the IBCFP and one director from each affiliated association. In 1991, that made the board a threesome: Denby Brandon, former chair of the IBCFP, became the first chair of the Board of Affiliated Associations; Oliver Welch, chair of the IBCFP in 1991, served as the second U.S. director; and Greg Devine, CFP, president of the Financial Planning Association of Australia, rounded out the group. Their tasks: Review affiliation proposals from other financial planning associations outside of the United States and monitor present and future agreements.

In September 1992, representatives of the IBCFP, IAFP Australia, and JAFP held the first meeting of the Board of Affiliated Associations in Anaheim, California. That same year, Tom L. Potts, CFP, chair of the IBCFP, traveled to France and Australia to speak to international audiences. He reported back to his U.S. colleagues: "Like planners in the United States, financial planners in [other] countries wish to increase the professionalism of their field, and they view the IBCFP as a role model. As we move toward a more global economy, it makes sense for the CFP mark to become more internationally recognized, and we foresee the possibility of affiliations with other countries in the future."

Despite Potts's confident prediction of more affiliates, there was debate about the future of the international effort. When the Board of Affiliated Associations held its first meeting outside of the United States, in Australia, in 1993, the topic was raised for discussion. "Where do we go from here?" Oliver Welch asked the group. "Do we stay as we are or go global?"

Internally at the IBCFP, there was even talk of disbanding the Board of Affiliated Associations altogether. At a strategic planning session in 1993, some IBCFP leaders raised the issue, contending that international activities were both a distraction to the board's domestic agenda and an expense the organization could not afford.

Tim Kochis, CFP, the IBCFP's treasurer that year, stood up to counter the opposition. "I argued that it would be a huge mistake to undo what we had accomplished so far and to abandon our international efforts," he recalled in 2009.

> *Consumers, planners, and financial planning organizations around the world were hungry for the CFP credential. They were knocking on our doors asking to be let in. I believed that it was up to us to continue to set the example for the establishment of professional standards in financial planning and to lead a financial planning movement internationally. There were no further objections, so that argument won the day.*

Bill Carter, the IBCFP's president, was among the majority siding with Kochis. "Tim made one of the most eloquent, impressive presentations I've ever heard," Carter recalled. "He challenged us by asking how we could

Open Doors

Throughout the 1980s and 1990s, the IAFP in the United States continued to welcome international members. The ICFP opened its membership to international CFP licensees in 1993; the first members were from Japan. When the IAFP and ICFP formed the Financial Planning Association in 2000, the new organization continued an open-door policy for international members, and by 2008, 41 countries were represented in FPA.

FPA also developed a variety of resources to help planners provide cross-border planning for clients. An online resource library, online conversation forums, annual conference sessions, and regional gatherings aided planners in better understanding the challenges and opportunities of working with clients across national borders.

pull back at the very time when the whole world was going global. If the motion to disband had passed, it would have changed the course of the international movement."

The next year, at a meeting in Japan, the Board of Affiliated Associations formally adopted a policy to promote CFP certification globally and took a new name: International CFP Council. The IBCFP adopted a new name, too: CFP Board. By 1995, CFP Board's staff included two employees tasked with managing trademark and international affairs, and by 1997, the first director of international operations, Don Bills, had been hired to run a small international department out of CFP Board's Denver office—a department that proved to be an ongoing expense for the organization.

Global Growth Accelerates

With a policy of expansion firmly in hand, the second half of the 1990s saw more countries joining the CFP certification movement. In June 1995, CFP Board authorized the United Kingdom's Institute of Financial Planning to grant the CFP mark in that nation—the first time a European financial planning organization had joined the International CFP Council.

In January 1996, authorization to grant the marks was awarded to the Financial Planners Standards Council of Canada; New Zealand's Association of Investment Advisers and Financial Planners followed suit shortly thereafter. (Only eight years later, in 2004, Canada could boast that it had the most CFP professionals per capita of any nation in the world.)

As organizations affiliated with CFP Board, they became members of the International CFP Council. Financial planning organizations from France and Germany joined the Council in 1997. South Africa and Singapore came on board in 1998, the same year that the European Community Trademarks Office issued a European Community trademark registration for the CFP mark.

By 1999, with the addition of Switzerland, the number of CFP licensees outside the United States had reached 18,067, roughly half of U.S. licensees. Canada led the way, with 10,677 licensees, followed by Japan with 2,454, Australia with 2,162, and South Africa with 1,834. As the twentieth century drew to a close, financial planning associations in 11 nations had CFP Board licensing agreements, and the CFP marks were registered or pending registration in 34 countries. CFP professionals—52,723 in all—now circled the globe.

As the number of affiliates grew, so, too, did the desire to be seen as a truly international movement, not as an operation of the U.S.-based CFP Board. International CFP Council members began to grow restless under a structure that required CFP Board's board of governors to ratify the council's decisions, even when the issue had little to do with the United States. "Especially in Europe, there seemed to be concerns about the U.S. origins of the CFP designation," JAFP's Sato said. "Some affiliates felt that we should become a separate, independent organization to be truly global."

CFP Board was not averse to the idea of spinning off its international arm, which had always been a financial drain on the organization, but it questioned whether a new organization could support itself. Patricia Houlihan, chair of CFP Board in 2000–2001, and chair of the International CFP Council in 2001–2002, recalled that despite those concerns, "the international movement was growing so rapidly that we needed to design a structure that would allow the CFP marks to become truly global." Her assessment of rapid growth hit the mark. Financial planning organizations in South Korea, Malaysia, Hong Kong, India, Brazil, and Austria recently had entered into agreements that allowed them to grant CFP certification in their territories. By the end of 2002, there were 73,618 CFP certificants, and 33,243 of them were from countries other than the United States (see Table 6.1 and Figure 6.1).

"I believe that financial planning for persons and families is as important as choosing your wife or husband and your profession for life."
—Louis Frankenberg, CFP, president, Brazilian Institute for the Certification of Financial Planners, 2000–2004

TABLE 6.1 CFP Certificant Growth 1996–2008

Date Affiliated	Country/Region	1996	1997	1998	1999	2000	2001	2002	2003	2004	2005	2006	2007	2008
Dec-90	Australia	782	1,030	1,480	2,162	3,011	3,885	4,725	5,198	5,336	5,310	5,308	5,524	5,430
Mar-02	Austria							19	54	82	88	110	139	182
Mar-02	Brazil							0	61	60	55	97	185	294
Jan-96	Canada		4,700	6,900	10,677	11,850	13,277	14,483	15,492	15,928	16,350	16,834	17,102	17,230
May-06	China										0	488	1,448	3,414
Jan-05	Chinese Taipei									0	148	345	514	580
Oct-97	France				172	283	540	850	1,200	1,297	1,433	1,471	1,344	1,394
Oct-97	Germany		23	227	349	451	601	694	880	921	973	1,009	1,102	1,092
Nov-00	Hong Kong						88	334	996	1,422	1,929	2,293	2,776	3,389
Oct-01	India						0	0	54	90	134	235	328	505
Nov-06	Indonesia											0	152	327
Oct-08	Ireland													0
May-92	Japan	810	1,025	1,276	2,318	4,007	5,860	7,967	10,037	11,614	13,061	14,751	15,012	15,802
Apr-00	Malaysia					9	24	961	2,580	2,320	2,581	2,689	2,588	2,508
Mar-96	New Zealand		265	268	226	240	253	268	287	307	346	385	397	400
Jun-00	Rep. of Korea						30	101	354	616	819	1,343	1,644	2,086
Dec-98	Singapore				3	3	91	212	370	505	539	548	537	671
Nov-98	South Africa				1,834	2,098	2,300	2,117	2,551	2,750	2,921	3,163	3,509	3,196
Apr-99	Switzerland				99	140	239	280	287	287	235	242	267	276
Jun-95	United Kingdom	60	63	80	131	190	215	232	284	400	510	610	760	900
	Total FPSB Council	**1,652**	**7,106**	**10,231**	**17,971**	**22,282**	**27,403**	**33,243**	**40,685**	**43,935**	**47,432**	**51,921**	**55,328**	**59,676**
	United States	30,129	31,939	33,120	34,656	36,307	38,408	40,375	42,973	45,755	49,117	53,031	56,511	58,830
	Grand Total	**31,781**	**39,045**	**43,351**	**52,627**	**58,589**	**65,811**	**73,618**	**83,658**	**89,690**	**96,549**	**104,952**	**111,839**	**118,506**

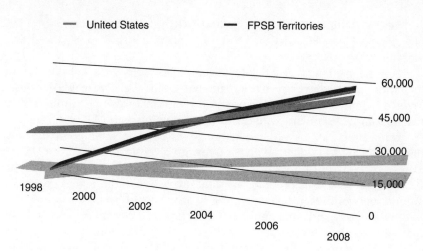

FIGURE 6.1 CFP Certificant Growth: United States and FPSB Territories
Source: Certified Financial Planner Board of Standards, Inc.

ISO Standard: Complement or Competition?

In 1999, representatives from CFP Board's International CFP Council visited Brussels to have a conversation with the European Commission about the adoption of CFP certification as the de facto standard for financial planning in Europe. The commission recommended that the CFP certification standards would carry more weight in Europe if they were associated with the International Organization for Standardization (ISO). CFP Board agreed to pursue the idea.

A Geneva-based federation of national standards bodies from 140 countries, ISO had long promoted the development of technical and quality standards worldwide for a wide array of products from photographic film to PVC conduit. However, this would be the organization's first effort to develop a standard for practitioners of a professional service industry like financial planning.

Two years later, in 2001, 16 countries sent representatives to the first meeting of ISO Technical Committee (TC) 222, Personal Financial Planning, for which CFP Board served as secretariat. The very creation of a financial planning TC was seen as groundbreaking because it acknowledged financial planning as a distinct practice, rather than placing it under the banking technical committee as some at ISO had favored.

The U.S. delegation, also referred to as the U.S. technical advisory group (TAG), comprised consumers, financial planners, and representatives from CFP Board, the Financial Planning Association (FPA), the American

Institute of Certified Public Accountants (AICPA), the National Association of Personal Financial Advisors (NAPFA), and the Society of Financial Services Professionals (SFSP).

For the next five years, ISO technical advisory groups from the 16 countries met to develop a standard that would be acceptable to those involved. During that period, some U.S. representatives began to question whether an ISO standard would end up competing with CFP certification.

Laura Brook, FPA's international relations director, summed up the way things appeared in 2003: "Many of those involved in ISO from the United States saw both an opportunity and a risk," she said. "If crafted well, a new ISO standard could help define a young profession and benefit consumers around the world. If mismanaged, the standard could become a competitor to the CFP mark and weaken the brand of financial planning." For all those reasons, FPA decided to remain involved in the discussion.

The standard that finally came before TC 222 for a vote in September 2005 was similar to CFP certification standards. One sticking point remained: ISO policy did not permit its standards to require third-party accreditation, or the ISO organization itself to offer certification or enforcement services. Thus, individual planners could purchase the ISO standard, perform a self-assessment of their capacity, and self-declare that they were in compliance with the standard. FPA, which generally supported the creation of a global standard, strongly opposed self-declaration of compliance in countries where financial planning certification bodies were in place. For that reason, FPA's representative voted against the proposed ISO standard when it came before the U.S. TAG—the only "no" vote among the U.S. delegation. CFP Board, which had administered the international secretariat, did not vote.

In November 2005, with 16 country votes placed, 12 were positive votes, including that of the United States. A month later, *ISO 22222-2005—Personal Financial Planning* was approved for publication.

Regulation and Legislation

In 2004, Malaysia became the first country in the world to require financial planners to hold a professional designation in order to practice.[5] The CFP designation was chosen to fulfill the requirement, along with the Chartered Financial Consultant (ChFC) designation. Steve L. H. Teoh, vice president of the Financial Planning Association of Malaysia, noted at the time that comprehensive financial planning was "still very young" in his country, and "it will take some time for it to mature." Nevertheless, he said, "I believe that the transition from a product-push market to a solutions-driven one will be relatively shorter than it took the currently more developed markets like the United States or Australia."

By 2004, CFP certification had also been recognized in legislation that included exemptions from licensing examinations in Hong Kong, Japan, and the United States. By 2006, South Africa and Canada (specifically, the province of Quebec and, more loosely, British Columbia) began regulating financial planners specifically as financial planners.[6]

FPSB: From Concept to Reality

In October 2002, a joint task force of CFP Board and the International CFP Council was formed to establish a new organization, Financial Planning Standards Board Ltd. (FPSB), to administer the CFP certification program worldwide, with the reservation that CFP Board would continue to own the CFP marks in the United States and administer the certification program there. FPSB's mission: to benefit consumers and foster professionalism in financial planning around the world by developing and enforcing international competency and ethics standards based on the four *Es*—education, examination, experience, and ethics. Specific certification standards for each country would be adapted to domestic marketplace, regulatory, and educational needs.

John S. Carpenter of Canada was named first chair of FPSB's board of directors. The first board had 10 members: 5 were nominated by CFP Board, 3 were from International CFP Council nominations, the ninth was reserved for the chair of the International CFP Council, and the tenth for the FPSB chief executive officer. In addition, representatives from all of the organizations offering CFP certification in their countries would serve on an advisory council to the board of directors (the FPSB Council).

The task force set 2003 as the target date for FPSB to be operational, but that goal proved overoptimistic. "FPSB was a concept that had to be fleshed out, and that took more time than anticipated," said Tim Kochis, who served on the first FPSB board of directors and chaired the board in 2005.

Throughout 2003 and most of 2004, the FPSB board of directors worked with CFP Board and the International CFP Council to establish FPSB and transfer the international CFP marks to the new organization. Raymond Griffin, CFP, of Australia, who chaired the International CFP Council in 2003, recalled: "Our American colleagues at CFP Board seemed at pains to hear firstly—and then to accept—that whether they liked it or not, in some parts of the world, the U.S. origins of CFP certification were an impediment to the CFP mark's expansion."

Kochis saw it differently. Far from being reluctant to spin off its international activities, many at CFP Board took the opposite view, he said, in part because the international program had always cost more in expenses than it gained in revenues. (Revenues came from a nominal affiliation fee and annual licensing fees based on the number of CFP certificants in a country; CFP Board then provided staff and financial support as new international entities established themselves.)

Furthermore, CFP Board had long been concerned that any failure to manage CFP certification properly in other parts of the world could expose the organization to liability on grounds of interfering with an individual's livelihood. Adding to the mix, CFP Board's attorneys insisted on an arm's-length negotiating posture between CFP Board and FPSB to safeguard CFP Board's not-for-profit status, which added to the complexity of finalizing the marks' transfer to FPSB.

"On October 13, 2004, the day we publicly launched FPSB at a meeting in London, I was in an anteroom with two cell phones to my ears," Kochis recalled. "On one line was the FPSB attorney. On the other were CFP Board's attorney and chairperson. We crossed t's and dotted i's up to the final minute."

Another hurdle was money—would FPSB have the financial wherewithal to survive on its own? CFP Board had agreed to sell its international CFP trademarks and operation in 36 countries to FPSB for $1.5 million, an amount that included CFP Board's legal costs and the cost of supporting the FPSB board of directors' functioning during 2003 and 2004. But how could a new organization come up with $1.5 million? FPSB solicited contributions from member organizations, which covered part of the sales price.

FPSB Korea, the Republic of Korea's affiliate, was the first organization to step forward with a monetary contribution. Eventually, most affiliates pitched in, but the organization would need to take out a loan to cover the balance. The sticking point: FPSB had no collateral other than the marks themselves. "We couldn't risk putting up the marks as collateral," recalled Noel Maye, who was hired from CFP Board as FPSB's first chief executive officer. "If the organization failed, we didn't want a bank to own the marks."

As he had done more than once over the years, Tim Kochis proposed a solution. He got a commitment from a San Francisco bank with whom he had done business to lend the money to FPSB. The bank had one condition, however: It wanted at least two U.S. residents to guarantee the loan.

Kochis agreed to put up his personal wealth as collateral. Then he called Elaine Bedel, CFP, a financial planner in Indianapolis, with a request: Would she be willing to do the same?

Bedel did not hesitate. She and Kochis had been friends and colleagues since the 1990s when Bedel chaired CFP Board's Board of Practice Standards and in 2002 when she was chair of CFP Board's board of governors. Like

Kochis, Bedel had always believed in the importance of establishing global financial planning standards based on the CFP marks. She had even resigned early from CFP Board to join FPSB's board in late 2003 so she could focus on helping FPSB get off the ground, serving on the transition team that created FPSB, as a member of its first board, and as chair in 2006.

"Both Tim and I were very confident that FPSB would succeed and that it was important to cut FPSB free from CFP Board," Bedel said in 2009. "But we also knew that it wouldn't happen without the loan. I felt very comfortable co-signing, and it worked out beautifully." Just three years later, Kochis's and Bedel's names were removed from the loan after several affiliates, as well as a few private individuals, assumed the debt. By 2008, FPSB had fully repaid the loan and established the beginnings of a trademark-protection reserve fund of its own.

Launched at Last

The final legal agreements were formalized between CFP Board and FPSB on the last day of November, and on December 1, 2004, FPSB officially opened for business. It would represent 17 financial planning affiliates that together had more than 45,000 CFP certificants outside of the United States. (See Appendix F for a list of FPSB affiliates.)

Maureen Tsu, CFP, FPSB chair, commented on the significance of the new organization in a 2004 press release: "This is a historic time for consumers of financial planning around the world and for the evolution of financial planning as an international profession centered around the CFP marks. The CFP marks have come to represent the gold standard for financial planning professionals."

Shortly after FPSB's inauguration, Australia's Raymond Griffin noted,

FPSB [has become] totally independent. That means that in those parts of the world where being global is most important, this can be stressed. In those parts of the world where its U.S. origin is most important, this can be stressed. With this framework, we have the best opportunity to help millions more people around the globe improve their life by a relationship with a Certified Financial Planner professional.

With FPSB's doors open at its Denver headquarters, financial planning organizations from another six territories soon joined the CFP certification movement: Chinese Taipei (Taiwan) in 2005, China and Indonesia in 2006, Ireland and Thailand in 2008 and the Netherlands in 2009.. The stories of two of the newest members, from China and Ireland, illustrate how financial planning was reaching into all parts of the world as the profession approached its fortieth birthday.

Profile: S. Timothy Kochis

When Tim Kochis stepped forward to personally guarantee the loan needed to start the new Financial Planning Standards Board (FPSB), he added another highlight to a decades-long record of service to the financial planning profession in the United States and around the world.

Fresh out of law school in 1973, Kochis, a Vietnam veteran, took a job in the financial planning department of a Chicago bank simply because "it was the best job offer I got." He soon discovered he'd found his calling.

In 1985, as a young member of the first Board of Examiners for the newly formed IBCFP (now CFP Board), Kochis successfully pushed to replace serial exams for CFP affiliation candidates with a single comprehensive examination; he contended that the single exam was an essential element of a professional credential. Later, as chair-elect of CFP Board, he convinced the organization not to abandon its international activities, despite the costs. He volunteered to sit on the first FPSB board of directors in 2002, chaired the organization in 2005, and served as an adviser and chair for FPSB's China Advisory Panel. In 2006, Kochis was awarded the inaugural Charles R. Schwab Impact Award for outstanding individual leadership in the independent advisory profession.

Kochis also made a mark on the academic front. At the University of California Berkeley Business School Extension, he co-created and taught one of the first accredited financial planning programs in the United States; an annual award for teaching excellence was created in his name. Actively practicing in 2009, Kochis was CEO of Aspiriant, a prominent wealth-management firm in San Francisco and Los Angeles.

In 1995, as president of CFP Board, Kochis reflected on his involvement in the new profession of financial planning. "When I was invited to become a member of the first Board of Examiners, I was neither a CFP designee nor a fervent believer in the credential," he wrote in CFP Board's annual report. "But I strongly believed that the public needed a way to identify competent, ethical financial planners, and that the best way to accomplish this was for the financial planning profession to coalesce around a single credential."

A Tiger in the East . . .

According to some sources, China has had the largest economy on earth for most of the recorded history of the past two millennia.[7] But that wasn't the case in the early years of the financial planning movement. Under the rule of communist leader Mao Zedong, China was in the midst of its Cultural Revolution, with a planned economy that was producing a gross domestic product (GDP) averaging at about 10 percent that of the United States.

Then, beginning in the late 1970s and continuing into the 1980s, reforms initiated by Mao's de facto successor, Deng Xiaoping, led to an export-oriented economic expansion that over the next few decades resulted in China's GDP growing to about 30 percent that of the United States.[8] By the time the global financial crisis hit in 2008, China had become a major source of financing for public and private overseas borrowing by the United States.[9]

With less government control over citizens' personal lives and a transition from a planned economy to a mixed one, the climate was conducive for a financial planning profession to take root in China. The first seeds were sown by Chinese-born academics and professionals living in North America who saw a need for a higher level of professional financial training in their homeland. Among them was Liu Feng, Ph.D., a professor of finance at McGill University in Montreal. In 1999, Liu and his colleagues proposed to the People's Bank of China, the central bank of the People's Republic of China, that they start a banking institute in Shanghai jointly funded by McGill, Shanghai Banking Association, and East China Normal University. The proposal was accepted and the institute opened, but the programs were not well received by the banking industry, and the institute failed after one year of operation. "The banking industry was still heavily monopolized by the government and financial institutions had no motivation to train their staff to become more competent professionals," Liu recalled in 2008. "They focused too much of their budget on computer hardware and office facilities, and not enough for education."

Despite that early failure, a feasibility study led by the McGill group concluded that there was a need for more professional financial training for bank employees and management. The deputy governor of People's Bank of China, Madame Wu Xiaoling, invited a prominent professor, Liu Hongru, to search for an internationally well-known educational program that would lead to a professional designation in financial planning. Professor Liu, who was known as the godfather of the Chinese finance industry, had been deputy governor of the People's Bank of China and founder of its graduate school, first chair of China's Securities Regulatory Commission, and one of the founders of the Chinese stock market. With his endorsement, and with the support of Dr. Cai Zhongzhi, an experienced banker and Liu Hongru's protégé, the group began to research the CFP designation, which they had learned about while attending conferences and university exchange programs in the United States.

In 2004, Cai Zhongzhi and Liu Feng attended the London inauguration of FPSB. The group, now formed as the Financial Planning Standards Council of China (FPSCC), presented its business plan to the FPSB and started a training program for candidates for CFP certification soon afterward. In 2006, with the elements of its CFP certification program in place, it became an affiliate member of FPSB.

Tim Kochis, who chaired FPSB in 2005, recalled the significance of the affiliation for both countries:

> *We had a very formal meeting with senior officials from the People's Bank of China and other regulators. We sat at low tables, with interpreters behind us, and observed all the formalities. FPSB, a creation of the West, wanted to demonstrate how important a relationship was with China. And the Chinese wanted to demonstrate how seriously they took this development by sending senior officials to the meeting.*

The Chinese introduced financial planning to China first by training bank employees in personal finance, so banks could offer it as a new service to their customers. According to Liu Feng, "We approached two of the largest banks in China, the Industrial and Commercial Bank of China and the Bank of China. We proposed an experiment that would involve three training classes of 180 individuals. We had to quickly prepare textbooks and recruit professors to teach the classes, including two Taiwanese professionals who could speak Mandarin, had teaching backgrounds, and had experience in practicing financial planning."

The first classes were a success. The banks were satisfied with the results, and another 300 students were recruited to the program. However, a problem soon arose: Many students found that the intensive curriculum was too difficult. In response, FPSCC split the program into two levels: an Associate Financial Planner level that required 108 hours of classroom time and a CFP certification level that required 132 hours.

By 2008, China had more than 26,000 Associate Financial Planners and 3,000 CFP certificants. The vast majority of CFP certificants—some 95 percent—worked for banks. Another 5 percent came from the insurance industry, mutual funds, securities, and accounting firms, plus a small number of individuals who had enrolled on their own to pursue a career change. The average age of CFP certificants was 32, with a nearly equal split between men and women. FPSCC had also started an education program for bank managers to help them better understand what their new financial planners could offer to customers.

Liu Feng summed up the progress financial planning had made in China:

> *Before the CFP certification program came to China, the emphasis was on selling products and basic banking transactions. The program has opened minds. Now, our graduates ask, "What's my client's point of view? What should I do for my clients?" And clients are coming into banks and asking to meet with CFP certificants or AFPs because they are performing*

much better than those who have not obtained these credentials. They were good bankers before, but now they have even more knowledge. Some banks are even requiring their senior managers to have the AFP or CFP designation to be considered for promotions.

We introduced a new model for financial planning. People regard it as a profession, like a doctor or an accountant. Still, we have a long way to go, because our financial planners are not really independent—they work for a bank or other employer—so there's the problem of conflict of interest. I'm not sure how long it will take for financial planners to become more independent in China. But Chinese citizens are starting to have more complex financial lives. There's huge room for financial planners to provide advice and help both the wealthy and ordinary people of China.

... And a Celtic Tiger

Like China, the Republic of Ireland would have been an inhospitable place for the CFP certification movement to take root in 1969. Gripped by poverty for most of its history, the country experienced high unemployment, mass emigration, burdensome taxes, and government instability well into the 1980s. Then, spurred by an influx of high-technology companies in the 1990s, Ireland became one of the fastest-growing economies in the world—a phenomenon known as the Celtic Tiger. By 2005, the Republic of Ireland's per-capita gross domestic product was the second highest in the European Union, behind Luxembourg.[10]

The transformation of the Republic of Ireland from one of the poorest countries in Europe to one of the wealthiest, coupled with the paradox of a citizenry that had "new money" but comparatively less understanding of how to manage it, made Ireland a likely target for financial planning services. But although there were thousands of financial advisers in the country, there was no financial planning profession as such before 2008. Rather, individuals involved in the sale of retail financial products for banks, brokerages, mutual funds, and insurance companies were subject to oversight by the government's Financial Regulator. In addition, beginning in 2007 those individuals were required to hold the Qualified Financial Adviser (QFA) designation, which was granted by the QFA Board, a joint venture of the Life Insurance Association Ireland, the Institute of Bankers in Ireland, and the Insurance Institute of Ireland.

Brian Toolan, a tax accountant and former president of the Life Insurance Association Ireland, recounted in 2008,

It was well respected by the government's Financial Regulator, and individuals with the QFA for the most part gave good advice, but it was not

comprehensive advice because it did not address all aspects of a client's
financial affairs. We wanted to offer a higher level of qualification and
create a profession of financial planning, as opposed to the occupation
of selling financial products. That was a quantum leap for us.

The CFP designation came to the attention of leaders of the Life Insurance Association and The Institute of Bankers in Ireland. "It provided
the level of qualification and professionalism that we were looking for and
emphasized comprehensive financial planning," Toolan said. "Plus, it was a
global mark that our citizens, who tend to be quite mobile, could take with
them anywhere in the world."

The two groups began working with FPSB to establish a CFP certification program in Ireland, formed FPSB Ireland, and earned affiliate status
in 2008. Plans were immediately initiated to offer a postgraduate education
program to candidates for CFP certification at University College Dublin's
School of Professional Finance, with the expectation of authorizing the first
Irish CFP professionals in 2011. This first group would largely come from
the ranks of QFAs, and consequently would, in most cases, have already
met the CFP certification experience requirement and part of the education
requirement.

By 2008, of course, the global economy was in a tailspin, and financial
planning advice couldn't come quickly enough to Ireland, which in midyear
earned the dubious distinction of becoming one of the first countries in
the world to formally declare itself in a recession. The country's banks
were reeling from bad debt, the stock market was plummeting, and real
estate—traditionally the investment of choice for the Irish—was losing value
fast. Toolan, however, saw these new Irish troubles as opportunities for CFP
professionals. "Nobody knows where to turn now," he said. "All asset classes
are in chaos here. But the more difficult the economic circumstances, the
more important good advice becomes. The opportunity is enormous for
financial planners in Ireland."

Conditions for Success

What made a country like Ireland fertile ground for a financial planning
profession? The answer lies in the link between democratic capitalism and
countries that had pursued the CFP designation.

Consider the nations that requested and obtained the right to grant
the CFP marks and build professional financial planning societies. Even
though they represented great differences in culture, human rights, and
religion, they also allowed at least some measure of freedom and private
ownership. The long-term success of a free society based on democratic

capitalism depends on its ability to keep increasing the number of people in the society who are owners and stakeholders in the society. CFP practitioners... facilitate the process by which each person seeks to achieve the ownership of the property, goods, and services he or she desires.

Laura Brook, international relations director at the Financial Planning Association, noted that several conditions were necessary for financial planning to take root in a country: a stable economy, a reasonable level of inflation, a trustworthy government, and an effective organization to support financial planners and promote their services to consumers. In addition, countries whose governments were less likely to throw out a financial safety net to their citizens fostered greater interest in personal financial planning. "That's why there's so much interest in personal financial planning in Asia," Brook said in 2008. "In many Asian countries, people feel an urgency to take care of themselves."

Noel Maye, FPSB's CEO, observed that same year:

> *A country becomes ripe for financial planning when a certain percentage of the citizenry is economically in a situation to access it and when government regulation is not so rigid as to prevent it from taking root. When a country takes a client-centered approach to financial regulation, the financial planning profession can help define what is a fair, reasonable, client-centered approach to financial advice, and what competencies an individual should have to set himself or herself apart as a financial planner."*

A Global Standard Emerges

In 2007, CFP Board in the United States, where financial planning had been born nearly 40 years earlier, took its place as a peer in the international community by becoming a full member of FPSB, the organization it had helped create. "It was like bringing the profession full circle," Elaine Bedel observed. A year later, the circle revolved yet again when the number of CFP professionals outside of the United States (59,676) surpassed for the first time the number of U.S. certificants (58,830).

In 2008, FPSB's Noel Maye summed up his take on the future of financial planning:

> *When FPSB members representing 23 countries and territories unanimously approved global competency and ethical standards for financial planning in Shanghai, it signified that CFP certification has emerged as the global standard. Going forward, we will see financial planning ideas*

from all over the world benefitting planners no matter where they live. And they will have this ethical framework front and center: "The client comes first."

No matter where people live, Tim Kochis said, one thing remains constant: "They increasingly recognize the need to take responsibility for their financial well-being. If we as a profession can be there to support their needs, that will be a wonderful accomplishment."

CHAPTER 7

Theory, Technology, and Process

The financial planning movement started with a clear purpose: to help ordinary Americans gain control over their financial lives. However, in the profession's early years that aim was not supported by much theory or research. The knowledge base grew incrementally with the movement itself, as financial planners and academicians discovered new ways to predict or explain investment success, spending behavior, and consulting effectiveness. Guest speakers at financial planning conferences and retreats discussed theories of behavioral economics, integral finance, and asset allocation; the *Journal of Financial Planning* introduced readers to leading economists such as Daniel Kahneman and Laurence Kotlikoff and financial analysts such as Morningstar's Don Phillips. As a result, financial planners now have a broad array of concepts and practice approaches from which to choose, and their education goes far beyond the on-the-job training of the early years to include undergraduate and graduate degree programs at colleges and universities in the United States and overseas.

Planners have also benefited from the democratization of computer technology, which has enabled even small firms and solo practitioners to streamline their operations and manage large amounts of information efficiently.

As the knowledge base grew and technological tools became increasingly sophisticated, planners could offer more extensive services to clients. At the same time, many planners began questioning whether financial planning represented something more than the sum of knowledge and technology: Did it touch an area of human need beyond the merely monetary?

The Technology Revolution

In the financial planning profession's first decade, computers were beyond the reach of most planners. (The exceptions were those planners who worked for large institutions that could afford mainframe computers.) The office of the typical financial planner of the 1970s was furnished with type-writers, adding machines, pens, rubber stamps—and reams of paper. The work was labor intensive and time consuming, and it limited the number of clients with whom a planner could work.

When the IBM personal computer (PC) went on the market in 1981, it brought some of mainframe computing's power to the desktop and promised to liberate planners from their dependence on paper files and handwritten forms. The spreadsheet program Lotus 1-2-3, introduced in early 1983, was the PC's first "killer application"; it quickly outsold the previous best-seller, VisiCalc. Also in 1983, Advent Software introduced Professional Portfolio, the first portfolio management software designed specifically for the PC. Around the same time, several companies, including Soft-Bridge, FastPlan, and Leonard Financial Systems, created programs aimed specifically at financial planners. Eager early adopters looked to these tools to automate routine back-office tasks, such as executing trades, and allow them to spend more time doing research and communicating with clients.

Not all financial planners waited for commercial software releases; some created their own analytical tools and proprietary software. Several became entrepreneurs. One of the earliest was Financial Profiles, Inc., founded in 1969 in Carlsbad, California, by August C. (Gus) Hansch, who received his CFP certification eight years later. His son, Thomas Hansch, CLU, CFP, joined the company in 1986. In its early years, Financial Profiles gathered and processed client information to generate financial plans; Hansch later developed a successful software program, Profiles+. In 2006, Financial Profiles was sold to Emerging Information Systems, Inc., which continued to support Profiles+ and other Financial Profiles products as well as its own NaviPlan product, originally introduced in 1990 as TIMS.

Money Tree Software was another early entry into the financial planning software market; like Financial Profiles, it was founded by a planner, Mike Vitkauskas, CFP. In 1979, Vitkauskas developed software for his own Corvallis, Oregon, practice; based on VisiCalc, it ran on an Apple II computer with 64K of memory. Two years later, when Vitkauskas was serving as president of the Oregon chapter of the IAFP, his fellow planners began requesting copies of the program. "I resisted until there was serious demand," he later recalled. The original release, MoneyCalc, included about 40 applications and templates on a single floppy disk. A later MS-DOS release was based on Lotus 1-2-3 and renamed Easy Money. The first standalone Windows version, Silver Financial Planner, was introduced in the late 1980s and was still being sold 20 years later along with a suite of other Money Tree products.

Yet another popular program, eventually known as dbCAMS+, was developed by David C. Huxford, CFP, in the late 1970s on a TRS-80 Model II with no hard drive—only a floppy disk drive. The program's name came from "database client asset management system ... plus a lot more," according to Huxford's son, Dusty, who began doing financial services programming in 1979. Dusty Huxford recalled checking the programs, written in BASIC computing language, "with a brand-new HP calculator, $300 retail":

We used a very fast 300 baud modem in which we laid the phone handset to send information to CompuTone/CompuServe—the precursor to AOL—which was the only available file-sharing service at the time. We "hosted" a bulletin board service (BBS); user group members would call in to get program updates and share files. We routinely wrote articles on technology and the need to embrace it. We encouraged advisors to "treat a computer like the telephone" and use it in everyday applications—a radically progressive stance back then.

Over numerous releases, dbCAMS+ became a sophisticated and scalable portfolio management system with more than 8,000 registered users.

David Huxford died at the height of his career in the 1994 crash of USAir Flight 427, along with all other passengers and crew. Dusty Huxford and his stepmother, Terry, continued running the Maryland-based business, Financial Computer Support, Inc., until September 2008, when they sold it to Morningstar, Inc., which rebranded dbCAMS+ and incorporated it into its Principia line.

The fast pace of computer innovation in the early 1980s was confusing to some planners—and irresistible to others. "Not all financial planners invested wisely in the early days," observed Marv Tuttle, former editor and publisher of the *Journal of Financial Planning*, who became the Financial Planning Association's executive director and CEO in 2004. "Some planners spent thousands on new products and then chucked them as soon as a new generation came along." To help planners avoid costly mistakes, professional journals began publishing not just *how-to*'s but also *why-to*'s.

By 1984, enough planners were using, or at least interested in, desktop computers that the *Journal of the Institute of Certified Financial Planners* could confidently publish an article titled "Computer Communications: A New Tool for Financial Planning." "Contrary to what you might think, you need not invest a fortune in computers and peripherals to go on-line with most communications services," the article assured readers.[1]

Even a Timex-Sinclair 1000, which recently sold for $49.95, can be used as the basis for your computer and a screen. If you already have a mini or microcomputer, it can be made to communicate....In addition to the computer, you'll need a modem, a serial card, and in some cases, a software package. When you want to communicate, you'll turn your computer on, dial up a number, and place the telephone receiver on the

*modem which allows your computer to talk through the telephone lines
with another computer. . . . It's possible that you can get into communicating with a minimum investment of $400.*

> *"When you want to communicate . . . turn your computer on, dial
> up a number, and place the telephone receiver on the modem which
> allows your computer to talk through the telephone lines with another
> computer."*
>
> —1984 article on computer communications
> for financial planners

The article went on to describe three of the "specialized information databases" available to planners with a computer modem: Dow Jones
News/Retrieval Service, CompuServe Information Service, and The Source,
from Source Telecomputing Corporation.

It took only a few years for some of the novelty and glamour to wear
off of office computing. In a July 1988 *Journal of the Institute of Certified
Financial Planners* article, David C. Huxford offered sympathy for the PC
user on the MS-DOS operating system:

> *Most planners I talk to are frustrated with their computer. Everyone says
> computers can do great things, but users feel the computer often gets in
> the way of administrative operations instead of facilitating them. Take
> the simple idea of keeping an appointment schedule in the computer. This
> is very simple to do and will work fine—if you only use the computer
> to keep the schedule. But as soon as you use the computer for another
> task, you lose access to the schedule. Using an appointment book is much
> more efficient.[2]*

Microsoft Windows would dramatically change all that. Although
Windows 1.0, introduced in November 1985, did not catch on, its successor, released two years later, was slightly more popular. With Windows 3.0,
released in 1990, planners finally could enjoy true multitasking capabilities.
Mike Ryan, CFP, said the development was a breakthrough:

> *Windows' graphics interface offered relatively foolproof programs, and
> financial planning—which had begun with a legal pad and a pencil and
> then a calculator and a spreadsheet—quickly became an environment
> in which financial plans were sold by the pound. I remember in the
> late eighties when comprehensive financial planning software vendors*

were almost as prevalent at industry meetings as tax shelter programs. It seemed that the first priority of anyone becoming a financial planner was to acquire a comprehensive planning program.

Within a few years, financial planners would have a new top priority: an Internet presence.

The Internet, originally called ARPANET, had been around since 1969, but its use had been limited to military and academic institutions. E-mail was still a business novelty in the late 1980s, when the first privately run Internet service providers began offering primitive search capabilities. In 1993, the National Center for Supercomputing Applications at the University of Illinois introduced Mosaic (later replaced by Netscape Navigator), the first true browser for the World Wide Web. Search engines proliferated, and some farsighted businesses began registering Internet domain names and establishing virtual homes on the Web.

One of the first financial planners with an online presence was Chuck Jones, CFP, of Portland, Oregon, who launched his firm's Web site in June 1995. In a June 1996 *Journal of Financial Planning* article, Jones recounted his online odyssey:

> *In October 1993, we decided we would try to be in a position by the year 2000 to do our clients' quarterly reports interactively and on what we thought would be a remote TV linkup. Two months later, my son came home from college and said, "Dad, you have to get involved in the Internet." We met with our in-house computer expert, who got really excited about the chance to be a pioneer in an exploding field, and away we charged.*

Jones urged *Journal* readers to "take the time to learn about the Web and set your goals before you charge off down the information superhighway."[3]

Even for planners who were slow to embrace the Web, the late 1990s were a time of near-miraculous technological change. The author of the June 1996 *Journal* article, Ed McCarthy, CFP, marveled:

> *Think about it: Pentium PCs with 16+ Mb of RAM and a 28.8 KB modem are standard. You use online services to retrieve your e-mail and update clients' investment portfolios each day. You run powerful PC-based analytical software and multimedia programs. Your client reports include colorful, informative graphics that you generate on a color laser printer. Prospective clients contact you after visiting your World Wide Web home page, and you can share ideas with colleagues across the country via computer bulletin boards....*

Remember when you had to manually enter each investment transaction into a client's records? You received paper statements weeks after the transactions occurred, and as your client base grew you had to devote increasing amounts of time to data entry. . . . Fortunately, most of today's client and portfolio management systems allow the exchange of data between the planner's PC and remote systems.

Perhaps inevitably, doubt and worry crept in. In an August 1999 article, writer Nancy Opiela reported in the *Journal of Financial Planning* that

[p]lanners say the Internet is having a profound impact on the profession, changing client relationships and providing plenty of fodder for discussion. Many planners report their clients pushing to get their portfolio information online. That makes [Marilyn] Bergen, CFP, of Capital Management Consulting in Portland, Oregon, uncomfortable. "We have concerns regarding confidentiality and security. The clients who are pushing us don't seem to have a care in the world. They don't see security as an issue."[4]

Interviewed for a December 2000 *Journal* article, Bill Carter, CFP, of Carter Advisory Services in Dallas, voiced another common concern: "Because of technology, the demands of the consumer have become greater. Today people think computers can do anything, so they want their answer by the end of the day and they don't think they are being demanding at all."[5]

The greater the demands on information technology, the greater the distress when that technology fails. After the 9/11 attacks, the failure of electrical and cell phone grids compounded the suffering of people in affected areas and those trying to contact them. Four years later, in September 2005, Hurricane Katrina demonstrated once again that no information system, no matter how well secured, is completely impervious to natural disasters.

S. Derby Gisclair, chief operating officer of institutional investment consulting firm Equitas Capital Advisors, LLC, in New Orleans, thought that because his firm was on the same grid as City Hall he'd lose power for only a couple of days—a week at most. He underestimated. "Our staff was

---

"Today people think computers can do anything, so they want their answer by the end of the day and they don't think they are being demanding at all."

—Bill Carter

scattered across the southeastern United States when Katrina hit," Gisclair recalled. "No one expected the catastrophic flooding that kept us out of our homes for months." Dave Thomas, the firm's chief executive officer, set up a temporary office in Baton Rouge; the firm's chief technology officer and IT consultants moved to Houston. Equitas ordered new cell phones for employees—the New Orleans area code was no longer reliable because of tower damage and heavy call volume; it also set up a virtual server in Houston and managed to get a high-speed data line in Baton Rouge. "We had a virtual presence in 36 hours, an office in Baton Rouge within a week, and within two weeks we had all our employees placed and working," Thomas said.

Not everyone affected by the storms was quite so fortunate. As another financial planner displaced by Katrina recalled: "We all learned to text message."[6]

Forty years after the first pioneering efforts at financial planning technology, planners had an array of specialized products from which to choose. According to *Financial Planning* magazine's 2008 software survey of more than 350 financial planners, "the single-most important factor in establishing and maintaining a successful financial advisory practice" was CRM (client relationship management) software, which helps planners stay in contact with clients. In the survey, 97 percent of planners said they used CRM products, although the largest segment claimed to use Microsoft Outlook—not a true CRM product—for this purpose. For financial planning, respondents put EISI products—Financial Profiles and NaviPlan—in the most-favored position. Money Tree, MoneyGuidePro, and SunGard also had their advocates. But 11 percent said they used no financial planning software. "Presumably, these folks are not doing financial planning work," the magazine editorialized, "because it is almost inconceivable that professionals are doing financial planning today without the help of some software application." Even more confounding, said the editors, was the 28 percent of respondents who said they used no form of portfolio management software. (Albridge and Schwab PortfolioCenter were the most popular choices among planners who did use portfolio management applications.) "We assume that some financial planners do not manage money, and others turn to third parties for portfolio management and reporting," the magazine concluded.

The Benefits of Diversification: Modern Portfolio Theory

Long before they knew it as *modern portfolio theory* (MPT), some early financial planners were putting a simplified version of MPT into practice. They called it "Don't put all your eggs in one basket."

Commonsensical though it seems when reduced to basic principles, MPT was revolutionary back in 1952, when Harry Markowitz, a 25-year-old economist with the RAND Corporation, published a paper titled "Portfolio Selection." The article, which concluded that portfolio diversification reduces risk and enhances expected return over time, became the cornerstone of MPT.

Before Markowitz's work, investors had focused on the risks and returns of individual securities. Markowitz looked instead at combinations of assets; he wrote that every possible asset combination could be plotted in risk-return space, and the collection of all such possible portfolios defined a region in that space. The line along the upper edge of this region is known as the *efficient frontier* (or the "Markowitz frontier"). For a given amount of risk, the portfolio lying on the efficient frontier represents the combination offering the best possible return.

Markowitz later wrote that the basic concepts of MPT had come to him while he was reading John Burr Williams's *Theory of Investment Value*, which proposed that the value of a stock should equal the present value of its future dividends:

> *But if the investor were only interested in expected values of securities, he or she would only be interested in the expected value of the portfolio; and to maximize the expected value of a portfolio one need invest only in a single security. This, I knew, was not the way investors did or should act. Investors diversify because they are concerned with risk as well as return. Variance came to mind as a measure of risk. The fact that portfolio variance depended on security covariances added to the plausibility of the approach. Since there were two criteria, risk and return, it was natural to assume that investors selected from the set of Pareto optimal risk-return combinations.[7]*

For their work on MPT, Markowitz and two fellow economists, Merton H. Miller of the University of Chicago and William F. Sharpe of Stanford University, were awarded the Nobel Prize in economics in 1990.

Financial planner Mike Ryan attended the first Ibbotson conference[8] on MPT in the late 1980s and later earned a CIMA (Certified Investment Management Analyst) designation through the University of Pennsylvania's Wharton School. But he observed that MPT had been practiced in the planning community as early as the 1970s:

> *The methodology had been developed in the academic community and applied to business following the severe recession of 1972–1974, when many pension plans found themselves severely underfunded. Institutional consultants who alone had access to the databases required to do this analysis dominated the field [but] financial planners quickly adopted the methodology in our practices.*

This was lucky on several counts. First, it greatly benefited our clients who were able to accomplish their financial goals with less risk. Second, it provided a revenue model for planners who wanted to move away from the commission model to a fee-based platform [assets under management] but were unsure how to replace the revenue stream. Charging fees can be onerous to clients. Debiting fees from an increasing asset base was painless and the margins were very healthy for the planners. The fact that financial markets began a decade-long bull market just as many planners were instituting this model was a great windfall.

Modern portfolio theory has not been without its critics. As the global economy skidded in 2007 and 2008, planners began questioning their traditional approaches. Kenneth R. Solow, CFP, a founding principal and chief investment officer of Pinnacle Advisory Group in Columbia, Maryland, told the *Journal of Financial Planning* in January 2009 that he was turning away from MPT and toward more iconoclastic thinkers such as Nassim Nicholas Taleb, whose works examine the role of randomness and "black swan events." "The idea that risk should be measured by standard deviation, which depends on normal distributions, is just one of the many false assumptions underlying modern portfolio theory and the capital asset pricing model," Solow said.[9]

The Probability Approach: Monte Carlo Simulation

Faster desktop computers gave financial planners access to a number of financial planning calculations that would have been impossibly time consuming if performed manually. Among them was the process called *Monte Carlo simulation*, which despite the name does not involve a roulette wheel. (The math formula behind Monte Carlo was developed by Manhattan Project scientists during World War II to forecast probable outcomes.) Applied to financial planning, Monte Carlo allowed a planner to evaluate a retirement portfolio to see whether it would last a lifetime. If a portfolio is run through 10,000 simulations and worked 8,000 times, there is an 80 percent probability that the retirement portfolio is sufficient. Adjusting the portfolio and rerunning the simulation may result in greater odds of a favorable outcome.

Many financial planning practitioners first learned about Monte Carlo simulation through an article in the October 1997 issue of *Journal of Financial Planning*, written by H. Lynn Hopewell, CFP, who at the time was president of The Monitor Group in Virginia. As the *Journal*'s first practitioner-editor, Hopewell assigned himself a topic that became one of the first articles to advocate using Monte Carlo simulation for financial planning. "Decision Making Under Conditions of Uncertainty: A Wakeup Call for the Financial Planning Profession"[10] provided detailed real-world examples of Monte Carlo simulation, and it accomplished its goal. "Almost overnight, planners began to adopt Monte Carlo techniques," Hopewell later recalled.[11] "[Lynn] didn't invent Monte Carlo, but he brought its *use* in the profession to planners' attention, essentially urging planners to add the methodology to how they plan," said Bruce Most, a *Journal* editor at the time of the article's publication. "These 'academic' underpinnings are an absolute requirement for a true profession."[12]

Monte Carlo had its detractors, primarily those who complained that the software was inadequate in extended bear markets. A common alternative to Monte Carlo simulation is the "flat rate" projection: assigning an expected rate of return to each investment in the portfolio. But flat-rate projections ignore the variability of the assumptions, said Dan Moisand, CFP, a Florida planner. He told Bankrate.com in 2003,

> *You can pick any number—if you average X percent each year, this is what it will look like. But in reality it doesn't work out that way. Monte Carlo helps bring in that variability and paints a more dynamic and realistic picture.*
>
> *The average rate of return has a fifty-fifty chance of happening. No one wants their retirement to come down to a flip of a coin. They want something bigger than a fifty percent chance of success.*[13]

The Balancing Act: Asset Allocation

During the late 1980s and 1990s, asset allocation became a hot trend in financial planning. While not uncontroversial, asset allocation was closer to the advisory roots of financial planning. Like modern portfolio theory, asset allocation builds on a commonsense concept: To minimize risk and maximize reward, assets should be divided into different classes—bonds, equities, real estate, and so on. Balancing the asset classes requires understanding a client's needs and objectives. Most asset models acknowledge that clients will have one of four objectives: preservation of capital, income, growth, or a balance of two or more goals.

Roger Gibson, CFP, whose 1989 book, *Asset Allocation*, has never been out of print (see the profile), liked to point out that asset allocation principles are ancient: The Jewish *Talmud*, written between 1200 B.C. and 500 A.D., contained the admonition, "Let every man divide his money into three parts, and invest a third in land, a third in business, and a third let him keep in reserve."[14] Diversification, Gibson observed, "is a time-honored investment principle."

Profile: Roger Gibson

Asset allocation was barely in the financial planning lexicon in the late 1970s when Roger Gibson enrolled in Carnegie Mellon University's graduate business program. Instead, many financial planners practiced market timing with their clients' portfolios, chasing the elusive target of "buy low, sell high." Gibson had always had a head for numbers: He'd been an undergraduate math major, worked as an operations supervisor for welfare programs in Pittsburgh, and received the top score in the country the year he took the CFP certification examination. (He had discovered his calling while working for the Social Security Administration: He'd picked up a copy of the *Christian Science Monitor*, read an article about the College for Financial Planning, and said to himself, "That's what I want to do.") The more he studied, the more he questioned market timing. He found himself asking questions: If market timing isn't possible, what's the best way to manage a client's portfolio? How can I mitigate the risks of the investment markets? Which strategy will maximize the likelihood of clients reaching their financial goals?

Exploring those questions led Gibson to develop his ideas about strategic asset allocation. When he received his master's degree, he put that theory into practice by passing up the corporate route most of his classmates chose and instead joined Allegheny Financial Group, a regional financial planning firm. "I was carried along by my enthusiasm," Gibson later recalled.

I wanted to develop a portfolio design process that actively involved clients in investment decision-making. In many ways, the greatest opportunity to add value is in the educational work advisors do with their clients—work that enables them to make better investment decisions.

Throughout the 1980s, Gibson took his message on the road, speaking at IAFP and ICFP meetings:

After a talk, I often had advisors approach me and express surprise that my clients would embrace an investment approach that made no attempt to side-step bad markets. . . . Financial planners were a natural audience for an approach that actively involved clients in the decision-making process. Financial planners have a strong

(*continued*)

Profile: Roger Gibson (*Continued*)

orientation toward client education, and the payoffs for educating clients about asset allocation are quite high.

In 1989, having freed up some time by changing his focus from financial planning to investment advisory work, Gibson turned his ideas into a book, *Asset Allocation: Balancing Financial Risk*. Boiled down to its essence, *Asset Allocation* was a primer on putting modern portfolio theory into practice. Gibson's premise seemed intuitive in retrospect:

Intelligent portfolio design involves a compromise between the competing objectives of greater returns on the one hand and avoidance of excessive volatility on the other hand. The compromise is reflected in the most important investment decision an investor makes: the balance between interest-generating investments and equity investments. Beyond that, a more broadly diversified approach that utilizes multiple asset classes can dramatically improve longer-term portfolio risk-adjusted returns.

"The concepts weren't new," Gibson explained, "but my timing was fortunate—mine was the first book on the subject." Now in its fourth edition, the book has been a best-seller since its original printing and has been published in Japan, Germany, South Korea, and China, and will soon be released in India.

In 2003, *Financial Planning* magazine named Gibson to its annual "Movers & Shakers" list; the article said many planners credited Gibson's insistence on diversification and realistic models with having "saved" their firms. The financial crisis of 2008 and 2009 was a critical test for asset allocation theory, Gibson acknowledged. "All major equity classes went down together once the global panic got under way," he said. "Strategic asset allocation mitigates risk; it doesn't eliminate it. As [former Federal Reserve Board Chairman] Paul Volcker said many years ago: 'You cannot hedge the world.'"

The asset allocation concept leapt to planners' attention in 1986, when an article by Gary P. Brinson, L. Randolph Hood, and Gilbert L. Beebower ("Determinants of Portfolio Performance") claimed that more than 93 percent of a portfolio's return could be explained solely by its asset mix, not market timing or security selection. The study became known by its authors' initials, BHB; it received the prestigious Graham & Dodd award for outstanding article in the *Financial Analysts Journal* and turned up in just about every advertisement, marketing brochure, and slide presentation in financial services.

But not everyone was convinced. William Jahnke had an economics degree from Stanford and an MBA from UC Berkeley; before becoming chairman and chief investment officer of Financial Educational Design Corp. in Larkspur, California, he had been manager of institutional portfolio development at Wells Fargo. And he didn't buy the BHB study. His article, "The Asset Allocation Hoax,"[15] in the February 1997 issue of the *Journal of Financial Planning*, concluded that investment policy mix explains only about 14 percent of a portfolio's total return. What's more, Jahnke accused financial professionals of taking liberties with the BHB study to market a wide range of investment products, some of which rarely related to a client's long-term goals.

The article stirred up controversy—immediately and for years to come. Brinson, Beebower, and Brian D. Singer rebutted Jahnke's conclusions in a later article, and the controversy quickly caught financial planners' attention. The debate was still simmering in 2006, when the *Journal* published a long "review and reconciliation" of the conflicting opinions.[16] The authors' conclusion:

[U]nless there is a strong belief in the ability to select active managers who will deliver higher risk-adjusted net returns, investors' focus should be on the asset allocation choice and its implementation using broadly diversified, low-cost portfolios with limited market timing.

Behavioral Finance

While asset allocation, asset management, and modern portfolio theory rely on probability formulas and mathematical models for their success, *behavioral finance*—which began gaining popularity in the late 1990s—turns the questions upside down. Rather than analyzing how portfolios perform, behavioral finance examines how *people* faced with money decisions perform. How tolerant are they of risk? How easy or challenging is it for them to make choices? And the big question: Which outcome is most likely to make a person happy?

Psychology was closely associated with early economic theory, including that of eighteenth-century writers Adam Smith and Jeremy Bentham. It later fell out of favor, to be replaced by theories that assumed people always act rationally with regard to money. A groundbreaking 1979 paper by two psychologists, Daniel Kahneman and Amos Tversky, shifted the discussion. In "Prospect Theory: An Analysis of Decision Under Risk," Kahneman and

> *"Your clients are far more distressed by prospective losses than they are made happy by equivalent gains."*
>
> —Daniel Kahneman

Tversky used the teachings of cognitive psychology to look at economic decision making—including the irrational variety.

In their prospect theory experiments, Kahneman and Tversky presented groups of subjects with this problem:

> *In addition to whatever you own, you have been given $1,000. You are now asked to choose between (A) a sure gain of $500 or (B) a 50 percent chance to gain $1,000 and a 50 percent chance to gain nothing.*

Another group was presented with this problem:

> *In addition to whatever you own, you have been given $2,000. You are now asked to choose between (A) a sure loss of $500 or (B) a 50 percent chance to lose $1,000 and a 50 percent chance to lose nothing.*

In the first group, 84 percent chose A. In the second group, 69 percent chose B. The two problems are identical in terms of net cash to the subject; however, the phrasing of the question causes the problems to be interpreted differently. "Put simply, your clients are far more distressed by prospective losses than they are made happy by equivalent gains," Kahneman said in a 2004 interview published in the *Journal of Financial Planning*.[17]

After Tversky's death in 1996, Kahneman collaborated with economist Richard Thaler on further research into "irrational" economic behavior. That work led to Kahneman's being awarded the 2002 Nobel Prize in economics. "The committee cited me for having integrated insights from psychological research into economic science," Kahneman wrote in his Nobel autobiography. "Although I do not wish to renounce any credit for my contribution, I should say that in my view the work of integration was actually done mostly by Thaler and the group of young economists that quickly began to form around him."[18]

Kahneman was a keynote speaker at FPA's 2004 convention. He observed, "All of us would be better investors if we just made fewer decisions."

Many planners found Kahneman's insights to be a welcome enhancement to their client services. Paula de Vos, CFP, of Synergist Wealth Advisors, LLC, in Carmel, California, told the *Journal of Financial Planning* that

planners provide value by being more dispassionate and objective, help-
ing clients control some of their prevalent instinctive behaviors that
can harm investment performance. Discussing behavioral finance with
clients leaves them more open to having personal discussions and mak-
ing the changes they need to succeed.[19]

Michael Pompian, CFP, CFA, an investment consultant in St. Louis, wrote a two-part article about behavioral economics for the *Journal of Financial Planning* based on his extensive study of 290 financial advisers in 30 countries. "The results were astounding," he summarized in the October 2008 issue of the *Journal*, saying that "93 percent of advisors believed that individual investors make irrational investment decisions, and 96 percent were successfully using behavioral finance to improve relationships with their clients."[20] Pompian proposed four "behavioral investor types" (BIT) to help advisers apply behavioral finance to their practices: Passive Preserver, Friendly Follower, Independent Individualist, and Active Accumulator. "By learning this process [of identifying an investor type] and applying it before creating an investment plan for a client, the client is more likely to be able to adhere to a plan ... and ... financial advisors build stronger relationships with their clients," Pompian wrote.

Life Planning and Interior Finance

The study and practice of behavioral finance proved to be excellent preparation for new forms of financial planning that emerged in the late 1990s. *Life planning* and *interior finance*—different names for essentially similar concepts—built on the principles of financial planning but greatly expanded the scope and depth of planners' services.

It was a development in sync with the spirit of the millennial era. Members of the post–World War II baby boom generation—77 million strong—were asking different questions about money, investments, work, and retirement from what their elders had, and financial planners sought relevant answers. Unlike previous generations, boomers tended to see retirement not as an abrupt end to work and income but as a dynamic new adventure. Many said they wanted to continue to work, but in new fields or under more flexible conditions. Many were comfortable with the language of therapy and of spiritual exploration; they were also more burdened with debt—from mortgages, cars, and credit cards—than their parents had been. A historically larger-than-ever percentage had experienced divorce and blended families. (For more about the challenges of serving baby boomers, see Chapter 9.)

One of the first planners to think strategically about these issues was Richard Wagner, JD, CFP, who in 1995 co-founded the Nazrudin Project as a think tank for exploring the multiple meanings of money (see the profile). Wagner preferred the term *integral finance* to describe his approach, which blended "exterior" premises about money power and money skills with "interior" premises about intimacy and social taboo. "Positively, money's virtues bring people together, encourage peace, and support creation and service," Wagner summarized in a 2002 *Journal of Financial Planning* article. "On the negative, we have substituted money for much that was inherently valuable."[21]

Profile: Richard B. Wagner

An undergraduate major in religious studies may not be the most obvious qualification for a career in financial planning. But for Dick Wagner, who co-founded the Nazrudin Project and formulated the conceptual basis of interior finance, the connection was perfectly logical. "Money is the second most frequently mentioned topic in the Bible," he noted. "Whether or not you believe in the Bible as an actual authoritative work of God, you have to respect it as a record of the priorities of people who worked pretty hard at being wise."

As he was about to enter a seminary, Wagner received what he terms "the anti-call." Instead, he earned a law degree at Lewis & Clark College in Portland, Oregon. Practicing law didn't live up to his idealistic expectations, however, and when he talked to some financial planners who were guests at his law firm's holiday party, something clicked. "I was thirty-one, and I realized I didn't know any happy fifty-year-old lawyers," Wagner said. "I also realized what an important role money had played in my own family and in the lives of people I knew." He left the law firm in 1982 and began working for a life insurance and financial planning firm; five years later he passed the CFP certification examination, and two years after that he and a colleague started their own firm.

From the start of his financial planning career, while he was developing his ideas about money and culture, Wagner was also deeply involved in financial planning organizations. He quit the IAFP in 1989 in protest over the failed merger and switched to the ICFP, where he quickly ascended the ranks, joining the institute's national committee and serving as president for the 1992–1993 term. In 1990, he published the landmark article "To Think ... Like a CFP" in the *Journal of Financial Planning*. In it, he compared the mindset of "established" professions like law and medicine with the comparatively "adolescent" thought processes of financial planners. Wagner came up with *interior finance* and *integral finance* to describe his ideal practice. He credits integral-consciousness pioneer Ken Wilber, author of *A Theory of Everything*, with nudging him toward that vocabulary; other influences included Jacob Needleman's *Money and the Meaning of Life* and the work of Belgian economist Bernard Lietaer, co-creator of the euro and the author of *The Future of Money*.

Wagner's Denver financial planning practice, WorthLiving, took its name from a Japanese planner who listed his clients' "worth living assets" as "family, art, religion, community, and education—the assets that make life worth living," Wagner said. His own aim, Wagner said, was "facilitating the vision and balance in our personal relationships with money."

And playing the role of gadfly: "It's such a miracle that financial planning has come to be what it is that I'm reluctant to be critical," he said. "But it's never wise to rest on our laurels." In particular, he said, he wanted to see more academic rigor and more emotional and spiritual training. "If economists are the modern equivalent of theologians," he said, harking back to his early academic experience, "then financial planners are the pastors. We serve an important community function in helping our clients understand their relationship with money."

Another life planning pioneer—and early collaborator with Wagner—was George Kinder, CFP, who began writing *Journal of Financial Planning* articles about what he called "money maturity" in 1996, and later turned the concepts into a book (see the profile). In April 1996, Kinder and Wagner collaborated on the first article in a new *Journal* section, "Money & Soul," that may have mystified more traditionally inclined readers. "Unfortunately, the emotional aspects of money generally have been neglected in our training as financial planning practitioners," they wrote. "Understanding them should be part of our profession's bag of skills. This is our focus in 'Money and Soul.'"[22]

Later that year, Kinder introduced *Journal* readers to his "seven stages of money maturity": Innocence, Pain, Knowledge, Understanding, Vigor, Vision, and *Aloha*—the last being a Hawaiian word Kinder interpreted to mean "simple human kindness around money." Kinder summarized the foundation of his philosophy in this way: "I believe that the existential dilemma of humanity is expressed in our relationships to money: How do we express the deep nature of our being in a world represented by dollar bills?"[23]

Profile: George Kinder

George Kinder has written that at one time he "assumed—as most of us do—that a sharp divide separates money and soul." When an economics professor at Harvard laughed at one of his papers, he "fled" to the English literature department. After graduating in 1970, he turned down a place in Harvard's literature Ph.D. program in favor of a move to the countryside, where he studied world religions, painted, and wrote. "I had heard the saying, 'Do what you love; the money will follow,'" he said. "But I couldn't find anybody to pay me to do what I loved."

Reluctantly at first, and at the urging of his concerned parents, Kinder migrated to the money side of the divide, drawing on his early interest in economics to become a stock analyst, a tax preparer, and eventually—after scoring third-highest in the state of Massachusetts on the CPA exam—a self-employed tax accountant and Certified Financial Planner professional in Cambridge. The practice gave him plenty of time to read, write poetry, and meditate. Still, the business thrived throughout the 1980s: "I found I had a knack for entrepreneurship," Kinder later said. He also had a talent for recognizing root causes. "Many of my clients were making bonehead investments, often on the recommendation of professional advisers," Kinder recalled. "Many of them were professors who'd been sold horrible tax shelters and been charged outrageous fees. I figured I owed them a chance at something better." His habit of asking clients to search their souls about their financial concerns earned him the affectionate nickname of "the tax therapist."

Then, in 1991, Kinder read a book that brought the "money" and "soul" parts of his life together: Jacob Needleman's groundbreaking *Money and the Meaning of Life*. The following year, he managed to get a speaking spot at the ICFP's Personal Economic Summit in Washington, D.C. "They put me on a panel on investments and savings," he recalled, "and I gave a pretty wild talk." Afterward, former ICFP president Madeline Noveck approached Kinder, shook her finger at him, and surprised him by saying, "You were the only out-of-the-box thinker at the whole conference! I want you back next year."

Kinder found another kindred spirit at that event—Dick Wagner, who was then serving a term as ICFP president. Wagner, who confided that he also had read Needleman's book, had the clout to bring Kinder's ideas to a wider audience. "It was like the ending of *Casablanca*," Kinder said, laughing. "'The beginning of a beautiful friendship.'" Together they formed the Nazrudin Project, a highly influential think tank dedicated to examining issues of spirituality and dysfunction related to money. After

Kinder's book, *The Seven Stages of Money Maturity*, was published in 1998, he was invited to give the keynote address at the ICFP annual conference. He went on to found the Kinder Institute of Life Planning, which offers five-day workshops that lead to a Registered Life Planning certification.

In 2006, Kinder won FPA's Heart of Financial Planning Distinguished Service Award for his work as an "innovator and influencer" in the profession. He has put his principles into practice in his own life: Although he maintains a demanding speaking schedule, he lives part of the year in Hana, Hawaii—"part of my life plan." His third book is a collection of poetry and photography. And he has never forsaken his literary studies. "To this day," Kinder said, "I take much of my guidance from William Blake, William Shakespeare, and Dante Alighieri."

By November 2000, there was enough interest in life planning that the National Endowment for Financial Education (NEFE) decided to sponsor a one-day think tank in St. Louis to explore the concept. Participants included CFP certificants; researchers and consultants in retirement planning and productive aging; a professor of gerontology and age-related employment issues; human resources consultants and executives; a wealth and philanthropy counselor; a minister and vocational specialist; a vice president of a major brokerage firm; and life planning specialists. "As the planning profession matures, there is at least anecdotal evidence that its emphasis may be starting to shift from financial planning to a more personal and holistic focus on [people's] financial *and* non-financial needs," the conveners wrote in a report published in 2002.[24] As a first step, they added, participants agreed "that a professional dialogue on life planning requires a thorough examination of its multi-faceted messages and a definition."

> *"As the planning profession matures, . . . its emphasis may be starting to shift from financial planning to a more personal and holistic focus on [people's] financial and non-financial needs."*
> —Report on NEFE life planning meeting, November 2000

One definition was proposed by Carol Anderson—a researcher, writer, and consultant on retirement preparation and life planning—and Joyce Cohen, the founder of Unconventional Wisdom, a firm specializing in creative aging, career transition, and retirement preparation. Life planning, they wrote in a research paper,

> *is a comprehensive approach to planning that is appropriate and useful for all ages—young adults as well as those nearing retirement. It is based on the philosophy that the most successful and satisfying retirement experiences are based on a series of thoughtful, future-focused decisions made throughout one's adult life.*

It was noted that the words *money, finances, wealth,* or *investments* don't appear in that definition. Or, as Ken Rouse, CFP, a principal with Ernst & Young's personal financial counseling division, put it in the introduction to his book, *Putting Money in Its Place*: "Welcome to a discussion of money that does not begin with money at all. It begins with you!"[25]

Participants in the NEFE think tank—titled Practical Applications of Life and Retirement Planning to Financial Planning—agreed on one big issue: that financial planners should take part in the evolution of the discipline. As one of them said, "We talk about this notion of 'life happens,' but life planning happens, too. It's already happening. And it's going to happen with us or without us."

In the years that followed, as life planning gradually became accepted in mainstream financial planning, planners continued to redefine and explore the concept and its practical applications. "Call it *spiritanality*, the new face of life, legacy, and retirement planning," wrote Lewis J. Walker, CFP, CIMC, CRC, in the May 2004 issue of the *Journal of Financial Planning*. "You will not find 'spiri-ta-nal-ity' in a dictionary. It is a coined expression recognizing a unique blend of personality and spirituality."[26]

From general observations about the value of life planning techniques, the profession gradually moved toward a more rigorous approach. Roy Diliberto, CFP, and Mitch Anthony, a nonplanner who had co-founded the Financial Life Planning Institute, developed a checklist for planners to use in tracking the events in clients' lives. Anthony identified more than 50 life transitions "with predictable and manifold financial implications," and Diliberto put the list to use in his Philadelphia planning practice. The two men reported on their success in 2003: Not only did it help Diliberto "avoid unpleasant surprises," it also "teaches our clients to be thinking about the future in areas that are not as obvious as retiring at a certain date or educating children"—such as the sudden illness or disability of a spouse or parent.[27]

Results of an even more rigorously designed study were published in June 2008, by Carol Anderson and Deanna L. Sharpe, Ph.D., CFP. Anderson and Sharpe worked collaboratively with members of the Life Planning Consortium, an ad hoc alliance of financial planners and communicators brought together by Andrea White, president of Arizona coaching

Loren Dunton, who founded with twelve of his colleagues what would become the IAFP and College for Financial Planning.

Reprinted with permission by the Financial Planning Association.

James Barnash, FPA president, 2005.

Cronin Photography, reprinted with permission.

Alexandra Armstrong, IAFP president in 1985.

Reprinted with permission by the Financial Planning Association.

P. Kemp Fain, Jr., an advocate of "one profession, one designation" and member of the first CFP class in 1973. He was the primary author of the famous white paper on unifying the profession.

Reprinted with permission by the Financial Planning Association.

Gwen Fletcher, financial planning pioneer in Australia in the early 1980s.

Reprinted with permission by the Financial Planning Association.

Dr. Daniel Kahneman: FPA Denver, 2004.

Dr. Kahneman, 2002 Nobel Prize winner in Economics, spoke on the necessity of professional financial planning. He and other researchers have demonstrated the vital importance of professional financial planning for the good of society.

Cronin Photography, reprinted with permission.

First graduating class, College for Financial Planning, 1973.

Reprinted with permission by the Financial Planning Association.

Lewis Kearns, chair of the board of regents of the College for Financial Planning, awarding CFP diploma to David King.

Reprinted with permission of Mrs. Bernice King.

Original IBCFP Board, 1985–1987.
Seated (left to right): Colin "Ben" Coombs, Daniel S. Parks, Dr. Tahira K. Hira, and E. Denby Brandon, Jr.
Standing (left to right): Charles G. Hughes, P. Kemp Fain, Jr., Raymond A. Parkins, Dr. William L. Anthes, H. Oliver Welch, and David M. King.

Reprinted with permission of the CFP Board.

First CFP International Organization meeting, September 25, 1992, in Anaheim, California.

Seated (left to right): Greg Devine (Australia) and Kazlo Tanaka (Japan).

Standing (left to right): H. Oliver Welch and E. Denby Brandon, Jr., chair.

Reprinted with permission of the IBCFP.

The London launch of the FPSB on October 13, 2004, a defining moment in the internationalization of the CFP marks. FPSB chairperson, Maureen Tsu and CFP Board chairperson, David Diesslin sign the official papers.

Copyright © 2002-2009 Financial Planning Standards Boards Ltd. All right reserved. Reprinted with permission.

The London launch, 2004. John Carpenter, FPSB Board past-chairperson; Francis Rim, executive director, Korean Financial Planners Association; chairman Byung Chul Yoon, Korean Financial Planners Association; Ian Heraud, Australia FPSB Council chairperson-elect and 2005 FPSB Board member; and K. P. Liu, executive director of Financial Planning Association of Taiwan.

Copyright © 2002-2009 Financial Planning Standards Boards Ltd. All right reserved. Reprinted with permission.

Henry Montgomery and David King at early ICFP Retreat.

Reprinted with permission by the Financial Planning Association.

ICFP retreat, 1985.

Reprinted with permission by the Financial Planning Association.

Ben Stein, widely known speaker and writer, with FPA president Elizabeth Jetton, FPA Denver, 2004.

Mr. Stein has been influential in popularizing financial education.

Cronin Photography, reprinted with permission.

General session.

Reprinted with permission by the Financial Planning Association.

FPA 2008 annual conference education session.

Reprinted with permission by the Financial Planning Association.

THE FINANCIAL PLANNER $

NEW HORIZONS IN FINANCIAL PLANNING

AUGUST
SEPTEMBER   **A MAGAZINE FOR PROFESSIONALS**

1972
one dollar

OFFICIAL PUBLICATION OF THE
SOCIETY FOR FINANCIAL COUNSELLING, INC.

International Association of Financial Planners   College for Financial Planning

The Financial Planner, 1972.

Reprinted with permission by the Financial Planning Association.

Journal *of*

FINANCIAL PLANNING

www.FPAjournal.org

Expanding the Body of Knowledge in the Financial Planning Profession

Also Inside:

10 *Questions with*
Hal Brill on SRI and Unhealthy Relationships with Money | Page 20

Contributions

When Should Retirees Retrench? Later Than You Think | Page 50

Benefits and Management of Inflation-Protected Treasury Bonds | Page 60

Data Dependence and Sustainable Real Withdrawal Rates | Page 70

FIRST AID
for Clients in Emotional Crisis
Page 28

FPA⹁ The Official Publication of
FINANCIAL PLANNING ASSOCIATION
The Heart of Financial Planning™

SEPTEMBER 2008 | VOLUME 21 | NUMBER 9

Journal of Financial Planning, 2008.

Reprinted with permission by the Financial Planning Association.

firm Financial Conversations. Anderson and Sharpe surveyed planners and their clients on key communication factors. (FPA co-sponsored the study, and CFP Board provided funding; the research relied heavily on CFP Board's practice standards as guidelines. Andrea White converted the survey instruments to an electronic format and created the data collection process.) The results were mixed, but generally encouraging for advocates of life planning. Anderson and Sharpe were able to identify "five communication tasks representative of a life planning approach that are directly related to higher levels of client trust and commitment in financial planning relationships." The tasks resembled the six-point financial planning process, with points four and five representing the most significant departures:

1. Planner and client mutually define scope of engagement before providing financial services.
2. Planner helps client identify personal and financial goals and objectives.
3. Planner uses a systematic process to help client clarify values and priorities.
4. Planner makes effort to explore and learn about the client's cultural expectations/biases, personality type/traits, and family history/values.
5. Planner explains how financial advice aligns with and supports client values, goals, needs, and priorities.

Interestingly, Anderson and Sharpe discovered that clients placed greater value on planners' efforts to learn about cultural expectations, personality types, and family history than did planners themselves.[28]

Did life planning, behavioral finance, asset allocation, and other theoretical underpinnings contribute to financial planning's acceptance as a true profession? To a degree; as Chapter 8 shows, other developments such as practice standards and educational requirements were probably more fundamental. But a more sophisticated body of knowledge certainly gave planners a wider range of tools with which to practice and helped them understand their mission more clearly.

A Proliferation of Practice Models

Financial planning was originally envisioned as a comprehensive service: not merely the creation of a financial plan but also the provision of integrated advice to clients about taxes, retirement savings, employee compensation and benefits, investments, and other issues. Most planners indeed offered comprehensive financial planning, but new tools and technologies gave them greater flexibility in the way they structured their businesses. Some became specialists, while others enlarged the concept of *comprehensive* to include what became known as life planning or integral finance.

Money management was one service that was rarely part of comprehensive financial planning in the early years, except among those planners who were affiliated with broker-dealers. According to a 1988 Securities and Exchange Commission report,

> A financial planner usually does not manage client assets. Instead, the planner's primary service is to prepare a financial plan for the client, and to offer advice as to the purchase or sale of specific financial products appropriate to the implementation of the plan.[29]

True, not all planners abided by that strict definition. The SEC report continued:

> With some financial planners the process ends with the presentation of a financial plan, for which the planner is compensated by a fee. In the more typical situation, however, once the client is presented with the plan, the implementation of the plan includes the purchase of investment or insurance products specifically recommended by the planner. Thus the planner may be affiliated with a broker-dealer, or with an insurance company, or both. And the planner's remuneration for the client may come more from commissions on the sale of products than from fees generated by the presentation of the plan.[30]

Planners who didn't want to be perceived as product salespeople often chose a fee-only practice model. Fee-only gained appeal in the 1980s, when desktop-computing tools became widespread and relatively sophisticated and planners could break away from broker-dealer affiliates (and their mainframe computers). Before then, fee-only planners were rare, said Elaine Bedel, CFP, president of Bedel Financial Consulting in Indianapolis:

> When I first opened my shop, people around the country told me, "You're a fool, Elaine. You're leaving all this money on the table [by not taking commissions]." And they probably were right, but it just wasn't comfortable for me. I came through a fee-only route to doing financial planning, where many others came from the insurance industry or the brokerage industry, and charging commissions was just part of what they did.[31]

In the late 1980s and early 1990s, a variation on the fee-only model emerged. Assets under management (AUM) put planners in the role of money managers, earning income from clients' assets being handled by the planner. The financial advantages to planners were obvious, but the trend worried some observers. In a 1995 *CFP Today* article, William

Anthes, then president of the National Endowment for Financial Education, cautioned that the jury was still out on whether this trend was wise, or one that planners would live to regret if faced with a protracted market downturn. "Don't forget you are a financial planner who provides comprehensive planning services to the public, not just a money manager," Anthes warned.[32]

In a February 1996 *Journal of Financial Planning* essay, Ed McCarthy, CFP, asked, "Are we losing our bearings?" In the 1980s, he wrote, "comprehensive financial planning was the standard by which practitioners measured their relationships with clients. . . . This in-depth analysis often resulted in the comprehensive financial plan, a hefty document that could easily run fifty pages or more of detailed analysis and advice." With the shift in focus to assets under management, "[m]any experienced planners acknowledge that they have not produced a written plan, particularly a comprehensive one, in years." The "darker side" of this migration, McCarthy wrote, was that some planners "are losing touch with their roots, and risk becoming a subset of the money manager universe."[33]

> *"Some planners are losing touch with their roots, and risk becoming a subset of the money manager universe."*
> —Ed McCarthy on asset management, 1996

Inherent in the AUM model was a conflict of interest: The planner stood to gain only if his or her clients' assets were in fact "under management." Even if, for example, a client might benefit from owning real property or precious metals, a planner might be reluctant to recommend their purchase and thus deprive himself of an AUM fee. There was another downside to the AUM model: It presumed that the value of a client's assets would always go up. That was generally the case during the long bull market that began in the 1990s, but during the severe recession that began in 2008, planners who followed the AUM model were forced to reconsider whether their approach would prove profitable in the long term.

Other financial planners' practices were a blend of fee and commission services, while a few worked on retainer and some—like Sheryl Garrett, CFP, of the nationwide Garrett Planning Network, whose goal was bringing financial planning to low- and middle-income people—worked on an hourly basis. (Garrett compared her business model to "a walk-in clinic that treats sprained ankles and dispenses flu shots—you're there for everyday kinds of issues."[34]) On the other end of the spectrum were wealth managers, who offered sophisticated investment strategies, estate planning, philanthropic advice, and other services to high-net-worth clients.

Still other planners brought a multidisciplinary approach to their work, teaming with other professionals—lawyers, psychologists, accountants—to focus on specific professions such as doctors, dentists, and engineers. One such development, probably not envisioned 40 years ago when financial planning was born, was Pride Planners. Founded by three CFP professionals in 1999, Pride Planners brought together planners who served gay, lesbian, and nontraditional clients and their families.[35] The group has held biannual conferences since 2001.

The rise of specialization and a sophisticated knowledge base appeared to many planners to be proof that the profession had finally come of age. At the same time, it was far from clear that the public shared that perception. Was increased diversity in fact preventing planners from reaching the consensus required for a coherent public image? That question, and others related to the definition of a profession, would continue to be discussed, debated, and argued about as financial planning entered its fifth decade.

CHAPTER 8

The Quest for Professional Status

From the beginning, leaders of the financial planning movement envisioned not simply a career but a profession. "I had a compulsion to upgrade the profession for the sake of both the practitioner and the public," said Lew Kearns, explaining why he put in hundreds of volunteer hours in the 1970s to develop the first CFP curriculum and serve as first chair of the College for Financial Planning. Jim Johnston, who worked with Kearns and Loren Dunton, "dreamed of a new financial professional who would provide better service to the consumer," as he said in 2008. They and their colleagues used *profession* freely with reference to CFP practitioners. When the Institute of Certified Financial Planners adopted its original constitution and bylaws in 1974, a code of ethics stipulated that "the honored ideals of the CFP profession imply that the responsibility of the CFP extend not only to the individual, but also to the society.... CFP certificants should obey all laws, uphold the dignity and honor of the profession, and accept its self-imposed disciplines...."

Forty years after financial planning's inception, had the dream of a profession been realized? Was financial planning on par with the traditional professions of law, medicine, and theology? Was it, in fact, "the first new profession in four hundred years," as some practitioners have called it?[1] For that matter, did financial planners in 2009 *want* their occupation to be regarded as a profession, with all of a profession's attendant obligations?

Opinion on all these questions remains divided. Bill Carter, who served on national boards of several financial planning organizations in the 1980s and 1990s, spoke for many when he observed in 2008, "We are in the baby stages of being a profession. But we don't determine if we are a profession. The public determines it. And now, when you ask consumers where they go for financial planning advice, the majority say they go to a CFP practitioner."

Of course, there are objective criteria as well. The commonly accepted characteristics of a profession include education, examination, experience, ethics and discipline, credential or license, clearly disclosed compensation, government regulation, public benefit and social purpose, and public recognition. Within financial planning, the first four characteristics—education, examination, experience, and ethics—became known as the "four Es." Together, they set the foundation for granting the fifth: the Certified Financial Planner credential.

The Education of a Financial Planner

A profession's members are assumed to have extensive theoretical knowledge and to possess skills based on that knowledge. A common body of knowledge, study, and training lies at the foundation of a profession. Jim Johnston knew this in 1969 and lobbied Loren Dunton to include an education component in their endeavor. "I thought that we could revolutionize the industry by teaching people to sit down with clients, talk about their goals, and look at the whole picture—not just recite a sales pitch, make a sale, and walk away," Johnston said.

Dunton was persuaded, and the following purpose was included in the charter for the new Society for Financial Counseling:

> *To establish an educational institute providing a certification program outside of either the mutual fund or insurance industry, to indicate the ability and desire in specific individuals to provide objective guidance and assistance to the public in the form of Financial Counseling.*

The educational institute they envisioned became the College for Financial Planning. Lew Kearns and other volunteers began hammering out the college's first CFP curriculum. Presented as a self-study guide, it was divided into six sections: fundamentals, money management, reviewing financial media, the investment model, considerations in effective financial planning, and counseling and consumer behavior. Brief by today's standards, this early curriculum was a groundbreaking effort at taking a more comprehensive approach to working with clients and their finances. And it outlined the core of what came to be known as the financial planning process.

The Financial Planning Process

Financial planners describe financial planning as a *process* that focuses on the client—not a product or a one-time event. Over the years, the definition of that process has steadily evolved.

1970s

Lew Kearns, Jim Johnston, Hy Yurman, and other volunteers on the college's education committee described the financial planning process in one of their lessons:

1. Collecting and evaluating financial and personal information
2. Counseling on financial objectives and alternatives
3. Installing the financial program
4. Coordinating the elements of the financial plan that involve others
5. Keeping the long-range financial plan current in light of internal and/or external changes

1980s

The International Association for Financial Planning (IAFP) published a six-step process in a 1983 brochure promoting the IAFP's Registry of Financial Planning Practitioners. This client-centered process was intended to serve as a guide toward a successful financial plan.

For clients, the key steps were:

1. Clarify your present situation by collecting and assessing all relevant personal and financial data.
2. Decide where you want to go by identifying financial and personal goals and objectives.
3. Identify financial problems that create barriers to achieving your goals.
   The planner's role comprised three subsequent steps:
4. Provide a written financial plan that meets specific standards.
5. Implement or coordinate the implementation of the right strategy to ensure that the client reaches his or her goals and objectives.
6. Provide periodic review and revision of the plan to ensure that the client stays on track.

(*continued*)

The Financial Planning Process (*Continued*)

1990s and 2000s

In 1995, CFP Board began developing standards for the financial planning process. In 2008, it refined its definition to include some or all of six elements:

1. Establishing and defining the client–planner relationship
2. Gathering client data including goals
3. Analyzing and evaluating the client's current financial status
4. Developing and presenting financial planning recommendations and/or alternatives
5. Implementing the recommendations
6. Monitoring the recommendations

Later volunteers worked to beef up the curriculum. New material on tax planning, tax shelters, pensions, and profit sharing was added, along with more case studies. Texts, supplementary readings, and teaching methods were repeatedly evaluated and reworked.

Under the leadership of William L. Anthes, who was recruited to become the college's president in 1979, coursework was refined, processes improved, academics hired, and the reach of the CFP curriculum expanded. The college also supported the concept of continuing education, but had no system for tracking graduates' CE activity until 1980, when the ICFP began to monitor and award continuing education credit on behalf of the college. The ICFP's policy required 30 hours of CE annually, enforced on the honor system; by 1986, the requirement had been increased to 45 hours. Failure to comply could cause a member's status to drop from "regular" to "associate," and the ICFP reserved the right to randomly check documentation.

To provide opportunities for continuing education, the ICFP began annual retreats in 1981, where experienced planners could receive instruction on subjects such as "management by computer" and "what the CFP [practitioner] should know about taxes." Five years later, a residency program was established for newly minted and less experienced planners, who were paired with CFP practitioner mentors during weeklong events that focused on solving case studies. The retreats and residency program remain core programs of FPA, formed in 2000 from the merger of the ICFP and IAFP.

Educational Opportunities Expand

With the establishment in 1985 of the International Board of Standards and Practices for Certified Financial Planners, Inc. (IBCFP—later renamed CFP Board), educational opportunities for future CFP licensees grew. In addition, because the IBCFP now owned the CFP marks, it could both grant and revoke the right of financial planners to use them. This signified the transition of the CFP designation from an education credential to a professional certification.

In 1986, the IBCFP established curriculum standards for colleges and universities that wished to register their program with the organization. The standards outlined a course of academic study that would cover certain personal financial planning topics. Within this framework, schools could develop their own programs and offer them at a certificate, bachelor's, or master's degree level. Students who successfully completed a registered program became eligible to sit for the CFP examination. By the end of 1987, 24 institutions besides the College for Financial Planning had registered programs with the IBCFP; they included Adelphi University, Georgia State University, Purdue University, San Diego State University, and Texas Tech University.[2]

The IBCFP also allowed individuals with certain credentials, such as CFA, CLU, or ChFC designations, a PhD in business or economics, or CPA or attorney licenses, to bypass the education requirement if they had been engaged in the practice of financial planning for at least three years. And the organization began reviewing transcripts for those who had completed coursework that corresponded to the CFP curriculum. If the transcript review was satisfactory, an individual could challenge the CFP examination.

In 1987, the IBCFP published the results of a study conducted by the College for Financial Planning: "Job Analysis of the Professional Requirements of the Certified Financial Planner." The study was based on a survey that asked more than 2,000 practicing financial planners to identify the tasks and topics of knowledge they used. The findings were grouped into six categories: fundamentals of financial planning, insurance planning, investment planning, income tax planning, retirement planning and employee benefits, and estate planning. (The categories have remained essentially unchanged since then.) A year later, in 1988, the IBCFP set a continuing education (CE) requirement for CFP licensees, based on the topic areas of the job analysis findings. Today, the requirement specifies 30 hours of CE every two years, including at least two hours on CFP Board's ethical and practice standards.

The results of the 1987 job analysis study formed the basis for a revised model curriculum for registered educational institutions in 1990, as well as for the content of the CFP examination. Subsequent job analysis studies have been conducted by independent research organizations approximately every five years. According to CFP Board, these periodic studies ensured that the organization's educational requirements continued to reflect the current practice of financial planning as well as the knowledge required by practitioners "to provide comprehensive financial planning advice to the public without supervision." A 2004 study, for example, identified 89 financial planning topics, including cash flow management, insurance needs analysis, employee stock options, investment strategies, income tax fundamentals and calculations, qualified plan rules and options, and estate planning for nontraditional relationships.

The new millennium also saw the first PhD program in financial planning, at Texas Tech in 2000. To help even more colleges and universities establish degree programs, CFP Board and the Academy of Financial Services (AFS), an academic organization, collaborated to develop a model curriculum in 2004. Academics who worked on the project were encouraged to go beyond CFP Board's topic list to capture the best thinking of academics and provide a high-quality curriculum for students preparing for a career in personal financial planning.

Another academic undertaking was aimed at advancing the body of knowledge in financial planning. Beginning in 1979, the *Journal of the Institute of Certified Financial Planners* (which later became the *Journal of Financial Planning*) published peer-reviewed articles for the academic and practitioner communities. By 1991, academic societies such as the Academy of Financial Services and the Association for Financial Counseling and Planning Education were also publishing financial planning research articles in refereed journals.[3] CFP Board supported these and other efforts with monetary awards for outstanding research papers and articles published in academic, practitioner, or consumer publications. In 1994, CFP Board also began providing stipends and grants for original research in personal financial planning.

In 2006, CFP Board reassessed its educational standards compared with other certification bodies. The results led to a number of recommendations, including requiring a bachelor's degree for candidates for CFP certification. The bachelor's degree requirement took effect in 2007.

By the end of 2008, there were 341 registered programs at 213 colleges and universities across the United States. Two hundred programs were at the certificate level, 91 were undergraduate programs, 46 were graduate programs, and 4 were doctoral programs.[4]

"We are among the very few who have ever had the charter to build a profession from scratch and to take responsibility for a foundation that can carry the weight of the future."

—Richard Wagner

Examination: Proving Mastery

A second building block of a profession is the ability to verify that those who wish to practice the profession have mastered a certain level of theoretical and practical knowledge. For most professions, this proof takes the form of an examination.

In 1972, the first CFP examination, consisting of 150 essay questions, was prepared by the College for Financial Planning's volunteer education committee. Exam-preparation courses were held around the country, taught by financial planning practitioners and people with relevant graduate degrees.

Because the college's curriculum was grouped into six subjects— introduction to financial planning, risk management, investments, tax planning, retirement and employee benefits, and estate planning—students took exams on each subject as they completed the coursework. This six-part serial exam format continued when the IBCFP opened the exam to qualified candidates from institutions other than the College for Financial Planning.

Within a few years, however, the IBCFP began to consider moving to a single, comprehensive examination as opposed to its series of six academic tests. IBCFP leaders P. Kemp Fain, Jr., and Tim Kochis were among those who advocated the change. Kochis recalled, "If we wanted the CFP mark to be respected as a professional credential, the exam needed to be a single and comprehensive exam."

The comprehensive 10-hour CFP Certification Examination was introduced in 1991. Bob Goss, the IBCFP's executive director, said the development was "a tremendous milestone for the CFP designation," adding, "The process will now be similar to the bar exam and the CPA exam." A November 1992 *IBCFP Bulletin* explained, "The purpose [of the examination] has changed from educational testing to a measure of competence to practice financial planning as defined by the 1987 job analysis study."

As of 2009, the exam continued to reflect the latest job analysis studies and was developed with the assistance of volunteer financial planners and academicians. Proposed exam questions were analyzed for relevance, fairness, validity, and reliability, and field-tested with financial planning practitioners. In 2008, 6,908 individuals took the exam. The pass rate since 1991 has averaged 57 percent.

Experience in the Practice

In the early years of financial planning, practitioners did not find it necessary to prove their abilities. Most already had years of related work experience under their belts before pursuing the CFP designation.

With the advent of the IBCFP, the need to demonstrate experience was addressed, and in 1989 the organization set another requirement for CFP certification: three years of personal financial planning–related experience for those who had a bachelor's degree, and five years of experience for those without a degree. The requirement was modified in 1999 to allow positions of supervision, support, and teaching of the personal financial planning process to count as relevant experience. In 2008, a CFP Board task force reviewed and affirmed the three-year work experience requirement. (The five-year requirement was no longer applicable because new certificants were required to have a bachelor's degree as of 2007.)

How to get this required experience remained a challenge. Anne Kern, then director of external relations at CFP Board, noted in early 2005,

We are seeing more people entering the field as a first career choice, and these individuals are looking for good entry-level positions. Many of the experienced planners tend to be associated with smaller independent planning firms, and it is difficult for them to hire many of these young graduates—people who have the academic background, but not the practical business experience needed to be successful in this field.

To help young planners gain experience, CFP Board encouraged veteran planners in both small and large firms to establish internship and entry-level positions. The board also voted to allow pro bono financial planning work, done under the supervision of a CFP practitioner, to count toward the experience requirement.

For its part, FPA supported young planners with online job listings, résumé-posting services, and sessions on career development at local, regional, and national conferences. Chapters worked to place new financial planners in internship positions through local members, and FPA's week-long residency program earned new planners credit for three months' work experience.

Ethical Standards: The Early Years

A fourth critical characteristic of a profession is its commitment to a high standard of ethical conduct. As the ICFP put it in a 1982 report, "Concepts of Professional Ethics":

A distinguishing mark of a professional is acceptance of responsibility to the public . . . Ethical conduct, in the true sense, is more than merely abiding by the letter of explicit prohibitions. Rather, it requires unswerving commitment to honorable behavior, even at the sacrifice of personal advantage.

The movement's pioneers understood the importance of an ethical standard. The charter of Loren Dunton's Society for Financial Counseling stated that its purpose included "to supply recognition to those who meet not only the legal, but also the ethical standards of financial counseling and conscientiously share their wealth of knowledge with the public."

The IAFP also adopted a code of ethics and agreement; to abide by it was a condition of membership. Likewise, the College for Financial Planning had an ethical code. In 1975, one of its objectives was "to pronounce, define, maintain, and promote ethical standards of professional conduct."

Also in 1975, the college demonstrated its willingness to enforce an ethical standard when it denied the CFP designation to a graduate because of legal and ethical problems. Only after he completed restitution requirements imposed by a California court and served his probation did the regents reconsider his application. "The CFP designation is a permissive thing, within the board's discretionary powers," said Lew Kearns, who was chairman of the board of regents at the time. It is not, he said, "a matter of right that arbitrarily accrues to any candidate successfully completing the college courses."[5]

A code of ethics was also an integral part of the ICFP's original constitution and bylaws adopted in 1974. But the code lacked teeth. "There is no way to discipline, suspend, or censure a CFP, even if he had committed grand larceny," complained David M. King, CFP, in 1975. (King would go on to serve as president of the ICFP in 1977–1979, chair of the college's board of regents in 1984–1985, and first chair of the IBCFP in 1985.)

By 1977, the code of ethics had been reworked several times, yet the only way to enforce it was to censure or expel members who violated its rules. The first expulsion occurred in 1978 when the ICFP learned that a member had lost his insurance license, been enjoined for various state securities laws violations, and was facing possible criminal charges. The member's right to appeal was noted in the records.

The ICFP continued to review potential violations of its ethics code until 1988, when it turned over ethics enforcement activities to the IBCFP, which had been established three years earlier to serve as the profession's standards-setting organization. Ben Coombs warned ICFP members that things would get tougher under the new IBCFP's jurisdiction. "The penalty for violations," he said, ". . . will involve not only a loss of member status [in the ICFP], but the possible loss of the CFP designation as well."

The College for Financial Planning was also ready to turn over its ethics enforcement activities to the new entity. William Anthes, the college's president, recalled having a box of complaints on his desk from the public about perceived misconduct on the part of former students. "To my knowledge, the college had never revoked the CFP marks from any graduate of the college," he later recalled, "but we knew the time was coming when we would have to address the issue."

Ethical Standards: A New Watchdog

When the IBCFP opened its doors in 1985, establishing and enforcing an ethical standard were top priorities. By June 1986, it had adopted a code of ethics based on seven principles: integrity, objectivity, competence, fairness, confidentiality, professionalism, and diligence. (The same principles were still in effect in 2009.)

As Coombs had predicted, the penalty for ethical violations did indeed become more severe: censure, suspension, revocation, or denial of the right to use the CFP marks. Dave King said in 1986, "The first thing we must do is to demonstrate our ability to protect the public from the actions of any CFP professional that violate the code of ethics."

> "The difference between business and a profession is the conscience of the profession."
>
> —Charles G. Hughes, Jr.[6]

The new organization set out disciplinary rules and procedures based on a system of peer review, and began investigating complaints in earnest. One of its earliest high-profile cases came in 1987: Tony Sorge, the College for Financial Planning's second president, who later had gained notoriety as an official of a corrupt California equities firm and had served a four-year prison sentence for mail fraud. The IBCFP permanently revoked Sorge's right to use the CFP marks. By 1991, 44 financial planners had had their right to use the CFP marks permanently revoked for ethics violations.[7]

Later refinements to CFP Board's disciplinary rules and procedures were made to ensure fairness and due process. The rules and procedures specified the opportunity for certificants in question to respond to complaints, introduce evidence and witnesses on their behalf, be represented by legal counsel, and appeal decisions.

In 2008, CFP Board reported that its Disciplinary and Ethics Commission was seeing an average of 80 cases a year. In 2007, 72 cases went to the commission for review out of approximately 1,300 matters that were initially investigated by CFP Board's staff for probable cause. Of the 72 cases, seven certificants had their use of the CFP certification marks revoked permanently, six had their certification suspended, and six were publicly admonished.

> *"Financial planning is a profession but not all financial planners are professionals."*
>
> —Lewis Walker

The balance—53 individuals—were either privately censured or had their cases dismissed. A total of 306 individuals had their right to use the CFP marks permanently revoked between 1987 and 2008.[8]

In 2009, the first non-certificant, "public" representative joined CFP Board's Disciplinary and Ethics Commission, which until that time had comprised only CFP certificants. CFP Board said the change reflected the practices of other established professions.

In a 2008 article in *CFP Board Report*, the organization said of its disciplinary process:

> *The variation in the judgment and penalties meted out by the Commission, and the existence of appeals procedures, speak to CFP Board's institutional concern with fairness and due process. The Commission's willingness, in extreme cases, to impose the maximum penalty of permanent revocation of the right to use the CFP marks speaks to CFP Board's commitment to upholding the integrity of the marks and to protecting the public.*

Ethical Standards: Strengthening the Code

In the early 1990s, the IBCFP embarked on a revision of its *Code of Ethics and Professional Responsibility*. John (Jack) Blankinship, CFP, who later became president of CFP Board (renamed from IBCFP in 1994), led the charge. "We wanted it to say more strongly than ever that a CFP certificant's responsibility was first and foremost to the client," he said in 2008. "It was the beginning of a fiduciary standard as we know it now."

As Blankinship traveled across the country to describe the new code, he often met with resistance. "Planners asked, 'Why are you doing this? It will increase my liability. I can't hold myself up to this standard,'" he later recalled. "It was clear that many of them viewed financial planning as a product delivery system, not as a profession that delivered advice to clients."

Bill Carter served with Blankinship on the committee that wrote the new code of ethics. He recalled that certificants hated the first draft. "It had too many 'thou shalt nots' in it," he said in 2008. "We had to go back and rework the language."

The code finally adopted in 1993 introduced a new level of disclosure requirements. Dick Wagner, chair of the ICFP that year, wrote:

> *The CFP community does not duck and run. Rather, the CFP community puts it squarely on the line with integrity and purpose. . . . CFP licensees stand for full disclosure, compliance with the law's spirit as well as its letter, and full acceptance of fiduciary responsibilities.*[9]

By 1995, the newly renamed CFP Board had adopted a mission statement that proclaimed its status as a "professional regulatory organization," and a new project began: the development of practice standards for the profession. The standards described best practices of CFP certificants when providing professional services related to the six elements of the financial planning process, including each standard's relationship to the code of ethics. Compliance with the practice standards was mandatory for certificants whose services included financial planning or elements of the financial planning process, although all financial planning professionals were encouraged to use the standards. By 2002, the final practice standards took effect; they remained in force in 2009. (For more on practice standards, see Chapter 4.)

Ethical Standards: A Fiduciary Obligation

The next significant revision of CFP Board's code of ethics began in 2005 and culminated with its adoption in 2008. A major addition was a fiduciary standard of care for financial planning services. The new code of ethics defined a *fiduciary* as "one who acts in utmost good faith, in a manner he or she believes to be in the best interest of the client."

The emphasis on fiduciary responsibility was both the motivation for the revision and the key differentiator between it and previous codes. But the issue of financial planners as fiduciaries had existed long before. In fact, the word *fiduciary* appeared in the IBCFP's first code of ethics, albeit only in the context of holding a client's property. "A Certified Financial Planner who holds a client's property, shall do so with the care required of a fiduciary," the code stated.[10]

But some planners maintained that fiduciary responsibility extended far beyond the holding of property. At the ICFP's 1985 Retreat, one element of the organization's regulatory position specified that a CFP practitioner, registered with the SEC as an investment adviser, was a fiduciary. The

ICFP reasoned that financial planning services would usually include invest-ment advice, which was covered under the "duty of care" stipulation of the Investment Advisers Act of 1940. "This was a breakthrough in thinking and the beginning of raising the standard of a CFP practitioner," Jack Blankinship later said.

Charles G. Hughes, Jr., CFP, president of the ICFP in 1987, made it clear that a professional financial planner puts the client's interest first:

> *The acceptance as a profession will be achieved when financial plan-ners assume and are perceived to have assumed the role of adviser fore-most. . . . Considering that modern-day financial planning is rooted in the sales business, however, makes accomplishing this separation [of ad-vice from product delivery] a formidable task. . . . It's a change in mindset and attitude. A little switch goes "click" in the head. The planner's view of himself, arrangement of his practice, and most important, the perception of the client, are fundamentally altered. It's a constant awareness—a burden almost—that the client comes first. . . . It's a difficult conversion, damn difficult. But the client and advisor both recognize when it has occurred.[11]*

Two years later, Blankinship, then president of the ICFP, insisted that CFP practitioners develop a "professional culture" that centered on fiduciary duty to clients. Blankinship drove home the point in several speeches during that time: "Others might act as a fiduciary . . . CFP practitioners must act as a fiduciary. The public expects it; the courts will expect it; we ourselves, must demand it."

It took nearly 20 years for Blankinship's vision of financial planners as fiduciaries to be codified. In CFP Board's revised *Standards of Professional Conduct*, Rule 1.4 spelled out the obligation:

> *A certificant shall at all times place the interest of the client ahead of his or her own. When the certificant provides financial planning or material elements of the financial planning process, the certificant owes to the client the duty of care of a fiduciary as defined by CFP Board.*

This raised the baseline duty of care from the previous code, which had stipulated "reasonable and prudent professional judgment," to a standard that required a CFP certificant to "at all times place the interest of the client ahead of his or her own." However, the fiduciary standard was reserved for financial planning services.

FPA took the obligation one step further. In August 2008, the board of directors passed a resolution supporting a standard of care for FPA financial planning members, whether or not they were CFP certificants:

All financial planning services will be delivered in accordance with the following standard of care:

- *Put the client's best interest first;*
- *Act with due care and in utmost good faith;*
- *Do not mislead clients;*
- *Provide full and fair disclosure of all material facts; and*
- *Disclose and fairly manage all material conflicts of interest.*

In a letter to members, FPA president Mark E. Johannessen, CFP, wrote, "The Standard of Care reflects FPA's belief that those of us who hold ourselves out as financial planners are fiduciaries, regardless of our business model, method of compensation, or professional designations."

Although some in the planning community objected to the new fiduciary standard, others applauded it. Robinson and Hughes wrote of FPA's standard of care in 2009: "Good-bye 'bait and switch!' Changing hats during the relationship as a means of skirting fiduciary responsibility is debunked as nothing more than the charade it really is."[12]

Profile: John T. Blankinship, Jr.

One word made many financial planners see red in the 1980s and 1990s: *fiduciary*. When they heard it applied to them, they heard "increased and unnecessary liability." And they weren't shy about expressing their antagonism. Jack Blankinship remembered giving speeches about financial planners as fiduciaries and seeing audience members stalk out of the room. Some, he recalled, even threw pennies and cherry tomatoes at the podium in protest.

But Blankinship never gave up or gave in. He was resolute about two core beliefs: that the CFP mark should be the one and only financial planning credential, and that CFP practitioners are fiduciaries. "My argument then and now is that the CFP mark is a mantle of responsibility that cannot be put on and taken off at will," he said in a 2008 interview.

Blankinship arrived at these strong views gradually. When he received his master's degree in economics from Southern Illinois University in 1964, the Navy veteran had no thought of becoming a financial planner. He went to work for Caterpillar Tractor Company's business economics department and later for a securities firm as a stockbroker. The securities firm sent him to work in its national training department in New York, where one of his projects involved developing a 40-page booklet "on how stockbrokers could take a more holistic approach when working with clients," he said. Around that time, Blankinship heard about the College for Financial Planning in Denver. "So when I opened my own firm in 1974, I decided to pursue the CFP designation," he said. "I wanted an education in all facets of financial planning, but I also thought that having the designation would help set me apart from the competition."

From that beginning, promoting the CFP designation became almost an "obsession," he said. "I felt compelled to be part of the CFP movement, as we called it—to be part of something big and grand as we worked to further a profession and give more stature to the CFP designation." Blankinship quickly rose through the ranks of financial planning organizations: president of the San Diego chapter of the IAFP in 1982–1983; president and chair of the ICFP, 1989–1991; president and chair of CFP Board of Standards, 1994–1995.

"Some people did not appreciate my fervor," he said. "When it came to the *fiduciary* responsibility of a CFP practitioner, I was definitely in the minority. We danced around the word for a long time. I would use it in my speeches, but the word never appeared in CFP Board's 1993 revised code of ethics, even though the code captured the idea that a CFP certificant's responsibility is first and foremost to the client."

Blankinship's view was vindicated 15 years later when CFP Board formally adopted a fiduciary standard as part of its 2008 revision to the code of ethics. "It tells the world that CFP professionals put their clients' interest above their own," Blankinship said. "It's something I've wanted for a long time."

A Single Designation

Professions typically seek to establish a registry or licensure to set apart their members as bona fide. Financial planning faced a dilemma: Which registry, membership, or designation could rightly identify an individual as a professional financial planner?

For many in the ICFP, there was only one answer: the Certified Financial Planner designation. Other planners—including early IAFP leaders—disagreed, asserting that it was not a designation, but rather competence and ethical behavior that conferred legitimacy.

Even the first CFP designees were not sure what to make of it. Ben Coombs, who was in the first graduating class of the College for Financial Planning, recalled, "I came to the college's conferment ceremony and the meeting that followed to find out what I was—what did it mean to be a 'CFP designee'?" he recalled.

Coombs and other ICFP members soon became ardent supporters of the CFP designation as the standard-bearer for a new profession. Among the advocates was P. Kemp Fain, Jr., also in the college's first graduating class. In 1987 Fain, then chair of the IBCFP, wrote a white paper that outlined why financial planners should coalesce around a single designation, the CFP mark.[13] The need, he said, was urgent: "Time is of the essence in order to avoid the continued proliferation of competing certifications and to eliminate public confusion regarding the validity of financial planning credentials."

Fain specified why the CFP mark should rise above its competitors. First, the IBCFP granted use of the mark only to candidates who fulfilled significant educational and experience requirements and passed a rigorous examination. Second, the CFP designation was already widely recognized as the "mainstream" certification of financial planning professionals. And third, it was the only financial planning certification with legal trademark protection. "The IBCFP is in an effective position to address the four essential components of professionalism: education, examination, experience, and ethics," Fain asserted.

"One profession, one designation," was the way Fain summed up his argument, and the phrase quickly became a rallying cry. (For more about Fain's landmark paper, see Chapter 4.)

A year later, in 1988, the Securities and Exchange Commission gave a nod to the credential when it noted, "The CFP designation appears to be developing as the most recognized designation in the field."[15]

Profile: P. Kemp Fain, Jr.

At a national meeting of financial planners in 1988, P. Kemp Fain, Jr., took the stage to deliver a speech titled "One Profession, One Designation." Fain laid out a scenario for transforming the CFP designation from an educational credential to a professional one. "There is some urgency to choose the correct path—toward professionalism—soon," he said, according to a *Financial Product News* report from the time.

Fain's son Paul, also a financial planner, remembers the declaration his father made: "Dad said, 'I will no longer be known as P. Kemp Fain, Jr., ChFC, CLU, CFP. I am P. Kemp Fain, Jr., *CFP*.'"

If anyone could influence his peers, it was Fain, a financial planning pioneer who had been the first enrollee in the CFP program and was in the first graduating class in 1973. He started the first local chapter of the IAFP (Knoxville, Tennessee). He helped found the IBCFP, served as its chair, and was a founder, president, and chair of the ICFP. "Kemp Fain was an early zealot in the movement," recalled Lew Kearns, first chair of the College for Financial Planning's board of regents. "He enthusiastically supported every step at every level. He was a real leader."

An engineer in his early career, Fain later worked as a stockbroker—the closest he could get at the time, he once said, to being a financial planner. He soon learned that brokers profited most from active trading. "Long term to them was 5 P.M.," he told the *Knoxville News-Sentinel* in 1987—the year he was named by *Money* magazine as one of the country's top 200 financial planners.

Fain was looking for a client-focused educational program when he met Loren Dunton. "I thought financial planning was the answer to our prayers," he said. "I was sold on the idea of a professional designation for financial planning."[14]

Fain told *Financial Planning* magazine in 1990 that "obtaining the CFP designation totally redirected the way I did things," and added that his clients' image of him changed from salesman to adviser in just a few years. Still, he noted, the profession had a long way to go. "Until there's a CFP in every village, it will be difficult to be perceived as a professional."

In 1993, the ICFP established the P. Kemp Fain, Jr., Award to honor contributions furthering the financial planning profession; the ICFP named Fain, who was battling cancer at the time, as the first recipient. He died a year later at age 54.

In 2008, Paul Fain said of his father,

Dad contributed enormous energy and hours to the financial planning movement. He missed a lot of ball games and family dinners because of it, but our family never begrudged it because we understood how much he wanted financial planning to grow and evolve to the highest standards of a profession.

And has it? "The landscape of financial services is still wide and some still use financial planning as a sales tool," Paul Fain said. "We are still on the journey toward rallying together behind a professional education program and a single designation, CFP, under a unified regulatory environment. But I think Dad would be pleased that it is going in the right direction."

Nevertheless, Fain's vision often collided with reality during the ensuing years. In 1990, an unnamed critic was quoted in his hometown newspaper, the *Knoxville Journal*, as describing the CFP designation as "a trademark in search of a profession." Even supporters of the designation had to admit to its limitations. Ben Coombs commented on the worth of the CFP credential the same year in an interview with *Financial Planning* magazine in its September 1990 issue: "It's either valueless or priceless," he said. "It depends on the commitment of the individual who holds it."

Tom L. Potts, PhD, CFP, wrote in 1992 when he was president of the IBCFP, "The single largest problem facing us in the years ahead is the need to set apart CFP licensees from those who are unethical or incompetent in their practice of financial planning."[16]

Coombs, Potts, and other proponents of the CFP designation persisted, however, and some significant victories were achieved over the years:

- In a 1994 U.S. Supreme Court decision (see Chapter 4), the justices quoted from CFP Board's brief about the value of the CFP designation and acknowledged the rigorous examination required of candidates before conferring the CFP designation.
- In 1995, the National Commission for Certifying Agencies (NCCA) accredited CFP Board's certification program, the first such accreditation for a financial services certification in the United States. CFP Board earned NCCA accreditation because it showed that its certification program was grounded in legal testing requirements and generally accepted certification standards.
- In 1997, the IAFP board of directors passed a unanimous resolution endorsing the CFP marks.
- A 1998 U.S. District Court ruling included the statement that the CFP marks were "distinctive and famous."
- In 2002, the U.S. Patent and Trademark Office approved the registration of *CFP* as a certification mark, giving the mark an increased level of protection afforded by federal registration for personal certification programs.

> *"CFP Board's high ethical standards and its active enforcement of its ethical standards, including the public release of disciplinary information, are key factors that differentiate the CFP certification from the many other designations found in the financial services industry."*
> —Marilyn Capelli Dimitroff, 2009 Chair, CFP Board

Competing Designations

The race for "one designation" had a packed field almost from the beginning, but two competitors to the CFP certification have stood out over the years. One was the Personal Financial Specialist (PFS), granted by the American Institute of Certified Public Accountants, Personal Financial Planning Division, to CPAs who demonstrated experience in personal financial planning services and met other credentialing requirements established by the AICPA.

A second competitor was the Chartered Financial Consultant (ChFC) designation, granted by The American College and established as a professional designation in 1982. The continuing popularity of the designation was evidenced by an 18 percent growth in the number of individuals earning the designation in 2008, compared with the previous year. A February 2009 American College press release proclaimed ChFC as "Financial Planning's Highest Standard," and described it as "the most robust and respected credential for financial planning professionals." (Omitted from that endorsement was the fact that the ChFC designation did not include a comprehensive exam, fiduciary responsibility, and ethics enforcement as did the CFP designation.)

But those designations were merely two of many. The Financial Industry Regulatory Authority (FINRA) listed more than 80 financial services designations on its Web site in 2008—along with a strong disclaimer that inclusion in the list in no way implied endorsement. The disclaimer stated, in part:

> *Not all designations carry the same significance or require the same amount of effort to obtain.... Some designations require formal certification procedures, including examinations and continuing professional education credits. Other designations may merely signify that membership dues have been paid. Still others are simply marketing devices.[17]*

Third-party accreditation of certification standards was seen as one way to distinguish legitimate designations from those that were little more than marketing gimmicks. As of 2008, only one financial services certifying body, CFP Board, had received third-party accreditation, although some other organizations had begun the process of earning it.

The Compensation Question

In their struggle to be recognized as a profession, financial planners for years have debated whether method of compensation is a defining element. The National Association of Personal Financial Advisors (NAPFA) has advocated for fee-only financial planning, along with fiduciary responsibility, since its founding in 1983. In contrast, the ICFP, IAFP, and later FPA, have taken the position that compensation, whether by fee, commission, or some combination, is not the critical issue. Rather, the issue was planners' integrity and commitment to fully disclose to the clients how they were compensated and to put clients' interests first.

In a November 8, 1987, article in the *Knoxville News-Sentinel*, P. Kemp Fain, Jr., explained that although he had evolved his practice from primarily commission-based when he started it in 1975 to primarily fee-based, an "honorable person" could give good advice either working on commission or a fee basis. The key, he said, was to "put the client's needs first."

Another focus of discussion was how to address conflicts of interest in a planning relationship. In an October 1989 issue of the *Journal of Financial Planning*, Lynn Hopewell, CFP, wrote,

> *Why do we have all these compensation labels [fee-based, fee and commission, fee-only, fee-offset]? One major reason is because they tip off clients to conflicts of interest associated with compensation. But are compensation-related conflicts the only important pieces of information to communicate?*

Hopewell advocated for a "master catalogue of conflicts of interest" with guidelines on how to deal with them, and concluded:

> *Professionalism, after all, depends not on whether the government licenses you, not on whether we have an SRO [self-regulatory organization], not on whether you have letters after your name, but rather on how you behave. We will become a profession only after we behave like one. Better handling of our conflicts of interest will improve our behavior.*

"Professionalism . . . depends not on whether the government licenses you, not on whether we have an SRO, not on whether you have letters after your name, but rather on how you behave."

—Lynn Hopewell

Richard B. Wagner, JD, CFP, addressed the issue of compensation head on in a 1990 article, "To Think...Like a CFP":

I suggest that the debate over commission-based planning is not that commission-based planners have harmed clients intentionally. Neither is it that commissions are evil and fees are good. Rather, the tragedy of the product diversion for both fee-only and commission planners is that it has blinded to the real implications and potential of our profession. In particular, we have neglected the development of how we serve.[18]

Madeline Noveck, CFP, chair of the ICFP in 1992, took a similar stance

The road a planner takes regarding compensation when structuring a practice is a business or marketing decision, not a moral decision...The question for professionalism is not third-party compensation, it is personal integrity, no matter what the manner of compensation.[19]

Still, the issue continued to divide planners. Some recommended better disclosure of compensation to clients. In 2000, CFP Board proposed changes to disclosure requirements in its code of ethics. The new rules would require a "reasonable" breakdown in compensation of fees and commissions—either in percentages or amounts—as well as the overall cost to the client.

The proposed changes became a lightning rod for debate. When they were posted on CFP Board's Web site, comments from planners flooded in. Those in favor of the new rules tended to identify their compensation method as fee-only; those opposed were mostly in the fee-and-commission or commission-only camps.[20]

In response, CFP Board reworked the requirement, backing away from specific percentages, amounts, and total costs. The new Rule 401, put into effect in 2003, stipulated that all CFP certificants must disclose conflicts of interest and compensation structure to clients. Rule 402 went one step further, requiring CFP certificants in a financial planning engagement to provide written disclosure of material information, including conflicts of interest and sources of compensation, prior to the engagement. However, the exact dollar amount of compensation—unlikely to be known at that point in the process—was not required to be disclosed then. What did need to be disclosed was the source of all compensation—commissions, percentage of assets under management, referral fees, hourly rates, and so on.

The same year, CFP Board clarified its definition of the term *fee-only* in Advisory Opinion 2003-1, stating that in order for a CFP certificant to describe his or her compensation as "fee-only," all compensation from all clients must be derived solely from fees. The definition was further refined in CFP Board's 2008 revised code of ethics. *Fee-only* meant that "client work comes exclusively from the clients in the form of fixed, flat, hourly, percentage, or performance-based fees."

As of 2009, CFP Board remained neutral on questions of which business models or compensation methods CFP certificants use in their practices. "CFP Board's *Standards of Professional Conduct* require CFP certificants to disclose information to clients about their compensation arrangements and any conflicts of interest associated with their choice of business model," explained Michael P. Shaw, managing director of professional review and legal. The most recent CFP Board study addressing the compensation methods used by CFP certificants in the United States, conducted in 1999, found that 40 percent were compensated by a combination of fees and commissions, 25 percent were fee only, 25 percent were commission only, and 10 percent were salaried. A 2009 study of FPA members found that 31 percent described their compensation as fee only, 19 percent said they were mostly or entirely fee-based, 35 percent reported a combination of fee-based and transactional compensation, 8 percent as mostly transactional, and 6 percent as salary based. (*Transactional* was defined as "commissions, 12-1b fees, etc.")

Government Regulation

Although financial planners in the United States in 2009 were subject to laws that affected aspects of what they did, such as providing investment advice or selling insurance products, they were not regulated as financial planners per se. As Jonathan Macey, JD, a Cornell law professor, put it in a June 2002 issue of the *Journal of Financial Planning*:

> To the extent that financial planning is a profession, it is a profession in which entry is virtually free to all. This is not to say that the activities of financial planners are unregulated . . . but what is regulated is not the core business of formulating comprehensive plans. . . . [W]hat is regulated are the individual modules or components of work that financial planners might do in implementing a financial plan. . . .[21]

If planners' core business was not regulated, should it be? Planners debated that question for decades, even while their organizations sought to assist and influence regulatory agencies in making decisions that affected financial planning.

The IBCFP, for example, saw its role in 1987 as "cooperating with regulatory bodies by participating in discussions regarding the proper role of government in the regulation of financial planners."[22] IBCFP leaders even hinted that its certification standards had potential to become the basis for regulation. Tom Potts, 1992 president of the IBCFP, wrote in the organization's annual report,

> *Ultimately, these [government] officials may turn to those with the education, experience, and ethics needed to serve the public well, and the IBCFP's comprehensive examination may become the standard in any government registration or licensing program.*

In 1993, the IBCFP (soon to be renamed CFP Board) began describing itself as a professional regulatory organization (PRO) for CFP practitioners. (Compared with self-regulatory organizations, or SROs, which are government-sanctioned regulatory bodies, PROs are not specifically defined or recognized in U.S. law.) In the IBCFP's 1993 annual report it explained its position: "It is CFP Board's hope that any future regulations will build on the organization's standards and experience in certifying professional financial planners."[23]

By the end of that year, CFP Board reported that it had met with regulatory agencies in more than half of the states to share the organization's expertise on certification and regulatory issues related to financial planners. As one result of these and similar efforts, several regulatory bodies made exceptions for CFP certificants in their licensing requirements. In 2003, for example, the National Association of Insurance Commissioners adopted an exemption for CFP certificants from pre-licensing education as part of its model regulation. Similarly, the National Association of State Securities Administrators (NASAA) granted a waiver to certificants from NASAA Series 65 and 66 competency exams for investment adviser representatives.

Despite some evidence of government recognition, it was apparent that financial planning still had work to do. When asked how regulators viewed financial planning, law professor Jonathan Macey told the *Journal of Financial Planning* in 2001,

> *They don't. They're very compartmentalized—securities regulators worry about securities and insurance regulators worry about insurance. They don't really know what financial planning is and they certainly don't view it as this holistic profession like those practicing it do.*[24]

By 2008, CFP Board had ceased using the PRO reference. "CFP Board was the only institution in the United States using it," explained Kevin R. Keller, CFP Board's CEO. He added that the term was misleading: "It gave some people the perception that CFP Board regulated the profession, rather than only individuals who hold the CFP designation."

That year, CFP Board had also relocated from Denver to Washington, D.C., partly to have more input in policy decisions that affected financial planning and the public's access to financial planning services. In its 2008 annual report, CFP Board stated:

> *Right now, as these words are written, decisions are being taken in the executive and legislative branches of the federal government that will affect the future of the financial planning profession and its ability to serve the public. As ideas about regulation of the profession arise and evolve, having not only a seat at the table in Washington, D.C., but also a loud, clear voice is critical to ensuring that CFP Board can continue to serve as a voice for the public and our certificants.*

As for the membership groups—IAFP, ICFP, and later, FPA—their status as 501(c)(6) organizations allowed them to lobby government officials on behalf of financial planners. As early as 1977, the IAFP and ICFP collaboratively drafted legislation for regulating financial planners, following the model of licensing laws in other professions. The draft never materialized into legislation, however.

In 1984, the IAFP established a Political Action Committee (PAC) and in 1986, the IAFP and ICFP participated in the first Congressional hearings on financial planning. Part of the effort was educational—most government officials did not understand what financial planning was. "They seemed to assume that we were all insurance people," recalled Alexandra Armstrong, CFP, IAFP's president in 1985.

The 1980s were also marked by discord between the two organizations. One flashpoint was the issue of a self-regulatory organization (SRO), which the IAFP supported as a way to have consistent regulation across state lines. The ICFP opposed a federally legislated SRO as "an infringement on the client–adviser relationship and a move away from the eventual acceptance of financial planning as a profession, rather than a trade or a business," explained Daniel S. Parks, JD, CFP, ICFP's 1984–1985 president. Instead, the ICFP advocated for wider registration and full disclosure under existing investment adviser laws.

The IAFP and ICFP eventually found common ground when the National Association of Securities Dealers (NASD) proposed that *it* serve as the SRO for financial planners. The IAFP backed away from its SRO proposal, and both organizations acknowledged the need to present a united front to regulators. (For more about this event, see Chapter 3.)

While the ICFP opposed the SRO concept, it did recommend that all CFP practitioners who provided investment advice as part of their regular services to clients should have their firms registered with the Securities and Exchange Commission as investment advisers. It also recommended uniform model legislation among states and took a favorable stance toward self-regulation in the absence of licensing.

When the IAFP and ICFP joined forces to create the Financial Planning Association in 2000, government lobbying efforts remained an important focus. A major victory took place in 2007 when a federal appeals court sided with FPA in forcing the SEC to vacate a rule that allowed broker-dealers to provide financial planning services without having to register under the Investment Advisers Act of 1940, which mandated a fiduciary duty. (For more information, see Chapter 5.)

The question of regulating financial planners, however, remained unresolved. The subject came up again in a roundtable discussion published in FPA's *Journal of Financial Planning* in 2007.[25] Asked whether there should be a change in the regulatory structure for financial planning, Charles Hughes replied, "The quick fix to marching down the road to becoming a true profession would seem to be licensing by the state."

The president of TDAmeritrade International, Tom Bradley, cautioned that while the future of regulation was a "profoundly interesting question, we do have to be very, very careful of over-regulation." Tom Potts, professor of finance and director of the financial services program at Baylor University and former president of the IBCFP, said he'd "like to see some sort of licensing, equivalent to being a CPA, being required to practice." Countered Hughes, "It seems to me the best position... is to think as broadly as possible and simply not be content with things as they are right now."

In 2008, FPA, CFP Board, and the National Association of Personal Financial Advisors (NAPFA) entered into a coalition to consider how financial planning could best achieve regulatory recognition. The three groups released a statement of understanding that said, in part:

[We] share this vision and will collaborate as Congress undertakes regulatory reform to achieve the following objectives:

Financial planning services are delivered to the public with fiduciary accountability and transparency, serving the client's best interest first and always.

Financial planning services are specifically regulated to distinguish and differentiate professionals who have met essential requirements to practice, including examination, education, experience, and ethics as modeled and enforced by the Certified Financial Planner certification. . . .

In response to the announcement, personal finance columnist Michelle Singletary wrote in the December 11, 2008, edition of *The Washington Post*,

I'm encouraged that the nation's three major financial planning organizations have said they are working together to promote more consumer protections. . . . One thing the government can do to regulate the

financial planning industry is get rid of the litany of three-letter alphabet-soup designations and require one certification. . . . A federally regulated and licensed designation for financial planners should make clear that a planner has the fiduciary responsibility to look out for your best financial interest—not the planner's bottom line.

Jack Blankinship observed that year, "It is my fervent hope that a sovereign body will decree that a CFP certificant is licensed to practice financial planning. Until that happens, we are not truly a profession, because a profession has barriers to entry."

What Is Financial Planning, Anyway?

In the December 2001 issue of the *Journal of Financial Planning*, writer Shelley Lee posed the question of what constituted financial planning. The question was neither new nor simple to answer, but if financial planning was on the road toward government regulation, it was a question to answer very carefully. In 2002, Jonathan Macey, JD, warned planners that they faced "a difficult problem of how to define 'financial planning' with suitable precision so as not to be over- or underinclusive."[26]

The ICFP had recognized the challenge 25 years earlier when the organization was attempting to draft legislation with the IAFP for the regulation of financial planners. "The biggest problem area is defining 'financial planning' and the duties of a financial planner," the minutes of a 1977 meeting noted.

In 2000, San Francisco planner Norman M. Boone, CFP, challenged his colleagues to rethink the definition of financial planning: "the process of determining whether and how an individual can meet life goals through proper management of financial resources." Boone argued that the definition was so broad and general that his plumber could do financial planning. "The possibility of government regulation of our industry provides another reason to rally around a single definition and lead the public to broad acceptance of it," he wrote. "Reaching a definition of financial planning and then spreading the word is the single most important thing that can be done to further our profession."[27]

Eight years later, CFP Board expanded on the definition in its revised code of ethics:

"Personal financial planning" or "financial planning" denotes the process of determining whether and how an individual can meet life goals through the proper management of financial resources.

> *Financial planning integrates the financial planning process with the financial planning subject areas. In determining whether the certificant is providing financial planning or material elements of the financial planning process, issues that may be considered include but are not limited to:*
>
> - *The client's understanding and intent in engaging the certificant.*
> - *The degree to which multiple financial planning subject areas are involved.*
> - *The comprehensiveness of the data gathering.*
> - *The breadth and depth of the recommendations.*
>
> *Financial planning may occur even if the elements are not provided to a client simultaneously, are delivered over a period of time, or are delivered as distinct subject areas. It is not necessary to provide a written financial plan to engage in financial planning.*

Serving a Social Benefit

Many definitions of *profession* include the concept of a higher social function or public benefit. The work of doctors leads to improved public health; the work of lawyers advances the rule of law and the equal distribution of justice. What about financial planning? Does the work of planners advance a social good?

As with questions of professionalism in general, responses have been divided between an enthusiastic "yes!" and a more cautious "not yet." FPA and CFP Board allude to a social function without referring to altruism. CFP Board's mission is "to benefit the public by granting the CFP certification and upholding it as the recognized standard of excellence for personal financial planning." FPA does not include "public benefit" among its stated goals, but has as its primary aim "to foster the value of financial planning and to advance the financial planning profession." It also supports members' pro bono activities, and since 2001 has had a director of pro bono services on its staff. (For more on FPA's pro bono work, see Chapter 6.) Some local and regional FPA chapters explicitly include a social benefit among their goals. The mission of the Financial Planning Association of Northern California, for example, includes helping the public "recognize the value of the financial planning process as a way to achieve their goals and dreams." The mission of the Financial Planning Association of San Diego is "to promote financial security for residents of San Diego County through excellence in financial planning." Other chapters, however, limit their mission to promoting the financial planning process or serving the needs of chapter members.

Social benefit has been addressed more directly by the National Endowment for Financial Education (NEFE) and the Foundation for Financial Planning. NEFE, created in 1992, is a private, nonprofit national foundation "wholly dedicated to improving the financial well-being of all Americans." Between 1992 and 1997, NEFE served as the parent entity of the College for Financial Planning; after it transferred ownership of the college to the Apollo Group in 1997, it used the proceeds of the sale—along with an endowment built up over the preceding years—to fund research and public service programs that address the financial education needs of large groups of Americans, including immigrants, disaster victims, and the poor. Through its High School Financial Planning Program, established in 1984 by the College for Financial Planning, NEFE provides, free of charge, a seven-unit student manual, a teacher's guide, and other tools that teach the principles of financial literacy.

The mission of the Foundation for Financial Planning—"to help people take control of their financial lives by connecting the financial planning community with people in need"—is realized through its support of pro bono advice and outreach activities. Grants from the foundation have underwritten a wide range of projects and activities, including a literacy demonstration project through the Center for American Indian Economic Development at Northern Arizona University; a home-study course in basic investing through Rutgers University; the public television series *Moneywise*, targeted at African-American families; and a financial literacy curriculum for young adults participating in City Year, Inc., a volunteer service program. In addition, a significant portion of the foundation's grants have supported FPA and its National Financial Planning Support Center, a 501(c)(3) organization that carries out FPA's pro bono efforts.

On the theoretical level, a few educators have attempted to connect financial planning with social purpose. At San Diego State University, the financial planning program description includes this endorsement of the profession's public benefit:

> *Financial planners need not be wonderwomen or supermen; but it wouldn't hurt. They must be able to deal with people sensitively in an area that most clients would rather not discuss. You must be able to instill the desire to take action in an area of life where fear and ignorance [are] rampant. Financial planning is very much a people profession. A planner must be able to understand complex social and economic trends, a huge variety of products and services, and the complexities of illogical tax law, unfathomable estate law and arcane investment theory. He must possess both the people skills and technical aptitude necessary to practice financial planning competently.*

Tom Warschauer, PhD, CFP, the director of the San Diego State program, has contributed a number of insights into the social benefit of financial planning. Writing in *Financial Services Review* in 2002, Warschauer compared financial planning to the more established profession of medicine: "If one views medicine as optimizing health and not merely fixing 'what ails' patients, the concepts of diagnosis, treatment, and prognosis really do apply. Financial planning could be seen as optimizing economic well being."[28] Warschauer also argued that financial planning "is essentially a middle-class need" and that "the most important factor in the growth of the financial planning profession is the size and affluence of the middle economic class."[29]

Perhaps this is true in principle. The reality, many experienced financial planners acknowledge, is different. "We have some of the trappings of a profession, but not the core," Richard Wagner said in 2009.

We have yet to develop a strong, consistent sense of mission, meaning, and purpose that would allow us to claim the same status as other authentic professions. But financial planners do have a mission: We help society and individuals work with the unprecedented forces generated by money. By honoring this mission, we serve an extraordinary, unprecedented, and meaningful purpose. By fulfilling this mission, we can become an authentic profession.

Public and Media Recognition

"Is financial planning a profession?" wasn't asked only by financial planners. The court of public opinion played an equally important role in the discussion. For much of financial planning's history, the answer was an emphatic "no"—a response that has changed only gradually, and especially within the last decade.

From the outset, the new profession had (and still has, many would argue) the challenge of explaining to the public what financial planning was in general, what a CFP professional was in particular, and why consumers should care in the first place. The origins of the financial planning movement, wrote Jeanne Robinson and Charles G. Hughes in their April 2009 *Journal of Financial Planning* article, "To Act . . . Like a CFP," lay in distribution—in other words, sales. "Certainly not everyone viewed financial planning as the most ingenious distribution system for financial products since the introduction of the commission," they continued. "Unfortunately, though, enough individuals and institutions did, making for a suspect beginning to the reputation of financial planners in general."

Throughout the 1970s and 1980s many business reporters and columnists wrote harshly about "self-described" financial planners. As late as

October 1987, nearly 17 years after the Chicago meeting that gave birth to financial planning's primary institutions, *Money* magazine warned its readers that financial planning was "an almost instant profession, with no government agency or professional association empowered to bar the door to the unqualified."

Yet opinion was already starting to shift, thanks in large part to early public relations efforts launched by the IAFP and the ICFP. (For details, see Chapter 3.) In addition to the caveat, the 1987 issue of *Money* featured a directory of 200 of the top financial planners in the country. More than 86 percent of the planners on the list were CFP professionals. An accompanying article advised readers to seek out planners who held the CFP designation.

Over the next decade, all of the major financial planning organizations stepped up their efforts to heighten public awareness and the perception of professionalism. The Personal Economic Summit, conducted in Washington, D.C., in 1993 by the ICFP, made financial literacy the centerpiece of its message. And the message began reaching influential ears. For example, in 1994 *Worth* magazine began including CFP professionals in its "Best 200 Financial Advisers in America" roundup; by 1996, the list included 173 CFP certificants.

Within a decade, any lingering doubts among members of the news and business media about the value of the CFP credential had largely disappeared. In the Adviser Network Directory section of its Web site, *Forbes* included a direct link to a CFP Board page, "Search for a Certified Financial Planner Professional." The *Wall Street Journal*'s financial columnist, Jonathan Clements, told readers in 2006 to "start by looking for someone with broad training in the financial planning field. The most widely recognized designation for a generalist is Certified Financial Planner, a designation held by some 50,000 people in the U.S."[30] Even Jane Bryant Quinn, the veteran *Newsweek* columnist who had written disparagingly of planners in the mid-1980s, gave her blessing in a 2008 column about how to find a financial planner:

> *The credible planners will have at least one of three designations on their business cards: Certified Financial Planner (CFP, the best-known credential), Chartered Financial Consultant (ChFC, for planners who use insurance to reach financial goals) or Personal Financial Specialists (PFS, held by certified public accountants). All three will have taken serious courses and passed difficult exams.[31]*

Among the public, recognition and acceptance of the CFP mark were less uniform, at least according to surveys taken by FPA and CFP Board. An early survey, undertaken for the nascent FPA by Knapp, Inc. and Wirthlin Worldwide in September and October 1999, asked 1,000 Americans in different income groups about the value of financial planning. The findings: The CFP credential was well known among a majority of respondents, and 70 percent considered the credential to be important. Respondents most frequently associated the CFP mark with specific skills and educational accomplishments.

FPA followed up in 2003 with another survey of 1,020 adults, this time asking them how confident they were in their financial future and whether they were likely to seek assistance—and from whom. Two-thirds of respondents said they were "very familiar" or "somewhat familiar" with financial planning services—a smaller percentage than those who were familiar with accounting, tax services, or insurance, but larger than those familiar with estate planning services. Of those surveyed, 39 percent said they had positive or very positive impressions of financial planning; nevertheless, only 24 percent had used the services of a financial planner.

FPA continued to survey consumers on an annual basis. In February 2006—before the U.S. and world economies showed signs of recession—the findings were only slightly more positive than they had been three years earlier. From the respondents, 25 percent of respondents said they had used the services of a financial planner in the previous year; 64 percent had used an insurance agent. About 18 percent said they were currently working with a financial planner, but only 12 percent said they were "somewhat" or "very" familiar with the CFP certification, compared with 15 percent in each of the two previous years. Those most likely to work with a financial planner were older (age 55 and up), more wealthy (28 percent reported household incomes of greater than $100,000), and more likely to be college graduates than the large majority who did not work with a financial planner.[32]

Two CFP Board studies conducted in 2004 generally confirmed FPA's findings. CFP Board split its focus, surveying upper-income consumers (with an average net worth of $567,000) separately from the "general market." Among upper-income consumers in particular, CFP mark certification had achieved a considerable degree of recognition and respect:

[It] continues to be the most recognized of financial planning credentials and trails only the CPA among all financial services credentials. More than half of upper-income consumers are aware of the CFP certification marks. In addition, clients of CFP professionals report being more satisfied in a variety of financial areas than clients of other financial advisers.

The figures among consumers in the general market were only slightly lower.

Two studies released in 2008 revealed both the challenges and the opportunities for financial planning. On the one hand, according to a study[33] of 654 U.S. households and six focus groups, commissioned by the SEC, both experienced and inexperienced investors had difficulty distinguishing between investment advisers and broker-dealers. Although study participants had a general sense of the difference in services offered by brokers and investment advisers, they were not clear about their specific legal duties. Even respondents who had employed financial professionals for years were often confused about job titles, types of firms, and payments made for services. Despite their confusion, however, respondents reported that they were largely satisfied with the services they received from their financial professionals, and they recognized the value of investment advice.

That positive impression was reinforced by the second 2008 study, commissioned by FPA, sponsored by Ameriprise, and carried out by the market research company Harris Interactive. Harris surveyed 3,022 people who had greater than $50,000 in household income or investable assets and identified three groups: self-directed, who never work with a financial planner; advice-supported, who meet occasionally with an adviser or planner; and comprehensive planning participants, who work with a professional financial planner and have a written plan. Even though the markets were volatile during the summer months when the study was conducted, and consumer confidence was near historic lows, the "comprehensive planning" group stood out for being "nearly twice as likely to report feeling confident about their financial future as those without paid, professional support."

The Quest Continues

When asked in 2009 if financial planning had achieved status as a profession, Jack Blankinship gave two sets of answers. Yes, he said, because CFP certificants must acquire and maintain proficiency in a body of knowledge, have a bachelor's degree, pass a 10-hour exam, fulfill an experience requirement, adhere to a code of ethics, and meet a fiduciary standard.

Then he turned to the negative side of the equation. The answer was no, he said, because anyone can hold out as a financial planner, no sovereign body regulates practitioners, no government authority decrees whether a person can practice financial planning, and no single credential is recognized above others as a practitioner's qualification to practice financial planning.

The score? The *nays* trumped the *yeas*. "Financial planning has yet to achieve the status of a profession," said Blankinship.

Ben Coombs concurred: "There is an accepted body of knowledge, a code of ethics and practice standards, and a disciplinary process. But there is no uniform acceptance of these standards among the general public and no public mandate that they be adhered to."

Other veteran planners were more sanguine. "Twenty years ago the public did not think of financial planning as a profession," said Mike Ryan. "Today, I believe we are indeed perceived by the public as a profession. Yet we are young and must strive diligently to maintain ever higher professional standards. What we have worked so hard to obtain can be easily lost."

Tim Kochis was even more emphatic. "The only people still asking that question are people within the profession. Everyone else—media and consumers—takes it for granted."

Perhaps planners in the years ahead will focus on the suggestion made by Robinson and Hughes in "To Act...Like a CFP":

> *We cannot self-proclaim that financial planning is a profession because this is, in the end, a status that can be conferred only by the public.. So perhaps it's time to leave the question of whether or not financial planning is a profession in the hands of the public. Acting as a professional, with all its attendant responsibilities, is in* our *hands.*

CHAPTER 9

The Next 40 Years

G lobal expansion, heightened professionalism, greater public recognition, a growing knowledge base: As the financial planning movement approached its fifth decade, these achievements appeared to portend continued successes. But the global financial crisis that began in 2008 cast a pall over this triumphant narrative and challenged planners everywhere to ponder their role in a financial system that might take years to recover.

Older financial planners had of course witnessed other market drops and cyclical turbulence. But many younger members of the profession had never known prolonged recession or had reason to doubt major financial institutions. How would they change their advice to clients, many of whom had suffered huge losses in the downturn? What would their role be in a changed economy already challenged by greater longevity and a huge cohort of Baby Boomers expecting to enter retirement? And given the dramatically changed economic circumstances, what, if anything, could financial planners do to bring about the profession's original goals of prosperity and financial security for all who would create and follow a good plan?

"Is Capitalism Working?"

As luck would have it, some of the worst financial news in the autumn of 2008 coincided with the timing of the Financial Planning Association's annual conference, which had started on October 4 in Boston. All week, global stock markets had been pummeled. The Dow Jones Industrial Average dropped 18 percent, the S&P 500 fell 20 percent, and U.S. markets closed lower, amid record-breaking volume, on five out of five sessions. At five o'clock on the morning of October 8, Mark Johannessen, FPA's 2008 president, checked the news as he was preparing to leave Boston for what should have been a media celebration of a milestone for FPA and the planning profession: the introduction of a new standard of care, calling for fiduciary duty for all financial planners. World markets were falling precipitously; the Indonesian stock market had already halted trading after a one-day drop of 10 percent. "It took my breath away," Johannessen later recalled. "Needless to say, it also took the focus off the standard of care."

On October 11, the head of the International Monetary Fund warned that the world financial system was teetering "on the brink of systemic meltdown." A deepening sense of gloom about the prospect of a long slump and a painful recession seemed to be the prevailing—possibly only—sentiment. Perhaps worst of all, public trust in financial advisers was severely shaken by several high-profile fraud cases. In December, money manager Bernard Madoff admitted to a Ponzi scheme in which tens of thousands of investors were defrauded of $50 billion. R. Allen Stanford, a Texas financier and founder of Stanford Financial Group, was accused by the SEC of an $8 billion fraud involving high-yield certificates of deposit issued by an offshore bank. A prominent New York lawyer, Marc Dreier, was charged in a $400 million hedge fund scam and two money managers in New York were accused of misappropriating at least $553 million. In all of these scams, victims included both individual investors and sophisticated institutions, including university endowments and employee pension funds.

So unnerving were the developments of 2008 and early 2009 that capitalism itself was called into question. *Knowledge@Wharton*, the respected newsletter of the Wharton School at the University of Pennsylvania, published "A Question Revisited: Is Capitalism Working?" by George M. Taber, the former business editor of *Time* magazine. Taber noted capitalism's Achilles heel: ". . . the business cycle of boom and bust, or put another way, greed and fear." It was "painfully obvious," Taber continued, "that bankers and other financial players had little or no understanding of the risk of investment derivatives that have been the centerpiece of the crisis."

George Soros, the billionaire investor and founder of Soros Fund Management, put it even more bluntly, telling a group of economists and bankers in February 2009 that the philosophy of "market fundamentalism" was now under question "as financial markets have proved to be inefficient and affected by biases rather than driven by all the available information."[1]

A "New Different" for Financial Planning

The seeds of the financial planning movement were planted in the late 1940s, at a moment of great economic ferment in America. Economic thinking was influenced by the work of Austrian-born economist Joseph Schumpeter, who had fled Nazism in the 1930s and taught at Harvard until his death in 1950. Schumpeter popularized the term *creative destruction*, by which he meant the process of radical transformation that accompanies radical innovation. More than a quarter-century after the war, radical innovation took the form of a small group of men who met in a nondescript Chicago hotel room, seeking a way to help people understand and achieve financial security. The economic climate seemed turbulent at the time: Between December 1968 and May 1970 the Dow Jones declined 36 percent. There would be four subsequent rough spots—declines of 45 percent, 27 percent, 36 percent, and 38 percent—between 1973 and 2002. But there was little similarity between those declines and recessions and the radical transformation under way in late 2008 and 2009.

"This event," said planner Harold Evensky, CFP, in early 2009, "is not like the technology bust of the early 2000s. It's also not the Great Depression. But it will have a permanent psychological impact on clients—and on planners."

> *"This event is not the Great Depression. But it will have a permanent psychological impact on clients—and on planners."*
> —Harold Evensky

Massive, fundamental changes in and challenges to the global economy were under way in 2008 and 2009, shifts that will remap the economic and financial landscape for years, and likely will alter the practices and business models of financial planners. This "new different," as some observers called it, included the beginning of a prolonged period of deleveraging as both consumers and businesses shed debt, a shift from consumption to savings, and fears about a return to inflation after a period of falling or lower prices. The U.S. economy's growth during the 1990s was largely based on an "artificial" driver—cheap, plentiful, and easy credit, for consumers and businesses alike. In the downturn, debt was transferred from consumers and businesses to the government, which could result in higher taxes during a future "payback" period. The United States also found itself entering 2009 in the classic "paradox of thrift," as described by the economist John Maynard Keynes: The nation's personal savings rate shot up to 5 percent in January 2009, up from 0.1 percent one year prior.[2] In a perverse twist, after years of being scolded for spending too much and saving too little, consumers were now blamed for not doing enough to reignite the economy. Meanwhile, the specter of inflation returned as huge infusions of government money sparked fears of price increases in 2010 and beyond.

At the micro level, individuals and families felt their own pain. According to the Federal Reserve Bank, Americans' net worth fell in 2008, erasing four years of gains; U.S. families lost $11 trillion. Retirement assets alone dropped by almost 25 percent in 2008, from $10.3 trillion to $7.86 trillion.

In the face of so many hard numbers and hard questions—How do I protect my buying power, not just get a constant return? How do I position my portfolio for growth when I'm only three years from retirement? Does diversification still work?—some planners and journalists looked for explanations in softer factors such as emotions and family experiences, the traditional purview of the "life planning" movement. "Workshops Raise Consciousness About Money," published in March 2009 in the San Francisco *Chronicle*, described how childhood messages about money continue to shape adult lives, crisis or not.[3] Veteran planner Deena Katz, CFP, wrote in *Financial Planning* magazine about why that strategy made sense:

> *In our practice, when faced with volatile markets and economic down-turns, we've always refocused the client on planning issues. "Yes, we know the market is fairly volatile right now," we say, "but let's look at your disability policy to ensure that you are well covered in the event of a personal disaster." After months of attempting to downplay market move-ments, this tactic won't work anymore. Clients who believe the world is coming to an end couldn't care less if we review their risk management.[4]*

Marion Asnes, former senior editor at *Money* magazine and now editor of *Financial Planning*, said investors may have realized that they were sleepwalking through their financial lives. Worse, said Asnes, some planners may have been sleepwalking enablers during the bull markets of the 1990s and the mid-2000s. "There are a lot of 'ifs' that clients didn't prepare for and planners didn't prepare them for," Asnes said in a 2009 interview. "And planners may not have prepared themselves either. It's easy to get lulled to sleep by your own success."

Mark Tibergien concurred. A respected industry guru and former Moss Adams consultant who is now CEO of Pershing Advisor Solutions, Tibergien said planners

> *are in the same position as their clients: they may not be able to re-tire when they planned. We're entering a massively unsettling period for advisers—margin compression, a tougher climate for managing growth, potential disaffection of clients. For the last ten years, the mantra was that [advisers] didn't need to really know the markets and investment management. They could outsource that—their value was in managing relationships. How many can now justify their fees for being a "relation-ship manager"?*

A Long Tail

In 2004, Chris Anderson, the editor of *Wired* magazine, coined the term *long tail* to describe the aggregation of many small markets to create a larger

Market Milestone: The Graying of the Baby Boom

Even before the recession of 2009, the march of the 77 million Baby Boomers toward retirement represented a tidal wave of both opportunity and crisis. Between 2010 and 2030, the population age 65 and over is projected to increase almost 80 percent: 20 percent of Americans will be older than 65 by 2030, compared with just one in eight in 1990.[6] One of the most dramatic future trends is the percentage of Boomers who will remain working well into their sixties and seventies. Between 1977 and 2007, employment of workers 65 and older increased 101 percent; employment of women in that age group rose 150 percent. And while the number of employed people age 75 and over is relatively small (0.8 percent of the employed in 2007), this group had the most dramatic gain, increasing 172 percent between 1977 and 2007. And seniors aren't necessarily choosing part-time work: Full-timers account for a majority, 56 percent in 2007, among older workers.[7]

one.[5] More recently—and more specific to financial planning—"long tail" described a large problem of long duration. For financial planning in 2009, the long tail consisted of more people with fewer assets and inadequate savings living longer than ever before, in many cases outliving their savings.

The long tail of longevity is most troubling to retirement experts. A third of women age 65 in 2009 can expect to live into their nineties, according to Alicia Munnell, PhD, professor of management sciences and director of the Center for Retirement Research at Boston College. "Thirty years of living requires an enormous amount of assets," said Munnell. "And people just aren't prepared." The 2009 National Retirement Risk Index (NRRI), produced by Munnell's group, painted a sobering picture. Even if they work to age 65 and annuitize all their financial assets, including the receipts from reverse mortgages on their homes, 61 percent of "late Boomers" (born 1955 to 1964) will be unable to maintain their standard of living in retirement.[8]

"Thirty years of living requires an enormous amount of assets, and people just aren't prepared."

—Alicia Munnell

In 2007, only 30 percent of workers of all ages contributed to a 40l(k) plan; the number was only slightly higher, 34 percent, for those age 50 to 59.[9] The average account balance for individuals in their fifties with a salary of $80,000 to $100,000 and job tenure of 10 to 20 years was $111,840 at the end of 2007, before the market collapse.[10] Although some in that age group still had defined-benefit plans, *40 percent had neither*.[11] Not that 40l(k) plans held up well during the collapse, noted Munnell: "Assets in defined contribution plans declined by $2.7 trillion from October 1997, at the peak of an expansion, to March 2009. This downturn really brought home the fact that employees bear all the investment risk in defined contribution plans. Everybody is having to re-think everything."

While planners have been aware for years of the challenges of a graying population, recent financial and economic trends may influence their practices in more significant ways. A larger percentage of their clients will be dealing with the grim realities of asset erosion from the downturn, more may need help with elder-care issues, some will still be helping their children (60 percent of empty-nesters surveyed by the Yankelovich organization in 2007 said they continue to give children financial support),[12] and many will be looking to planners to help them with one of the most vexing issues for the next couple of decades: health-care costs. Research done by Fidelity Investments in 2009 indicated that the cost of health care in retirement rose 50 percent since 2002—a 65-year-old couple who retired in 2009 would need about $240,000 to cover medical expenses in retirement *apart* from Medicare insurance.[13] Other estimates placed the figure even higher: $295,000 for health-care premiums and out-of-pocket expenses during retirement, with a person living to age 95 potentially spending as much as $550,000.[14]

Even the most sophisticated and astute of veteran planners has run into the unexpected consequences of the market collapse. Harold Evensky, who practices in Coral Gables, Florida, said that firms like his had large numbers of clients with relatively high net worth who had been comfortable self-insuring for long-term care risk. "Now they aren't," said Evensky. "It's a ramification I really hadn't thought through until recently." Even clients with significant assets were reevaluating their long-term care risk: The 2009 NRRI reported that nursing home care required an additional expenditure of up to $77,000 per year in 2009 dollars, a financial drain that less than 15 percent of the senior population could withstand.[15]

Planners' clients aren't alone in facing these dilemmas. The planner population is rapidly aging, too. According to CFP Board, in 2008, 30 percent of CFP practitioners were age 50 to 59; 15 percent were over age 60. But by 2017 the 60-plus age bracket is expected to grow to 38 percent. And in 2027, the 2007 pool of CFP practitioners will have declined by 42 percent due to death, and almost two-thirds of those remaining will be older than 60.[16] In the broader financial services world, the numbers also are shrinking. In

2001, there were 674,000 FINRA-registered representatives (some of whom also are CFP practitioners); by 2009, that number was down to 659,000. In addition, the number of life-licensed agents declined by 20 percent between 1998 and 2007.[17]

> "In 2027, the 2007 pool of CFP practitioners will have declined by 42 percent due to death. Almost two-thirds of those remaining will be older than 60."

Who will serve the complex needs of aging Baby Boomers? Will graying clients facing longer lives and inflation understand the difference between safety and certainty? Will "asset liquidation" describe the typical planner's practice? Can planning weather a post-crisis "go-to-cash" investment philosophy? More important, what will "retirement" even look like?

Here Comes the Age Wave

On January 1, 2011, the first baby boomers will turn 65. In their sixties and beyond, members of the post–World War II generation will challenge the financial planning profession and the culture at large to redefine products, services, and indeed the very concept of retirement. They've already challenged society's notions of what aging and getting "old" means—even if they sometimes want it both ways.

A 2008 survey of 4,000 people across the generations, conducted by Charles Schwab Corporation and market research firm Age Wave,[18] revealed that on average people believe "old age" begins at age 75. But they also firmly believe that Social Security benefits should start at age 63. "Surprisingly, study respondents believe they should qualify for 'old age' benefits twelve years before they become 'old,'" said Ken Dychtwald, PhD, president and CEO of Age Wave.[19] That attitude is more than unrealistic, he said: "As life expectancy has continued to elevate, we can't expect to retire at sixty-three or sixty-four and sustain ourselves for another twenty years." To harbor that expectation, said Dychtwald, is to head for "a train wreck."

> *There's been an absence of financial accountability and self-reliance on the part of the overwhelming majority of the population. Is our [baby boomer] generation financially responsible? No. Unfortunately, we've come to glorify indulgence and immediate gratification. And we can't expect the government to do it all. The hard truth is that government will fund less and there will be more triaging—with Social Security, and*

also for Medicare, which poses an even bigger challenge. There will be more limited benefits for people of higher net worth. Older people will increasingly have to fend for themselves. They'll need to know how to do it and be disciplined to do it.

(The Charles Schwab–Age Wave study also found that boomers are most widely viewed as having a positive effect on society, most socially conscious, most productive, but *not* as most self-indulgent. That dubious honor was reserved for Generation Y, those born between 1983 and 2002.[20])

Compounding the distress, Dychtwald said, has been a massive trust deficit, as the public lost faith in Wall Street and the financial media. "At the very time that people need help, guidance, discipline, and good counsel more than ever, they don't know who to turn to," he said.

Dychtwald has studied aging and retirement for 35 years. In his first book, *Age Wave*,[21] he began a national dialogue about what retirement really means to the Boomers and what aging America means for business, society, and culture. In his 2009 book, *With Purpose: Going from Success to Significance in Work and Life*,[22] he said that the future of age has never looked better.

"We have created a model about what we want to be when we grow up which might be wrongheaded," Dychtwald told the *Orange County Register* in early 2009. "I think what's going on is not just a crashing of the economy but seeing unsustainable companies and lifestyles disappear. I've never seen more people in more varying circumstances asking important questions of themselves and loved ones: What really matters to us? What kind of life do we want to lead?"[23]

Dychtwald said one response may be a healthy shift in financial offerings, with more emphasis on insurance products and less on stocks and bonds. Even as the stock market was plummeting, said Dychtwald, "the insurance industry was coming up with new products—new annuities, new long-term-care products." The public may soon start regarding insurance companies as their pension providers, he added.

Maslow Meets Retirement

"Retirement is an unnatural condition," wrote trainer and consultant Mitch Anthony in his groundbreaking 2001 book, *The New Retirementality*.[24] Financial planning, he said, can help individuals "stop making a living and start making a life." Anthony called his philosophy "Maslow meets retirement" and based it on the psychiatrist Abraham Maslow's hierarchy of human beings' needs: physiological, safety, psychological, esteem, and self-actualization. In 2009, Anthony partnered with planner Lewis Walker,

CFP, to form Life Transitions Advisors, LLC, "using the Maslow Conversation as the centerpiece of financial planning's focus for the next twenty years."

Walker and Anthony have said that planners circa 2009 and beyond are in the "life transitions management profession," and must focus on Boomers' needs and desires for the latter part of their lives. But it's not just a client exercise in narcissistic navel-gazing, according to Anthony:

> *We all eventually will need to engage in a conversation about developing an income stream that lasts as long as we do and that outpaces the inflation that threatens to rot our nest egg, slowly but surely. The best way I know to accomplish this task is to work Maslow's hierarchy of needs (with money in mind) and walk through the process of designing an income for life.*[25]

According to Walker, the conversations aging Boomers need to have with their financial advisers will be "hard work." "Planners will have to learn how to have 'right brain' discussions, going from data manipulation to emotional connections. And many more of those conversations will be with women. In fact, I believe financial planning in the coming decades will be very driven by women's concerns." Walker noted the work of futurists Amy Oberg and Joe Bourland, who maintain that men will need to develop new skills in a society being reshaped by older women. "In the rising service economy, the skills required include interfacing, caring, empathy, and counseling. These high-touch skills have been considered female skills, so changes in the economy may be especially difficult and confusing for men in the years to come."[26]

"I believe financial planning in the coming decades will be very driven by women's concerns."

—Lewis Walker

Dychtwald agreed that aging clients will be looking for more help with life transition issues. "Several years ago we asked the pre-retiree generation what they wanted from a financial adviser," he said. "The answer: someone to help me envision my future and how to fund it. That means a deeper familiarity with the issues of adulthood, retirement, divorce, grandparent-hood, and all the other stages of life. And that's not the current expertise of the financial planning industry. When I go to financial planning confer-ences, all the workshops are about products and selling. Ask planners what an empty-nester might be feeling compared to a new grandparent, and they look like deer caught in the headlights."

Bob Veres, a consultant, author, and longtime "sage" of the profession, said he sees the future that Walker envisions for Boomers, and subsequent generations, as "the Age of Fulfillment." Yes, the planning profession will inevitably and increasingly tie the planning service to personal client goals and preferences, said Veres. "The truest thing you can say about the profession is that it is now, and will always be, trending toward making the technical part of the service more and more personally relevant and individually focused," he said. "Our society is moving, by fits and starts, away from a consumer-based or consumption-based model to a fulfillment-based dynamic. The financial planner will become the key source of advice and counsel for people who wish to move into the Age of Fulfillment."

Walker maintained that the financial planning practice of the future will go well beyond financial management and more to a "resource platform." "Planners will be expected to have answers or sources of expertise on geriatric care, property maintenance, pet care, travel, and philanthropy," he said.

Others were skeptical. "The Internet is a resource center," said Mark Tibergien.

Why would I pay thousands of dollars a year for that? Information is the easiest thing to get. Now, if that extends to clients being willing to pay for judgment, analysis, recommendations, and guidance on how both planner and client are using that information to manage my financial life, that's different. Ultimately, clients want their financial professional to function just as their doctor, accountant, or lawyer does. It's basically, do something.

Redefining the Model for Advice

For the first time since Hewitt Associates began tracking 401(k) accounts in 1997, workers in February 2009 held less than half of their 401(k) money in stocks (48 percent, as opposed to 69 percent in 2007). Most money now sat in fixed-income and cash instruments, including money market funds.[27]

"In essence, we've lost our biggest client: the market," said Harold Evensky. "As clients become more conservative, and many will, you certainly can't charge a traditional AUM fee for a heavy-on-cash portfolio," he said.

> *"We've lost our biggest client: the market. You can't charge a traditional AUM fee for a heavy-on-cash portfolio."*
>
> —Harold Evensky

Yet Evensky isn't convinced that flat retainer fees will be the wave of the future, even as clients' needs shift more to life transitions. In fact, his firm tried introducing a retainer, "and we were completely unsuccessful in explaining and educating on it. We just seemed incapable of making it work." Nevertheless, he said he believes that planning firms will have to serve clients with larger asset bases *and* increase the size of their firm to serve more as family-office-conversation-facilitator. "Firms simply have to be a lot bigger in order to make services such as exploratory conversations cost efficient," he said. "Even though we have some difficulty with the necessary resources, what we're able to deliver is still much more than a practice of a couple of planners can."

Although the 2008 report "Fast Forward: The Advisor of the Future," from Pershing Advisor Solutions and Moss Adams LLP, focused on registered investment adviser (RIA) firms, its findings are relevant for other members of the financial planning profession as well. The report predicted that by 2012 most RIA firms will nearly triple in size and that revenue will grow by $35 billion, fueled by the unprecedented demand for independent, objective financial advice. The firms that will "fast-forward," according to Mark Tibergien, principal author of the report, will successfully address the "three Cs": change, capacity, and culture.

Change will result in a typical firm recruiting and retaining 11 new people by 2012, with some of the new hires operations and management staff. The resulting environment will require "a systematic internal process for the development of talent, a well-structured compensation model, and a career path that is fulfilling to all employees in the firm." Capacity not only must be created, it also must be maintained in order to be ready to capture opportunities when they arise. "In the future, the increased sophistication of clients and the increased service time caused by the wave of retiree clients will require firms to seek more leverage in their service model and eliminate inefficiencies in their service process," said Tibergien. And culture will require firms to honor the principles that made them successful while simultaneously integrating additional employees and responding to clients' more influential role in defining the advisory relationship.

"RIAs will shift from a focus on generating high income to creating a significant and lasting presence in the market, and generating opportunities for a large number of people," commented Tibergien, who called this a shift "from income to significance." In short, the business evolution of financial planning will be to a true business.

"Fundamentally, most planning firms have been small businesses not professionally managed," Tibergien said. "The bull market camouflaged a lot of sins."

The new model of business as a *business* will require a different definition of *adviser*, according to Tibergien. While today's adviser is "investment-centric," according to the Pershing report, tomorrow's will need to be "client-centric." Managing risk will take the place of managing money. Generating return will shift to balancing cash flows. Financial planning will move to life planning, and planners' preference for a do-it-yourself business model will shift to depending on specialists and strategic partners.

In fact, said Bob Veres, planners might not merely need to leverage specialists, they might *become* specialists. "Planning firms may define their ideal clients non-geographically," he said. "Instead of working with 'people in the Philadelphia area,' a firm will have a planning clientele, with communication by videophone, of 'owners of dry cleaners'—or any other subcategory you can think of. Specialization will become more intense and focused when firms are liberated from a particular geographic area."

While the "new different" for post-recession financial planning may translate to success for some advisers—and a rise in the number of people seeking qualified financial advisers—other planners "are at the precipice of being weak leaders to their clients," said Tibergien.

> *More importantly, advisers need to use this opportunity to re-think whether their business is positioned correctly, including financially. And the profession as a whole needs to start re-focusing on training people in business development. The sales muscle has atrophied. When advisers saw 80 to 90 percent of their revenue coming in predictably, from assets under management fees, they didn't need to worry about the dirty word "selling." Now they do.*

The Final Frontier: Reaching the Mass Market

Statistics on the use of planners and investment advisers were mostly encouraging through the early and mid-2000s. A 2008 report from Pershing Advisor Solutions indicated that a growing proportion of overall household financial assets were professionally managed. The report cited a 2006 FINRA-funded investor survey showing that 60 percent of responding individuals indicated their involvement in savings and investments had increased, and a 2006 survey by the Investment Company Institute (ICI) estimating that 73 percent of mutual-fund investors consulted a financial adviser before purchasing a mutual fund. In addition, total professionally managed assets under management represented nearly 60 percent of total household financial assets in 2005, up from 55 percent at year-end 2000.[28] Many consumers, said the report, have yet to seek the services of an adviser, but will in the future, as the need for a financial adviser becomes increasingly standard.

But "standard" for whom?

In 2007, the College for Financial Planning released results of its alumni survey that indicated that the "typical client" of its alumni-planners was a two-income couple, each of whom was between 50 and 59 years old, with a combined gross annual income of between $100,000 and $149,999, discretionary income of $10,000 to $20,000, and a net worth of $1 million to $1.5 million.[29]

Social class, a debatable, even controversial, term, is often defined by numerical measures such as wealth or income. In 2005, sociologists William Thompson and Joseph Hickey used U.S. Census Bureau information to describe four distinct classes.[30] The "lower class" has a high school education, makes $7,000 a year, and is either unemployed or works only part-time. Clerical, service, and blue-collar workers making between $15,000 and $25,000 are the "working class." The "lower middle class" has a bachelor's degree, works in professional support and sales, and makes between $32,000 and $50,000. Professionals with a graduate degree make $72,500 to $100,000 and constitute the "upper middle class," while chief executives and politicians, making more than $200,000, are the "upper class." The top 5 percent of households in household income distribution, according to the U.S. Census Bureau's 2006 figures, make $167,000 and up; the top 20 percent make $92,000 and up.

By those measures, and applying the College for Financial Planning's "typical client" profile, most planners serve clients positioned within the top 20 percent of the population in household income. In 2009, practicing financial planners did not come close to serving 20 percent of the U.S. adult population of 218 million people.[31] Clearly, financial planning has largely been built around a client base of upper-middle-class white America.

Since its inception, financial planning has been pulled between its stated purpose—to help ordinary Americans gain control over their financial lives—and the compelling need of planners to earn a livelihood. Generally, the more affluent the client base, the healthier the planner's income—whether that income was based on assets under management, commissions, an annual retainer, or a fee-and-commission arrangement. A common perception, verifiable or not, has been that financial planners serve the top 2 or 5 percent—the "high-net-worth" clients who, it is argued, have complex financial challenges that need the sophisticated expertise of a skilled, well-trained financial planner. Where, then, does that leave "ordinary" middle-class Americans? How can financial planning expand into the mass market—the teachers, physical therapists, caterers, journalists, and contractors who represent a diverse and deserving client base?

One financial planner who has devoted much of her career to the mass market question is Sheryl Garrett, CFP. Garrett founded Garrett Planning Network in 2000 after working for a wealth management firm that, in her words, "felt like a high-demand, on-call, 24/7 concierge service." She envisioned something very different: a service provided on an hourly, as-needed, fee-only basis. Nine years later, the network comprised just over 300 independent planners throughout the United States and in 13 other countries; each planner paid an entry fee ($10,100, spread over the first year) and a yearly renewal fee. In exchange, network members received coaching, on-line training (for which they could earn continuing education credits), and free admission to an annual conference.

Garrett defined her market as individuals who fall between the broad definitions of poverty and semi-affluent—about 86 percent of all Americans. More important, she said, "middle-class is a mindset—and a healthy one for the financial planning profession. Middle-class people have realistic expectations about their financial goals and the conviction they *will* achieve them." A key element of her approach—one that helps control costs—is collaboration between client and planner: Most of the engagement involves "truly getting to know clients and their goals, and helping them overcome resistance or inertia," while much of the implementation of the plan is left to the client. This method, which Garrett acknowledges owes much to the principles of life planning (covered in Chapter 7), "is rewarding for the client and healthy for the practitioner."

But a network with only 300 planners can't begin to address the needs of the huge middle-market population. Achieving that goal, Garrett said, would require as many as 400,000 planners, each serving 300 clients at the modest fee of $500 each. The scope of service would necessarily be limited at first, Garrett said, but "most people simply don't need the $5,000 plan at the beginning of the engagement—they want answers, help, guidance."[32]

In the meantime, the Garrett Planning Network scored a coup, and got closer to its own goal, when it was chosen to be the only financial planning resource serving the 380,000 members of the Military Officers Association of America (MOAA). Planners took a series of webinars on the culture of military families; in addition to offering planning services at a discount, the Garrett Planning Network shared tips on a wide range of subjects—including credit, charitable giving, divorce, and money management—on the MOAA Web site.

While models such as the Garrett Planning Network were beginning to make a dent in the mass market, certain demographic groups remained underserved. Most conspicuous in their absence from financial planning's roster were Latinos and African Americans, who together made up about 28 percent of the U.S. population and whose share of the population will almost certainly increase in the next few decades.

The problem was addressed directly in a 2007 "open letter to the financial services industry, government policymakers, employers, and community leaders," in "The Ariel-Schwab Black Paper." Written by John Rogers, Jr., Charles Schwab, and Mellody Hobson, the letter asked government, employers, and communities to foster a cultural shift toward wealth-building for future generations of African Americans and measures "to ensure equal access to the broad benefits of life in the world's wealthiest country":

> *At the very heart of this great and wealthy nation lies a terrible irony and pressing challenge: despite our wealth and in the face of decades of social progress, we are not doing enough as individuals and collectively as a nation to assure the long-term financial security of our citizens in retirement. Few other issues touch our population as broadly, yet for some, the challenge is even greater. For middle-class African-Americans, the march toward financial security has been an uphill journey marked by half steps, pauses and, for some, retreat. . . . [M]iddle class [b]lacks may not be able to realize a key part of the American dream: a comfortable and secure retirement after a job well done.*[33]

The tenth annual Ariel-Schwab Black Investor Survey revealed that while African Americans are on equal footing with whites when it comes to accessing and enrolling in employer-sponsored defined contribution plans, they save far less each month and have a considerably smaller nest egg—just $53,000 in household savings for retirement. The comparable figure for whites was $114,000. Thirty-nine percent of blacks surveyed said real estate was the "best investment overall" compared with 37 percent who picked stocks or mutual funds. Among whites, just 28 percent chose real estate compared to 55 percent who chose stocks and mutual funds.

In one of the earliest years, 1999, the study helped identify why blacks' and whites' attitudes and behaviors toward investing differ so greatly. In general, African Americans are introduced to savings and investing tools later in life and are drawn toward conservative investment vehicles because of the feeling of security those investments provide.[34]

The situation among Hispanic Americans is even more discouraging. According to the National Council of La Raza (NCLR), a Latino advocacy group, between 35 and 42 percent of Latinos did not even have a banking relationship in 2009. Those Latino families had not made the leap from depending on wages, and consequently have been left behind in the asset-based economy. NCLR said in its 2009 Policy Agenda that while many financial educators offer classes, videos, brochures, and Internet-based seminars for Latinos, there is little evidence to suggest that low-income Latino families are benefiting from such efforts. NCLR said its research shows that to improve their economic well-being, Latinos living in the United States need customized, one-on-one financial counseling at the community level, "and there are virtually no such programs that fulfill this need today."[35]

Los Angeles planner Louis Barajas, CFP, has devoted much of his planning career to this challenge. An author, frequent guest on CNBC and CNN, and former FPA board member, Barajas said studies show that the Latino population is increasing as a proportion of the total U.S. population, and that a high percentage is poorly prepared for old age. According to a 2004 AARP research report,[36] "Hispanics age 65 and older have fewer retirement income sources than others in the same age group; fewer Hispanics have income from Social Security, any kind of pension, interest earnings, or dividends.... For older Hispanics, Social Security is not only their primary source of income, it is a source of income they rely on far more than retirees as a whole." That circumstance is far more dire than that of African Americans, who, according to the Ariel-Schwab study, have access to and participate at healthy rates in employer-sponsored retirement plans.

Barajas has been passionate and outspoken about planning's need to reach into the Latino population, and not with pro bono efforts. "I'm convinced it's the wrong tactic," said Barajas. "Pro bono is fine when there's a catastrophe, but for groups mired in entrenched, cyclical problems, we need a permanent situation, not a temporary one." And he hasn't been reticent in criticizing the planning community's own views: "Most in our profession think 'diversity' means having an attorney, an insurance agent, and a CFP in the firm. They don't get ethnic diversity."

> *"Pro bono is fine when there's a catastrophe, but for groups mired in cyclical problems we need a permanent solution, not a temporary one."*
> —Louis Barajas

The numbers support Barajas's charge. According to CFP Board's most recent figures, compiled in 2002, only about 1.1 percent of CFP practitioners identified themselves as Latino or Hispanic; fewer than 1 percent were African American. FPA has an active diversity task force, but as of 2009 it was "exploring the issues and looking for solutions," said FPA executive director Marv Tuttle, and had not begun a strategy phase.

Barajas said he envisioned a day when the focus on Latinos' "buying power" was supplanted by a focus—spurred by financial planning—on turning them into savers:

> *I'd also like to see us figure out ways to help Latinos actually earn more, because the old maxim about setting aside 10 percent of your pay just doesn't cut it for people who are making low wages and just trying to survive. Financial planning could help by working with Latinos on strategies to increase their income and, very important, on the need to delay gratification ... Many Latinos tell me they want to enjoy life now. I think this partly comes from not having enough hope for the future*

and not enjoying financial dignity. Financial planning can give them hope. How the financial planning world is going to do this is a big question—there are few Latino planners to serve as role models for a next generation, those that could serve this population. I would like it to be easy to ask the question, "Have you considered a career in financial planning?" and for there to be good role models to point to.[37]

The Importance of Scale

Like Sheryl Garrett, Mark Tibergien also can envision a day when the $50,000-a-year teacher will benefit from expanded availability of financial planning:

Will [the teacher] be able to say he or she has a financial planner? Not necessarily. But I think they'll be able to say they have a financial plan. Firms such as Schwab and Fidelity will likely crank up the retail side of the business because not only do they recognize the need of the mass market, they also have the scale to offer a packaged solution.

To believe in the future of the financial planning profession is almost necessarily to accept that planning needs the large institutions, especially to allow many more people to access and benefit from planning. In 2009, approximately 30 percent of current CFP professionals were associated with about 30 of the largest employers in the financial services industry, and both FPA and CFP Board hold an annual meeting for financial services firms. Two large firms, Merrill Lynch and IDS, were financial planning pioneers. In the early 1990s, Merrill Lynch was turning out 150,000 financial plans a year; the planning effort was sophisticated, thorough, and used the accepted six-step process. IDS, the predecessor to Ameriprise, offered financial plans to its representatives' clients as far back as the 1970s.[38] Many independent broker-dealer firms—Financial Service Corporation (founded in 1965 as Mutual Funds of America), Capital Analysts (founded in 1969 as insurance-owned within Fidelity Mutual), Raymond James & Associates (founded in 1962), and LPL (founded as Linsco in 1969)—have a history as long as financial planning's. Some started primarily as mutual fund sales channels and evolved into firms that supported financial planning.

According to the Financial Services Institute (FSI), an advocacy organization for the independent channel, with 118 broker-dealer firm members as of 2009, the typical independent financial adviser affiliated with its broker-dealer members provides financial planning advice and investment management services primarily to the middle market, or "Main Street" investors.[39] But even if every one of the approximately 150,000 FINRA-registered representatives affiliated with independent broker-dealers that support financial planning offered "full" financial planning services (and many limit their services to investment management), there still might not be enough advisers to adequately serve most Americans in the future. The planner/adviser population is shrinking due to its own graying (and, according to some, due to the risk and expense brought on by increased regulation in the 2000s) and the financial planning education programs registered with CFP Board turn out only about 5,000 graduates per year. The financial professional feeder system of former days—primarily life insurance companies and major wirehouses—also seems in 2009 to have withered, with fewer large firms willing to hire neophytes and train and support tomorrow's financial planners. Or, as Mark Tibergien put it, "Everybody wants to adopt a 21-year-old. And with Wall Street's current situation, it's not likely to be the place for the profession to see dramatic growth."

Raymond James has long been considered a champion of financial planning within its large-firm structure. "We have believed since our founding that investing without a thorough understanding of one's own financial situation, as well as an understanding of the various tax laws affecting investing, is ill-advised," said Tom James, chief executive officer. "There is no higher calling for a financial professional than dedicating oneself to attaining the financial well-being and objectives of every client. A financial planner is integral to a client's financial health."

Raymond James has three broker-dealers and more than 5,000 financial advisers. An early adapter of asset-based pricing, it developed numerous platforms for supporting financial planners, as either independent contractors or employees. About 1,256 of its advisers are employees. (Raymond James also was the first investment and planning firm to introduce a client's bill of rights; the 14 rights are followed by 12 client responsibilities.) The employee model is one that could help solve the adviser scarcity problem: A company is more likely to invest more heavily in the professional development of its employees. While most independent broker-dealers do offer education and marketing support, they have more to lose after making sizeable "people development" investments when affiliated advisers can change their broker-dealer affiliation easily—taking their clients with them. If more independent broker-dealers adopted a Raymond James–type model with an adviser-employee channel it might also promote the wider availability of planning to consumers. But large firms still carry the taint of a "sales" culture, anathema to financial planning's quest for true professional status.

The "efficient self-destruction" of the wirehouse retail delivery model, said Bob Veres, is both positive and negative for financial planning. It's positive because the decline of retail brokerage eliminates a competitive force and—more importantly—an alternative business model that made it appear as if "service" were free to the customer. But on the negative side, "those firms provided training for new advisers getting into the business, and gave them experience in their formative years," Veres said. "In addition, the advertising budgets of the larger brokerage firms created demand for the planning service. Millions of consumers got their first taste of financial advice because they responded to a brokerage advertisement. If the experience wasn't positive, they were motivated to seek out an alternative, and many planning firms thrived in this ecology."

At one time, banks were viewed as the likely channel for delivering financial planning services to the mass market, but by 2009 that potential seemed mostly unrealized. Tom Potts, PhD, CFP, professor of finance and director of the financial services program at Baylor University and 2009 president-elect of FPA, forecast banks being in planning in a big way. "But I was wrong," said Potts:

> *Banks have such a broad retail reach and it seemed to me that a template could be created at a reasonable cost to offer products and services to middle-income individuals. The "typical" bank customer doesn't have complex issues such as figuring out stock options or planning for a complicated estate. But banks that tried it just didn't do a good job—likely too much emphasis on "cross selling" and its conflicts of interest—and it didn't work out. Accountants also eyed offering financial planning, viewing it as a way to realize increased revenue, but they too pulled away when they discovered there was a lot more to financial planning than they thought.*

Another option for reaching the large underserved market is the workplace delivery model. The global professional services firm Ernst & Young, for example, offers a telephone service, the EY Financial Planner Line; staffed by 80 CFP professionals, the helpline is available to two million employees of 40 companies and organizations. About 3.6 million people are eligible for planning advice without a fee from financial services giant TIAA-CREF, which provides its telephone services mostly to people earning less than $200,000 a year.[40] Ayco, a Goldman Sachs company, offers the Ayco AnswerLine through its Money in Motion Personal Finance Program. Ayco's 1,340 associates, many trained as JDs, MBAs, CPAs, and CFP professionals, deliver personalized, comprehensive financial counseling to nearly 12,000 senior executives at 410 Fortune 1000 companies.[41]

Bob Veres suggested another future model for achieving scale: "Advisory firms will work collaboratively with thousands of clients at once, all of them paying a subscription fee for access to the adviser's retirement planning and goal-calculation software and, more importantly, for as-needed advice on moving forward in the goals they select," he said. "Collaboration will replace delegation as the model of the future: more clients per adviser, more of the work handled by the consumer. Instead of retainers, the model for the masses will look more like subscriptions."

> *"Collaboration will replace delegation as the model of the future: more clients per adviser, more of the work handled by the consumer."*
> —Bob Veres

New Technologies: Web 2.0 and Beyond

In past decades, computer technology liberated planners from routine work and allowed them to expand their client base. Evolving technologies will continue to play an important role in financial planning's next phase of development and in its service to the mass market—even though it isn't yet entirely clear how, and even though some planners have hesitated to embrace newer options made possible by the interactive Web.

Their hesitation is misplaced, warned Nicholas Nicolette, CFP, a principal at Sterling Financial Group in New Jersey. "We, as financial planning advisers, need to continue to dedicate ourselves to lifting up our core competencies," Nicolette told *InvestmentNews* in April 2009, adding that using advanced tools will allow planners to better serve a larger number of clients.[42]

> *I get very frustrated when I attend [conference] sessions and see an adviser who has made the effort to attend a conference and then seems to just get frustrated and says, "I don't need to understand how that technology works; just make it easy to present." And then they just seem to give up.*
>
> *The bottom line is that financial planners need to learn to deal with complicated technology issues and how to integrate them with our holistic approach.... They need to make investments to expand technology competencies within their firms. It's all about raising the level of professionalism.*

The other side of the equation is that it has become easier for consumers to find do-it-yourself financial solutions from technology. Indeed, they've been directly targeted by financial Web sites and software companies offering sophisticated platforms originally developed for planners. In April 2009, Boston University professor Laurence Kotlikoff, PhD, released a consumer version of his "economics-based, consumption-smoothing" software, ESPlannerBASIC, formerly available only to professionals. Designed to help individuals build a lifetime financial plan, ESPlannerBASIC included calculations of how much people should spend, save, and insure each year to achieve a stable living standard through retirement.

More than ever, financial planning tools are coming to consumers via the Internet rather than in off-the-shelf software. The National Endowment for Financial Education (NEFE) introduced Decumulation.org in 2009 to help individuals design customized retirement income plans. MyFinancialAdvice.com has provided financial counseling over the telephone and e-mail.

Some planners are communicating with clients and potential clients using Web 2.0 technology: the Internet as interactive platform. Blogs, wikis, and file sharing, as well as networking sites such as Facebook, LinkedIn, and Twitter, have the potential to reach large numbers of people unmoved by more traditional forms of marketing. The profession as a whole has encouraged experimentation: The *Journal of Financial Planning* introduced readers to *blogs*—short for *Weblogs*—in 2005, defining *blog* as "a Web site with fresh and regular commentary, analysis, musings—usually distinctly 'individual'—and links to sources cited, usually other blogs."

Although some ambitious planners were quick to answer the siren call of the new social media, Web 2.0 has presented pitfalls as well as potential. For example, LinkedIn, a popular site for business networking and job searching, encourages members to solicit and post recommendations from colleagues, clients, and employers. Proceed with caution, warned Bill Winterberg, CFP, a former software engineer who switched to advising financial planners on technology issues. Writing in March 2009 in his blog, FP Pad, Winterberg told readers that "investment advisers registered under the SEC who use the 'Recommendations' feature of LinkedIn.com may be in violation of Rule 206(4) of the Investment Advisers Act of 1940."[43] That rule stipulates that publishing "any advertisement" that refers "directly or indirectly, to any testimonial of any kind concerning the investment adviser or concerning any advice, analysis, report or other service rendered by such investment adviser" shall constitute "a fraudulent, deceptive, or manipulative act, practice, or course of business."

California financial planner Cathy Curtis, CFP, credited LinkedIn with increased publicity for her small firm. A Dow Jones Newswires reporter found Curtis's LinkedIn profile by searching for "financial planning contacts," then visited Curtis's Web site and called her. As a result, Curtis was quoted in two *Wall Street Journal* stories. Curtis also maintained a business page on Facebook, the popular Web site that was created in 2004 as an online network for college friends and quickly evolved into a more general social-networking platform. In addition, Curtis, Winterberg, and other financial planners joined Twitter, the short-communication tool—messages are limited to 140 characters—that facilitates conversation among people who "follow" one another.

Twitter and other social media may be particularly useful for planners who are targeting Generation Y as future clients. This generation, often referred to as "digital natives," is the product of the Internet era and their social interactions (and, frequently, their business ones, too) have been shaped by cell phones, instant messaging, texting, and Facebook, making them the most connected of all generations.[44]

Whatever the ultimate models for the next phase of financial planning, there will always be an important role for face-to-face interaction, said magazine editor Marion Asnes. When all is said and done, she said, "People want you to remember the name of their kid and their dog."

The Next Generation of Planners

If the final frontier for broader acceptance of the financial planning profession is reaching the underserved mass market, the future course of the profession itself may be decided by about 150 planners age 36 and younger in FPA's NexGen group, representing the 24 percent of CFP professionals in that demographic.

Conceived in 2004 as a way for younger planners to participate in the larger community of established planners, NexGen was spearheaded by Aaron Coates, CFP, Michael Kitces, CFP, April Johnson, and Dave Demming, Jr., CFP. "When I went to my first FPA Retreat, in 2003, it was a group of older planners—and me," said Coates, who was 30 at the time. "I was amazed at the high-profile 'names' I got to interact with. They took me right into their circle and shared their knowledge with me. But I was only one young planner and I wanted others to have that experience. Without it, we weren't catching what could be passed on from the first generation."

By September 2004, NexGen became official, holding its first gathering at FPA's annual conference in Denver and launching a membership campaign that increased its size from four members to 30. But development of NexGen did not go as smoothly as Coates had hoped. In fact, it was met with skepticism, suspicion, and even hostility—especially after an article titled "The Great Divide," by 25-year-old planner Angela Herbers, CFP, was published in *Investment Advisor* magazine in February 2005.[45] The article, which Herbers called "a view from the bottom up," brought into the open the dissatisfactions she and her contemporaries were experiencing in the planning profession. She wrote:

This gap between successful planners and the next generation is wider than most people realize, and it's growing. The cultural differences are leading new planners into careers fraught with obstacles, disappointment, and frustration. The crisis doesn't just involve newcomers to the profession. I believe that the implications for the established planning community are much worse: The failure to find a place for these young professionals results in low productivity, high employee turnover, and unattractive exit strategies that cost firm owners millions of dollars every year. If the situation doesn't change, some of the best and brightest young planners are likely to leave the profession, and there will be fewer new graduates to fill the void. It is a serious crisis that threatens the future of financial planning.

By the time the fledgling NexGen group met at FPA's 2005 Retreat, the frustration of the younger planners was matched by that of their elders. "They viewed us as renegade upstarts who felt 'entitled' to a share of older planners' practices without paying our dues like they and others who were pioneers in the profession," said Coates. "They had some anxiety—after all, there was no model for passing down the profession and their practices. We just wanted good dialogue and interaction about where we fit in." Eventually, bruised feelings healed and "word got out that older planners could really take advantage of what *we* could offer," said Coates.

FPA's leadership supported the NexGen concept, even sponsoring the annual NexGen conferences beginning in 2006. By 2008, NexGen was beginning to coalesce into what Coates and the original group had envisioned: creating a new circle of pioneers for the next generation of planners, an environment for collaboration among the generations of planners, and a national stage to showcase leadership by younger planners. "We can come into the golden age of financial planning together," said Coates.

But with accredited degree programs turning out only 5,000 new planners each year, the newest of the new planners and the current 14,000 or so CFP certificants under age 40 will have a difficult time carrying financial planning to millions of Americans starved for the benefit. And that's *if* the younger generation can hang on through the downturn of 2008 and 2009.

According to a January 2009 article in *InvestmentNews,* young advisers now face a longer and rockier road to ownership as succession plans get shelved, firms' values drop, and the job market for young planners tightens:

[O]pportunities to buy into an advisory firm may not even exist, or at least they won't be as abundant as they were before the downturn. The recent turmoil in the financial markets may compel adviser-owners to hold on to their stakes and go back on promises they made to begin selling off part of their firms. . . . That's because they are simply not interested in selling their stock at lower valuations as firm assets have declined.

Valuations declined in the last two quarters of 2008 by 20 to 25 percent.[46]

Despite the rather bleak outlook closing out the first decade of the twenty-first century, young planners could take heart in the results of a survey done by Succession Planning Consultants: 78 percent of advisers expect to employ an internal succession plan, compared with 66 percent in a similar survey done in 2005. "For a young adviser, getting your foot in the door and internal succession are key," said David Goad, president of Succession Planning Consultants in Newport Beach, California. "When an individual looking to sell brings in a young adviser who is in front of the client base over a period of time, the clients are more accepting of a younger adviser."[47]

The shortage of next-generation advisers worries Mark Tibergien, who foresees a talent war for professionals and an unhappy ending for consumers who need help:

> *Unless the profession meaningfully addresses this issue, it runs the risk of fewer and fewer providers becoming even more selective about who they work with and driving the cost of financial advice higher. Everybody needs to do more to make this a compelling profession for young people to choose.*

All Eyes on Washington

The biggest wildcard in the mix of forces that will shape financial planning in the future is held not by planners but by elected officials. "Politicians," said Harold Evensky, "are the big unknown, both in terms of regulation and in terms of what they will continue to do with the economy."

Barely 30 days after the September 2008 implosion of Lehman Brothers, Merrill Lynch, and AIG, the U.S. House of Representatives held its first hearing on reforming financial markets regulation. Numerous experts urged lawmakers to carry out substantial but carefully planned changes. Joseph Stiglitz, the 2001 Nobel laureate in economics, proposed an active government role: "The deregulatory philosophy that has prevailed during the past quarter century has no grounding in economic theory nor historical experience," he said. "Quite the contrary, modern economic theory explains why the government must take an active role especially in regulating financial markets."[48]

Lobbying and politics tempered the pace of change, but key players in Congress made it clear that reform was high on their agenda. House Financial Services Committee Chairman Barney Frank (D-MA) said his panel was determined to separate out the function of systemic risk protection and investor/consumer protection. Senate Banking Committee Chairman Christopher Dodd (D–CT) said reform was a top priority of his panel. While many of the early hearings focused on the broader financial markets, it wasn't long before it became clear that financial planning and planners would be included in the sweep of a major regulatory reform, in large part due to President Obama's appointment of Mary Schapiro to lead the SEC.

Until her appointment, Schapiro, an attorney and career regulator, had headed the Financial Industry Regulatory Authority (FINRA), an industry self-regulatory organization (SRO). In that role, Schapiro oversaw regulation of registered representatives of broker-dealer firms, many of whom were practicing financial planners subject to a lower "suitability" standard for client engagements than the fiduciary standard imposed on registered investment advisers (RIAs), who must register with the SEC under the Investment Advisers Act of 1940.

After her appointment, Schapiro signaled that she was serious about creating a combined and consistent regulatory structure for both broker-dealers and investment advisers. Testifying before the Senate Banking Committee in March 2009, Schapiro said the SEC was "studying to recommend legislation to break down the statutory barriers that require a different regulatory regime for investment advisers and broker-dealers, even though the services they provide are virtually identical from the investor's perspective." Although only Congress has the authority to create an SRO, under the 1940 Act FINRA has the authority to adopt regulations that would establish fiduciary standards for broker-dealers and their affiliated representatives.[49]

Schapiro expressed the view that investors prefer the fiduciary duty as the standard of care; her successor at FINRA, Richard Ketchum, called for "a fiduciary standard that works for both broker-dealers and advisers." But the major professional organizations were disturbed that his position didn't go far enough. In April, CFP Board, FPA, and NAPFA responded in writing to an article in *The Wall Street Journal*; the groups registered their "serious question" about Ketchum's comment:

> *A single standard could work but only if it is a bona fide fiduciary standard—one that requires placing the client's best interests first and foremost. . . . Anything less than the fiduciary standard that is currently in place for investment advisers or for financial planners who hold a CFP certification would reduce, not enhance, the level of care that consumers need to restore their lost trust in the delivery of financial advice. Such a standard would require significant changes in the business practices and models of broker-dealers. We cannot pay lip service to the concept of reforming the financial system by adopting a uniform standard of care that in practice reduces the duty of care that advisers are currently required to provide their clients.[50]*

Most in the industry acknowledged that the regulatory system circa 2009, a hodgepodge of federal and state regulation on the various "subsets" that make up financial planning, had serious flaws and that a single SRO that focused on the overall act of financial planning would be the ultimate desired result. What alarmed many planners was the suggestion that FINRA might be the sole SRO.

Given Schapiro's background as head of FINRA and the agency's broker-dealer "suitability" standard, Harold Evensky, for one, was not optimistic about the eventual outcome. "There's a significant possibility that planners will wind up under FINRA and *not* with a fiduciary standard," he said. "FINRA will say, 'My goodness, look at the depth of our existing regulation, all 14,000 pages of it. Why should we not just include financial planners under us?'" Indeed, that appeared to be the position of Ketchum, who told the Senate Banking Committee that "FINRA is uniquely positioned from a regulatory standpoint to build an oversight program for investment advisers quickly and efficiently."

Mark Tibergien worried that if FINRA became the regulatory authority for those who give advice to the public, it would "dumb down" the standard to *suitability*, rather than enhance it to *fiduciary*. Broker-dealers (and their lobbyists) don't want another layer of compliance, a huge cost center for firms. "But RIAs," said Tibergien, "will counter with this argument: 'Why would you dilute or reduce standards when we've just gone through a maelstrom of activity with lower standards resulting in bad advice and investors getting wiped out?'"

Others saw the silver lining in either version of regulatory reform. "Will Congress give FINRA regulatory control over independent RIAs? Will Congress mandate fiduciary standards, or move everybody to a lower common denominator or suitability standard? Either one could be positive for the profession," said Bob Veres.

> If the regulators move to a compliance standard, then those who adhere to fiduciary standards might be able to use this to positive marketing advantage. If a fiduciary standard is imposed, retail brokerage will at once become less profitable and more risky from a liability standpoint—reducing competitive pressure on planning firms.

"If the regulators move to a compliance standard, then those who adhere to fiduciary standards might be able to use this to positive marketing advantage."

—Bob Veres

Any new regulatory structure built around an SRO that would monitor and enforce standards for the development and delivery of financial planning advice separate from the investment management part would carry new costs. A higher standard of care would require ways to monitor, measure, and train. "I would expect to see some type of a fiduciary audit, either peer review or some other methodology to evaluate how planners are developing plans and delivering advice, and some protocol for inspection," Mark Tibergien said. "If the mission and purpose of a new SRO are clear—raising standards—it will have to have teeth."

The ultimate outcome is unclear, especially given the Obama Administration's intense focus in 2009 on shoring up the economy and the banking system and figuring out a way to help homeowners in danger of foreclosure. As in all moments of political and economic upheaval, the rush to regulatory reform may result in unintended, even disastrous, consequences. Said Tibergien, "All major reform has come after a crisis—the 1933 act after the Depression, Sarbanes-Oxley after Enron. Did those changes materially improve our lives or were they addressing a problem that somebody would simply figure out how to circumvent? Sometimes regulatory reform just adds layers without solutions."

Financial Literacy: A Radical Notion

Psychologists used the jargon of their profession to describe how clients thought and felt during the market meltdown and ensuing recession of 2009: mania and overoptimism behind the housing bubble, addiction to debt caused by lack of self-control, and shock and betrayal on the part of those Americans who had thought they were making safe investments but now faced a frightening, uncertain future. The language of psychology helped reveal that behind all the statistics about falling home prices and other indicators of economic decline lay *people*.[51]

People were now learning some hard truths, according to Don Phillips, managing director at Morningstar. "Investors have realized this isn't a game," Phillips said. "Many had had a mindset that this was all about creating the biggest pile of cash. There's no such thing as wealth without work. Investing is hard, humbling, and it requires sacrifice. The upside is that people will have a better appreciation for financial advisers and the counsel they provide."

That's an outcome that personal-finance journalist Terry Savage would welcome. Savage started her career as a stockbroker and later became a founding member of and the first woman trader on the Chicago Board Options Exchange. Nevertheless, she was seen as, in her own words, "a novelty, just a girl talking about money" when she first appeared on Chicago television in 1984. Five years later, she began writing a regular column for the *Chicago Sun-Times*. Her columns from the early days bear a striking resemblance to those of 2009.

"We were going into a recession in 1989, too," said Savage:

And people were beginning to realize that their financial future depended on them making so many more decisions than their parents had. But the issues were the same—choices for 401(k)s, getting a good mortgage, the wise use of credit. My advice has been consistent for twenty years: Your future is your responsibility, spend less than you make, get out of debt, do your own homework on advice and advisers, invest for the long term in a diversified portfolio. The biggest difference then was that I wasn't able to offer Web sites as resources.

There was another similarity: In her first book, *Terry Savage Talks Money: The Common-Sense Guide to Money Matters*, published in 1990 (Longman), Savage recommended the services of a CFP professional, mentioning the ICFP, IAFP, and NAPFA.

Since the original publication of that book, Savage said there had been a proliferation of extremely complex financial products that were difficult for investors to understand. Yet she was more concerned that by 2009 there still weren't enough qualified financial planners to serve the majority of consumers seeking experienced, ethical advice:

Financial planning needs a national charter, national credentials, and national recognition, and I don't mean a public relations campaign. The planning profession needs to elevate the discussion of planners as a "national trust" so that they are a key component of the American financial system. I'm hopeful that we'll get a commitment on planners and their role in financial literacy from the very top—the presidential level. And the message can't be just "use credit wisely." With Americans looking for direction and leadership and our lawmakers looking to construct a new regulatory system, now is the time to seize the moment.

Savage said she envisioned a day when personal finance would be a required course in high school. "We can't teach personal financial

---

"Financial planning needs a national charter, national credentials, and national recognition, and I don't mean a public relations campaign."

—Terry Savage

responsibility remedially," she said. "The lessons that teach the most cost the most. Today, we're getting some very expensive lessons."

Morningstar's Don Phillips seconded Savage's judgment. He expressed dismay that public officials, policymakers, and media commentators often profess their financial ignorance openly, and that sports and entertainment celebrities—"people who have long track records of making disastrous decisions about finances"—are held up as role models. "The solution has to be education," said Phillips. "I can see personal finance classes in high school or in college, perhaps mandated by the government, with the CFP designation as a prerequisite for teaching. Or the government may require employers to teach their employees about investing."

Because he's spent a lifetime in higher education, Tom Potts said he believed financial literacy is best instilled during the college years. "High school may be a little early," he said.

But by the time young people are in college, they are having to make decisions on budgeting and spending. The key is to get to individuals early enough that they can make life-changing modifications in their views of and decisions about money.

What is going to be most effective in dramatically changing financial literacy in this country? It's either the age or the delivery system or the message—or all three. Think if this country spent just some of the billions in [federal] stimulus money on literacy. It could head off a lot of future problems.

Government support for financial literacy also has the support of the esteemed economist and Yale University professor Robert Shiller, author of *Irrational Exuberance* (2000). In a column published in *The New York Times* in mid-January 2009,[52] Shiller suggested that in evaluating the causes of the financial crisis of 2008–2009, we mustn't forget "the countless fundamental mistakes made by millions of people who were caught up in the excitement of the real estate bubble, taking on debt they could ill afford. Many errors in personal finance can be prevented. But first, people need to understand what they ought to do. The government's various bailout plans need to take this into account—by starting a major program to subsidize personal financial advice for everyone." While he applauded the small steps already taken—the Treasury Department's Office of Financial Education, begun in 2002, and President George W. Bush's Advisory Council on Financial Literacy in 2008—a more ambitious effort is needed, Shiller said, including subsidizing professional advice for lower- and middle-income people, much as we do with Medicaid and Medicare.

"Professional financial advice is now generally accessible only by the relatively wealthy," Siller wrote. "Changing this would be an important corrective step. Giving the general public access to trained advisers would be a boon for the nation in this time of doubt and distrust."

Like Phillips, Potts, and Savage, magazine editor Marion Asnes foresaw a time when financial literacy will be taught, learned, and *used* by a majority of the population, as ingrained as technological literacy. She acknowledged that financial literacy's benefits would be hard to measure. "It's like the effectiveness of a vaccine," she said. "You don't know until you've died of old age without ever having smallpox that the vaccine worked."

Don Phillips said he expects that the planning profession will reach parity with law, accounting, and medicine in terms of recognition in the public's eyes as an essential profession. Most importantly, said Phillips, "The most radical thing that could happen is we'll become a nation of financial literates. It's within the realm of possibility."

That would be a fitting, and shining, testament to the "unlikely revolution" started by a tiny group of visionaries in an inauspicious hotel meeting room near Chicago's O'Hare Airport on December 12, 1969.

Epilogue

As financial planning enters its fifth decade, it is clear that much of its potential and promise are being realized. From virtually nothing, it has become by the early twenty-first century a highly desirable, worthwhile, and important profession. From 42 new CFP professionals in the first graduating class of the College for Financial Planning in 1973, it has grown to more than 120,000 CFP certificants in 20 nations around the world. From a primary product-selling field, it has evolved into a sophisticated process for achieving life goals and addressing all the *what-ifs* for financial security. It has increased the number of individuals who can say, "My child went to college, my business prospered, my retirement was secured." It has given rise to many organizations—including the CFP Board, the FPSB, and the FPA—that have coalesced into powerful forces for professional standards and consumer protection. It has even become an environment for discussing "money wholeness." But, the unholy trinity in the financial services field of conflicts of interest, greed, and corruption are still alive and well.

Much remains to be discussed, analyzed, and advanced, including this: How can financial planning become a better and more accepted profession?

The challenge to seize the moment after 40 years of development can be understood as a clarion call to planners themselves, societal leaders, and the public they both serve. Increased core competence and ever higher ethical and fiduciary standards are at the heart of how financial planning can continue to improve and evolve in the decades to come. But these are not the only issues. Many unresolved questions still demand serious and thoughtful dialogue: How, for example, to expand financial planning to more individuals, improve personal and societal productivity, enhance career paths for entering planners, seek to reduce and productively respond to periods of economic crisis and market turmoil, and better protect the public from unethical "planners."

The profession must also embrace a healthy debate on capitalism as a public good, not just an economic system. In his classic book, *The Spirit of Democratic Capitalism* (American Enterprise Institute/Simon & Schuster, 1982), the philosopher Michael Novak affirmed that capitalism is good because, of all the economic systems devised by humankind, it is the one that lifts the greatest numbers out of poverty—it grows and produces, bringing more services, more creativity, more opportunity, and more life to the citizens of a capitalistic society. Post–financial crisis of 2008 and 2009, an evolving and improving democratic capitalism are part of the hard work that must be done by the next generation of leaders. Financial planners must be among them.

In keeping with the spirit of the pioneers who pushed and challenged others, we pose the following questions as a challenge to the financial planning profession:

- How can the financial planning profession best seek, research, and implement even higher levels of ethical financial planning and fiduciary standards, increased personal and societal productivity, and better coping strategies for market breaks and recessions?
- How can the financial planning profession best expand freedom and values that build better democratic capitalism ownership societies that are more equitable for all the members of society?
- What can the CFP Board, the FPSB, the FPA, and other financial planning organizations around the world do to expand and improve the value of the CFP mark and continue to improve the services of those who hold the mark?
- What should be the financial planning profession's target for the number of CFP professionals in the world at the end of the next forty years?
- If the goal is reached, what percent of the world population that need and desire the services of a CFP professional, can access them?
- What are the most effective programs for accelerating the growth of the total number of CFP certificants?
- How can the CFP examination be further improved to better prepare a new CFP professional?
- What more can be done to improve the CFP education program as preparation for the CFP examination? How can continuing education be improved?
- What are the best new programs to help new CFP practitioners more quickly assimilate into the workforce?
- What more can be done to protect the public from unethical financial services practitioners and better cope with the unholy trinity of conflicts of interest, greed, and corruption in the financial services field?
- How can the profession better inform the public of the services CFP professionals provide?
- How can the FPA and other financial planning membership organizations around the world increase their membership and financial strength and expand services and visibility?

- What are the best ways to expand financial planners' ability to serve all social and ethnic groups?
- What should be the increased role of the financial planning profession in supporting NEFE and other financial public education organizations improve financial literacy and maturity world-wide?
- What are the best ways to expand and improve financial planning's ability to connect, interact with, and enhance the values of life planning?

Quality answers to these and other questions and quality programs to implement these answers can act as a catalyst for a new golden age of financial planning. We urge the financial planning profession to explore these and similar questions and seek quality answers and implementation programs.

Financial Planning Leadership through the Years

Presidents of the International Association for Financial Planning

J. Chandler Peterson, JD, CLU, CFP	1975
Richard F. Venezia, CLU	1976
William B. Shearer, Jr., JD	1977, 1978
C. Robert Strader	1979
Ronald A. Melanson, CLU, CFP	1980
Kay H. Baird, CFP, CPA	1981
C. William Hoilman, CLU	1982
John M. Cahill, CLU, CFP	1983
Bill E. Carter, CFP, ChFC, CLU	1984
Donald R. Pitti	1985
Alexandra Armstrong, CFP, CMFC	1986
Charles B. Lefkowitz, CFP	1987
Larry W. Carroll, CFP	1988
R. Neil Barnes, CFP	1989
Robert A. Hewitt, Jr., CFP, ChFC, CLU	1990
Stephen J. Arpante	1991
Robert J. Oberst, Sr., PhD, CFP	1992
M. Anthony Greene	1993
Ross Levin, CFP	1994
Martin Jaffe, CFP	1995
Gregory D. Sullivan, CFP, CPA/PFS	1996
Peggy Ruhlin, CFP, CPA/PFS	1997
G. Joseph Votava, Jr., CFP, CPA/PFS, JD	1998
Richard P. Rojeck, CFP	1999

Presidents of the Institute of Certified Financial Planners

W. Robert Hightower, CFP	1973, 1974
Jordan N. Kokjer, CFP	1975
Nicholas C. McDaniel, CFP	1976
David M. King, CFP	1977, 1978
Terrance M. Gill, CFP	1979
Henry I. Montgomery, CFP	1980
Betty D. Jones, CFP	1981
Graydon K. Calder, CFP	1982
P. Kemp Fain, Jr., CLU, CFP	1983
Daniel S. Parks, JD, CFP	1984
Colin B. Coombs, CLU, CFP	1985
Lewis J. Walker, CFP	1986
Charles G. Hughes, Jr., CFP	1987
Eileen M. Sharkey, CFP	1988
John T. Blankinship, CFP	1989
Diane V. Schaak, CFP	1990
Madeline I. Noveck, CFP	1991
Richard B. Wagner, JD, CFP	1992
Terry J. Siman, JD, CFP	1993
Marysue J. Wechsler, CFP	1994, 1995
John S. Longstaff, CFP	1996
Judith W. Lau, CFP	1997
Robert J. Klosterman, CFP, CLU, ChFC	1998
Elissa Buie, CFP	1999

Presidents of the Financial Planning Association

Roy T. Diliberto, CFP, CLU, ChFC	2000
Guy M. Cumbie, CFP	2001
Robert Barry, CFP	2002
David B. Yeske, CFP	2003
Elizabeth W. Jetton, CFP	2004
James A. Barnash, CFP	2005
Daniel B. Moisand, CFP	2006
Nicholas A. Nicolette, CFP	2007
Mark E. Johannessen, CFP	2008
Richard C. Salmen, CFP, CFA, CTFA, EA	2009

Certified Financial Planner Board of Standards, Inc. (CFP Board) Chairs, 1985–2009

David M. King, CFP	1985, 1986
P. Kemp Fain, Jr., CFP, CLU, ChFC	1987, 1988
E. Denby Brandon, Jr., CFP, CLU, ChFC	1989, 1990
H. Oliver Welch, DBA, JD, AIP, CPM, CPA/PFS, CFP	1991, 1992
Tom L. Potts, PhD, CFP	1993
Bill E. Carter, CFP	1994
John T. Blankinship, Jr., CFP	1995
S. Timothy Kochis, CFP (president)	1995*
Donna G. Barwick, JD, CFP	1996, 1997
Harold R. Evensky, CFP	1998, 1999
Patricia P. Houlihan, CFP	2000, 2001
Elaine E. Bedel, CFP	2002
Frederick E. Adkins, CFP	2003
David H. Diesslin, CFP	2004
Glenn M. Pape, CFP	2005
Barton C. Francis, CFP, CPA/PFS, CIMA	2006
Karen P. Schaeffer, CFP	2007
David Strege, CFP, CFA	2008
Marilyn Capelli Dimitroff, CFP	2009

IBCFP Board of Affiliated Associations Chairs

E. Denby Brandon, Jr., CFP, CLU, ChFC	1992
H. Oliver Welch, DBA, JD, AIP, CPM, CPA/PFS, CFP	1993

---

*Under CFP Board's reorganization structure, adopted in 1995, the lead volunteer position became "chair" and the compensated organization executive became "president and CEO," eliminating the transition from volunteer president to chair.

International CFP Council Chairs

Tom L. Potts, PhD, CFP	1994
Bill E. Carter, CFP	1995
John T. Blankenship, CFP	1996
S. Timothy Kochis, CFP	1997
Donna Barwick, CFP	1998
Harold Evensky, CFP	1999, 2000
Patricia P. Houlihan, CFP	2001, 2002

Financial Planning Standards Board (FPSB) Chairs

John S. Carpenter	2003
Maureen M. Tsu, CFP	2004
S. Timothy Kochis, CFP	2005
Elaine E. Bedel, CFP	2006
Margaret Koniuck, CFP	2007
Selwyn Feldman, CFP	2008
Stephen O'Connor, CFP	2009

The History of Financial Planning Timeline

1924
Mutual funds are introduced.
U.S. first-class stamp costs 2 cents.

1933
The Securities Act of 1933 is passed, with the aim of protecting investors from a repeat of the 1929 stock market crash.

1934
The Securities Exchange Act of 1934 creates the Securities and Exchange Commission (SEC).

1939
The National Association of Securities Dealers (NASD) is created in response to 1934 Securities Act amendments.

1940
The Investment Advisers Act of 1940 establishes guidelines for regulating the investment industry.

1952
Economist Harry Markowitz publishes "Portfolio Selection," forming the basis for modern portfolio theory.

1962
Congress passes the Self-Employed Individuals Retirement Act, establishing Keogh plans.

1963

Financial Services Corporation founders John Keeble and Richard Felder create their first financial plan, producing about 300 plans a month by 1968.

1969

June 19: Loren Dunton forms the Society for Financial Counselling Ethics.

December 12: Loren Dunton and James Johnston meet with 11 other financial services colleagues, forming the International College for Financial Counseling and International Association of Financial Counselors (IAFC).

President Richard Nixon signs the Tax Reform Act of 1969.

ARPANET, the original name of the Internet, is used by the military and academic institutions.

Neil Armstrong is first person to set foot on the moon.

More than 600,000 U.S. and allied troops occupy Vietnam.

1970

P. Kemp Fain, Jr., attends the IAFC's first sales workshop and organizes the first IAFC chapter in Knoxville, TN.

Fain becomes the International College for Financial Counseling's first enrollee.

The International College for Financial Counseling becomes the College for Financial Planning.

The IAFC has 114 members in Canada, 24 in Germany, 6 in Spain, 5 in Switzerland.

The United States slides into an 11-year bear market.

The Beatles break up.

Unemployment is at 3.5%.

U.S. first-class stamp costs six cents.

1971

Hy Yurman and Jerrold Glass write *A Financial Planner's Guide*.

NASD creates Nasdaq, the first computerized stock-trading market.

Mao Zedong invites the U.S. Ping-Pong team to visit Beijing.

U.S. Supreme Court rules that busing of students may be ordered to achieve racial desegregation.

U.S. voting age is lowered to 18 by the 26th Amendment.

Intel introduces the microprocessor.

1972

A CFP exam, consisting of 150 essay questions, is prepared by the College for Financial Planning's volunteer education committee.

NASD president Gordon S. Macklin notifies member firms that they are not to use *financial planning* or *financial planner* to describe the work of broker-dealer representatives.

Bruce Bent and Henry Brown invent the money market mutual fund.

Five men are apprehended by police in an attempt to bug Democratic National Committee headquarters in Washington, D.C.'s Watergate complex.

The CAT scan is developed in England.

The compact disk is developed by RCA.

1973

IAFP formally separates from the Society for Financial Counseling.

College for Financial Planning confirms its first class of 42 Certified Financial Planner designees.

Thirty-six of the first class of CFP designees meet to form an alumni association, the Institute of Certified Financial Planners (ICFP).

OPEC responds to U.S. support of Israel in the Yom Kippur War by imposing an oil embargo; fuel prices quadruple.

A ceasefire is signed, ending involvement of American ground troops in the Vietnam War.

President Nixon accepts responsibility, but not blame, for Watergate.

1974

IAFP holds its first convention, "Expanding Horizons."

New York Stock Exchange authorizes members with certification from the College for Financial Planning to use the CFP mark on business cards.

OPEC ends the oil embargo.

Gold is $180 an ounce.

Nixon resigns U.S. presidency.

President Gerald Ford signs the Employee Retirement Income Security Act (ERISA).

Individual retirement accounts are created.

Inflation rate is 12.3% (from 5.6% in 1969).

1975

Society for Financial Counseling dissolves.

President Ford proposes a $2.3 billion aid package to rescue New York City from financial disaster; the proposal passes soon after.

Saigon is captured by the North Vietnamese army, North and South Vietnam are unified, the Vietnam War ends.

Apollo and Soyuz spacecraft launch for U.S.–Soviet linkup.

1976

The United States celebrates its bicentennial.

U.S. first-class stamp costs 13 cents.

Khmer Rouge leader Pol Pot becomes prime minister of Cambodia after Prince Sihanouk steps down.

Nineteen-month civil war ends in Lebanon.

1977

Unemployment is at 7%.

Inflation hits 11%.

Department of Energy is created.

The United States and Panama sign the Canal Zone Treaty.

1978

ICFP, for the first time, expels a member, based on violations and possible criminal charges.

Pope John Paul I dies unexpectedly after 34 days in office, succeeded by Karol Wojtyla of Poland as John Paul II.

Framework for Peace in Middle East signed by Egyptian president Anwar Sadat and Israeli premier Menachem Begin.

U.S. inflation is 12.4%.

Baseball player Pete Rose sets a National League consecutive-game hitting-streak record of 44.

1979

Bill Anthes is hired as president of the College for Financial Planning.

IAFP approaches ICFP about folding it into the IAFP; ICFP president David M. King and other ICFP leaders decline.

Bernice Newmark is hired as a part-time ICFP executive director, embarks on a cross-country road trip to recruit ICFP members.

First issue of the *Journal of the Institute of Certified Financial Planners* is published.

Daniel Kahneman and Amos Tversky tie psychology to financial decision-making in "Prospect Theory: An Analysis of Decision Under Risk."

Margaret Thatcher is elected first woman British prime minister.

Mother Teresa receives the Nobel Peace Prize.

President Carter approves a $1.5 billion federal bailout loan for Chrysler.

1980

ICFP's headquarters return to Denver, Colorado, from Florida.

College for Financial Planning sues Adelphi University for attempting to grant the CFP mark without authorization.

Inflation is at 13.5%.

Gold is $880 an ounce.

Iraqi troops hold 90 square miles of Iran after invasion; eight-year Iran–Iraq War begins.

1981

ICFP hires Dianna Rampy as its first full-time executive director.

ICFP holds first Retreat at St. John's University in Collegeville, Minnesota.

The IBM PC is introduced to the public.

Sandra Day O'Connor is first woman appointed to U.S. Supreme Court.

DuPont acquires Conoco for $7.9 billion.

U.S.–Iran agreement frees 52 hostages held in Teheran since 1979.

1982

IAFP establishes the Registry of Financial Planning Practitioners.

U.S. bull market kicks in, caused in part by anti-inflationary policies and deregulation.

Barney Clark receives the first implant of the Jarvik 7 artificial heart.

The Boeing 747 is introduced.

U.S. first-class stamp costs 20 cents.

1983

The National Association of Personal Financial Advisors (NAPFA) is created.

IAFP promotes a six-step process for financial planners to follow when working with clients.

Lotus 1-2-3 arrives on the technology scene.

Professional Portfolio is the first portfolio management software designed for PCs.

Unemployment is at 10.8%.

Sally Ride is the first woman in space.

U.S. deficit of $189 billion is projected.

1984

IAFP establishes a Political Action Committee.

Financial Products Standards Board is created by the ICFP.

College for Financial Planning teams up with the Cooperative Extension Service of the U.S. Department of Agriculture to form the High School Financial Planning Program.

"Computer Communications: A New Tool for Financial Planning" is published in the *Journal of Financial Planning*.

ICFP hosts its first international retreat, in London, with the last in 1987 in Switzerland.

Average wage is $20,147 per year.

Bell System is broken up.

Russia announces boycott of Los Angeles Olympic games.

1985

IBCFP is created and assumes ownership of the CFP marks.

College for Financial Planning's enrollment peaks at 10,103 students.

Membership in the IAFP peaks at 24,000.

Microsoft Windows 1.0 is introduced.

President Ronald Reagan signs Graham-Rudman bill mandating budget control.

DJIA tops 1,300 for the first time.

Barbie dolls surpass in number the American population.

Reagan and Gorbachev agree to step up arms control talks and renew cultural contacts.

1986

IAFP and ICFP take part in the first Congressional hearings on financial planning.

IBCFP adopts a code of ethics and standards of practice, along with a set of disciplinary rules and procedures.

Financial Independence Week is hosted through a collaboration of the IAFP, ICFP, and College for Financial Planning.

Gary Brinson, Randolph Hood, and Gilbert Beebower publish "Determinants of Portfolio Performance," claiming that more than 93% of a portfolio's return can be explained by asset mix.

Tax Reform Act is passed.

Inside trader Ivan Boesky pays $100 million fine.

Nuclear accident at Soviet Union's Chernobyl power station.

1987

January: DJIA closes above 2,000.

IAFP proposes merging with the ICFP.

IBCFP uses results of a study conducted by the College for Financial Planning to outline six areas of knowledge for financial planners.

P. Kemp Fain, Jr., presents the "one profession, one designation" concept in his white paper, "Unifying and Professionalizing the Financial Planning Segments of the Financial Services Industry."

Twenty-four educational institutions along with the College for Financial Planning have IBCFP-registered CFP programs.

Money magazine introduces a list of the 200 "best financial planners."

October 19: DJIA drops more than 22% on Black Monday.

New York Stock Exchange is computerized.

President Reagan presents first U.S. trillion-dollar budget.

Prozac is released for use in the United States.

1988

A joint organization committee agrees to an IAFP/ICFP unification package.

ICFP testifies for the first time before a U.S. Senate Congressional committee.

IBCFP establishes continuing education requirements.

SEC states that the CFP designation "appears to be developing as the most recognized designation in the field."

Benazir Bhutto is chosen as Pakistan's first Islamic woman prime minister.

Ted Turner starts Turner Network Television and buys MGM's film library.

George Bush, Sr., is elected U.S. president.

1989

IAFP votes down IAFP/ICFP unification package.

Registry of Licensed Practitioners is created by the ICFP.

Federal grand jury indicts junk-bond dealer Michael Milken on 98 counts of racketeering and fraud.

National Savings and Loan Corporation's taxpayer-funded bailout is more than $153 billion.

The Series 65 exam, covering investment adviser laws, is introduced.

April–June: Tiananmen Square pro-democracy demonstrations last for seven weeks, culminating in military response and civilian deaths.

November 9: The Berlin Wall is opened, with demolition formally completed October 3, 1990.

Oil tanker *Exxon Valdez* strikes a reef, spilling 10.8 million barrels of crude oil into Prince William Sound.

1989–1992: English scientist Tim Berners-Lee develops the first Web server and Web site.

Fraunhofer-Gesellschaft receives a German patent for MP3 (MPEG Audio Layer III) technology.

1990

Institute for Tax Studies is created by the College for Financial Planning.

College for Financial Planning has 25,000 enrolled students and close to 40,000 alumni.

IBCFP ratifies an agreement that makes IAFP Australia the first organization outside the United States to grant CFP certification.

Harry Markowitz, Merton Miller, and William Sharpe receive the Nobel
   Prize in economics.
Microsoft releases Windows 3.0.
Americans with Disabilities Act becomes law.
The Soviet Union is dissolved.
First McDonalds in Moscow opens.
Iraq invades Kuwait.

1991

IBCFP introduces a single, comprehensive exam for CFP certification.
Robert P. Goss is hired as executive director of the IBCFP.
IBCFP establishes a subsidiary Board of Affiliated Associations.
The United States launches Operation Desert Storm in the Persian Gulf
   War.
Slovenia and Croatia declare independence from Yugoslavia.
Federal Reserve lowers interest rate to 5.5%.
Talk-show host Jay Leno succeeds Johnny Carson.
DJIA closes above 3,000 for the first time.

1992

NEFE is formed as a holding company by the College for Financial
   Planning.
IBCFP and Japan Association of Financial Planners sign a license and
   affiliation agreement.
USSR becomes Commonwealth of Independent States.
Bill Clinton is elected U.S. president.
Unemployment is at 7.1%, highest in five years.
Copy of first *Superman* comic book (1938) sells for $82,000.
Chrysler, Ford, and General Motors report record losses.

1993

ICFP celebrates its 20th anniversary with a focus on financial literacy,
   hosting the Personal Economic Summit in Washington, D.C.
ICFP adopts the IBCFP's Code of Ethics and Professional Responsibility,
   agreeing to follow all future ethics rules established by the IBCFP.
ICFP opens membership to international CFP professionals.
ICFP establishes the P. Kemp Fain, Jr. Award.
IBCFP describes itself as a professional regulatory organization, stops
   PRO reference in 2008.
Intel's Pentium processor is unveiled.
Car bomb explodes in World Trade Center in New York City.
National Center for Supercomputing Applications, University of Illinois,
   introduces Mosaic, first true browser for the World Wide Web.

1994

Sylvia Ibanez is ordered by the Florida Board of Accountancy to stop using her CPA and CFP credentials in any advertising; she takes her case to the U.S. Supreme Court and wins.

CFP Board (formerly IBCFP) provides stipends and grants for financial planning research.

Worth includes CFP certificants in its "Best 200 Financial Advisers in America."

Netscape and Yahoo! are in business.

Mexican peso collapses.

Major League Baseball players go on strike.

1995

IAFP restructures IAFP Foundation as an independent entity and renames it the Foundation for Financial Planning.

CFP Board acquires IAFP's Registry of Financial Planning Practitioners.

NEFE becomes a private foundation.

CFP Board's CFP certification program is accredited by the National Commission for Certifying Agencies.

Richard Wagner and George Kinder form the Nazrudin Project to explore aspects of what is popularly known as life planning.

Netscape's share price jumps from $28 to $54 in its first day of trading.

Federal 55-mph speed limit is repealed.

DJIA closes above 4,000.

A $42 billion loan to Mexico is authorized by President Clinton to prevent default.

1996

Registry of Financial Planning Practitioners is retired.

National Securities Market Improvements Act is passed.

Worth's "Best 200 Financial Advisers in America" list includes 173 CFP certificants.

DJIA tops 6,000, up 100% in four years.

Actor George Burns dies at age 100.

Ted Kaczynski is arrested as the Unabomber.

The first issue of 10-year exchange fund notes is launched.

1997

NEFE becomes private foundation, sells College for Financial Planning and other programs and divisions to the Apollo Group.

IAFP endorses the CFP marks.

IAFP president Peggy Ruhlin writes "If I Ruled the World," in which she expresses her wish that the IAFP and ICFP merge; Ruhlin and ICFP president Judy Lau meet to discuss the possibility.

IAFP board votes unanimously to endorse the CFP marks.

IAFP and ICFP form a project team and hire a consultant who recommends creating a new organization.

H. Lynn Hopewell brings Monte Carlo simulation to the financial planning community with his article, "Decision Making Under Conditions of Uncertainty: A Wakeup Call for the Financial Planning Profession."

DJIA closes above 7,000.

Gold is $334 an ounce.

Tiger Woods wins the Masters golf tournament.

1998

U.S. District Court rules that the CFP marks are "distinctive and famous."

Foundation for Financial Planning awards its first grants.

IAFP/ICFP project team presents a core ideology at a joint meeting of the boards.

DJIA tops 9,000.

Chrysler and Daimler-Benz merge.

Russian debt default sets off global stock market plunge.

Belfast Agreement is signed by British and Irish governments, aimed at resolving conflicts in Northern Ireland.

Unemployment is lowest since 1970.

1999

CFP Board's board of governors proposes Associate CFP as a mark for entry-level practitioners, later withdrawing its proposal.

IAFP and ICFP boards approve memorandum of intent for creation of a new organization to be called the Financial Planning Association.

ICFP members vote to form the Financial Planning Association, with 81% voting in favor.

There are 52,723 CFP certificants worldwide.

Portable MP3 players appear.

U.S. Senate opens impeachment trial of President Clinton, later acquitting him and rejecting censure move.

Nelson Mandela, first black president of South Africa, steps down.

War erupts in Kosovo after Yugoslavia's president Slobodan Milosevic clamps down on the province, massacring and deporting ethnic Albanians.

The world anticipates possible technological consequences of Y2K.

2000

Financial Planning Association is launched, with more than 30,000 members and 100 chapters.

FPA holds Success Forum in Boston, its first large-scale annual convention.

Robert Goss resigns from CFP Board.

First PhD program in financial planning is offered, at Texas Tech University.

America Online agrees to buy Time Warner for $165 billion.

Charles Schulz, creator of the *Peanuts* comic strip, dies.

2001

Lou Garday becomes CEO of CFP Board.

September 11: Al-Qaeda terrorists hijack four U.S. jets, flying two into the World Trade Center's twin towers and one into the Pentagon. The fourth plane crashes in a field in Pennsylvania.

To help those affected by 9/11, FPA creates the National Financial Planning Support Center, with support from the Foundation for Financial Planning.

President Bush signs new tax-cut law, the largest in 20 years.

Budget surplus dwindles; Congressional Budget Office attributes rapid change to the slowing economy and the Bush tax cut.

2002

CFP certificants number 73,618 worldwide.

FPA holds its first Financial Planning Week.

U.S. Patent and Trademark Office approves registration of *CFP* as a certification mark.

Financial planning organizations in Hong Kong, South Korea, and Malaysia are authorized to grant CFP certification.

Citing charges of investor fraud, New York State Attorney General Eliot Spitzer orders brokerage firm Merrill Lynch to pay $100 million and agree to business reforms.

Enron, Tyco, and ImClone join the list of corporate scandals.

Daniel Kahneman is awarded the Nobel Prize in economics.

Nasdaq closes at 1,185. Stock market records a $4.4 trillion loss in value.

2003

CFP certificants number 80,973 worldwide.

CFP Board implements Rule 401, requiring CFP certificants to disclose conflicts of interest and compensation structure to clients.

CFP Board clarifies definition of *fee-only* in Advisory Opinion 2003-1.

U.S. Department of Homeland Security officially begins operation.

U.S. invades Iraq.

Space Shuttle *Columbia* explodes, killing all seven astronauts.

President Bush signs 10-year, $350-billion tax cut package, third-largest tax cut in U.S. history.

Harley-Davidson celebrates 100 years of motorcycle manufacturing.

Lance Armstrong wins his fifth Tour de France.

2004

Financial Services Institute is formed to serve broker-dealers.

NexGen holds its first gathering, at FPA's annual conference in Denver.

Financial Planning Standards Board is officially launched to oversee CFP certification in countries outside of the United States. Congress extends tax cuts due to expire at the end of 2005.

Wired editor coins the term *long tail* to describe the economics of abundance.

An undersea earthquake erupts in the Indian Ocean, triggering a tsunami that kills more than 225,000 people in 11 countries.

2005

With 12 of 16 country votes placed being positive, ISO 22222-2005— Personal Financial Planning is approved.

Hurricanes Katrina and Rita ravage the Gulf Coast in August and September.

With support from the Foundation for Financial Planning, FPA members offer pro bono assistance to Gulf Coast hurricane survivors.

California Republican congressman Randy "Duke" Cunningham resigns after pleading guilty to taking at least $2.4 million in bribes.

2006

FPA's National Financial Planning Support Center receives a $244,865 grant from the Foundation for Financial Planning to support pro bono programs.

In its lawsuit against the SEC over the Broker-Dealer Rule, FPA files a brief in federal court, saying that the SEC improperly created a new exemption for the brokerage industry that defies Congressional intent and puts the investing public at risk.

The *Journal of Financial Planning* celebrates 25 years of publication.

Financial Planning Standards Council of China becomes an affiliate member of FPSB.

Israeli prime minister Ariel Sharon suffers a massive stroke and he is replaced by acting prime minister Ehud Olmert.

Jack Abramoff, a lobbyist with ties to several members of Congress, is sentenced to six years in prison by a Florida judge on fraud charges.

The International Astronomical Union votes to redefine the solar system, and Pluto loses its status as a planet, reclassified as a dwarf planet.

2007

A bachelor's degree is required for CFP certification.

Kevin Keller is hired as CFP Board's CEO.

CFP Board moves from Denver to Washington, D.C.

U.S. Court of Appeals for the D.C. Circuit rules in favor of FPA in its lawsuit against SEC over SEC's broker-dealer exemption rule.

NASD becomes the Financial Industry Regulatory Authority (FINRA).

U.S. housing market starts to falter as a result of risky lending practices.

Romania and Bulgaria are admitted to the European Union.

President Bush says the $2.9 trillion budget will eliminate the federal deficit by 2012 without increasing taxes.

DJIA falls 416 points, or 3.3%, after the market in China drops nearly 9%.

Federal Reserve puts $72 billion into the U.S. financial system over two days to steady the volatile markets that plummeted in response to losses in the American mortgage market.

General Motors reports a $722 million fourth-quarter loss in 2007 ($920 million profit in the fourth quarter of 2006).

Former U.S. vice president Al Gore and the UN Intergovernmental Panel on Climate Change are awarded the Nobel Peace Prize.

2008

FPA, NAPFA, and CFP Board form the Financial Planning Coalition to protect and educate the public in the name of financial well-being, and to influence financial services regulation.

Financial planning pioneer Donald Pitti receives FPA's P. Kemp Fain, Jr. Award. As part of the revision to its code of ethics, CFP Board's newly adopted fiduciary standard takes effect.

FPA's board of directors passes a resolution supporting a Standard of Care for its members, clarifying the role of a fiduciary adviser.

FPSB hosts a meeting of representatives of financial planning organizations from around the world to adopt common global competency, ethical, and practice standards.

MSNBC includes financial planning in its "Top Twenty Jobs of 2008."

By year-end, number of CFP professionals outside of the United States
(59,676) surpasses for the first time the number of U.S. certificants
(58,830), for a total of 118,506 CFP certificants in 23 countries.

Summer Olympic games are held in Beijing.

Highest recorded price of regular unleaded gas in the United States is
$4.14 in July.

U.S. government places Fannie Mae and Freddie Mac under government
conservatorship.

U.S. banking system falters with the collapse of financial giants such as
Lehman Brothers, AIG, and Washington Mutual.

Global economic crisis unfolds with numerous bankruptcies, buyouts,
bailouts, massive market losses, and skyrocketing unemployment.

U.S. Senate passes bailout plan, House approves, and President Bush
signs the measure into law.

October 9: In the most active day in New York Stock Exchange history,
DJIA closes below 9,000 for the first time in five years.

Finance ministers from Group of 7 industrialized nations create a plan
to stem escalating financial crisis.

Bush administration announces plans to invest $250 billion, part of the
$700 billion bailout package, in nine of the largest U.S. banks.

Barack Obama is elected U.S. president.

Insurance giant AIG reports a $61.7 billion loss for the fourth quarter of
2008.

Fed cuts interest rates from 1% to .25% to zero.

Bush unveils $17.4 billion rescue plan for auto industry.

2009

Two FPA members testify in separate Congressional hearings on the
effects of market volatility on retirees and plan sponsors.

Mary Schapiro, former FINRA head, is appointed to chair the SEC.

US Airways Flight 1549, en route from New York City to Charlotte, NC,
is forced to land in the Hudson River; all 150 passengers and 5 crew
members survive.

President Obama signs the Lilly Ledbetter Fair Pay Act, expanding
workers' rights to sue in pay disputes.

February: Gold is $1,000 an ounce.

February: President Obama announces intent to withdraw most
American troops from Iraq by August 31, 2010.

March: Financier Bernard Madoff pleads guilty to running a Ponzi
scheme estimated at nearly $65 billion.

March: U.S. unemployment rate is 8.1%, with 651,000 jobs lost in
February.

March: DJIA drops below 6,600, with stocks at lowest close since April 1997.

March: U.S. Treasury Secretary Timothy Geithner presents a $2.5 trillion bailout plan, including a new entity that would partner with private investors to buy troubled assets.

March: U.S. government sets strict conditions for General Motors and Chrysler to receive additional aid, requests resignation of GM's CEO G. Richard Wagoner, Jr.

Barbie turns 50 years old.

U.S. first-class stamp costs 44 cents.

Quick-Reference Guide to Organizations and Designations

AFCPE, Association for Financial Counseling and Planning Education: A nonprofit professional organization for financial counselors and educators, offering two certifications: Accredited Financial Counselor and Certified Housing Counselor.

AFS, Academy of Financial Services: A membership association focusing on financial planning and financial services research, financial services curricula at universities, and interaction of financial services professionals and academicians.

AICPA, American Institute of Certified Public Accountants: A membership association founded in 1887, creating the Uniform CPA Exam, monitoring compliance in the accounting profession.

American College, The: Founded by Solomon S. Huebner in 1927, first offering the CLU program, later creating the ChFC and CASL (Chartered Advisor for Senior Living) designations.

Board of Affiliated Associations: Formed in 1991 by IBCFP, comprising two directors from the IBCFP and one director from each affiliated international association. Forerunner of current Financial Planning Standards Board.

CAE, Certified Association Executive: Certification offered by the American Society of Association Executives, a membership organization founded in 1920.

Certified Financial Counselor: Proposed name for new designation in 1969.

CFA, Chartered Financial Analyst: Designation program first proposed by Benjamin Graham in 1942 and offered by CFA Institute.

CFP, Certified Financial Planner: Certification owned by the Certified Financial Planner Board of Standards, Inc. (CFP Board).

CFP Board, Certified Financial Planner Board of Standards, Inc.: New name for IBCFP effective February 1, 1994. Founded in July 1985 by the College for Financial Planning and Institute of Certified Financial Planners as an independent certifying body to establish and enforce education, examination, experience, and ethics requirements for CFP certificants.

CFP Board's Board of Practice Standards: Created in 1995, composed of CFP practitioners to draft practice standards, identifying six elements of the financial planning process.

ChFC, Chartered Financial Consultant: Granted by The American College and established as a professional designation in 1982.

CIMA, Certified Investment Management Analyst: Designation designed for investment consultants, offered by the Investment Management Consultants Association (IMCA).

CLU, Chartered Life Underwriter: A professional designation for individuals specializing in life insurance and estate planning.

College for Financial Planning: Originally the International College for Financial Counseling (name change occurred in mid-1970), the first institution to offer the CFP certification program.

CPA, Certified Public Accountant: Designation created and offered by the AICPA.

FINRA, Financial Industry Regulatory Authority: Formed in 2007 from a consolidation of the NASD and NYSE Regulation, Inc.

Foundation for Financial Planning: Originally created in 1981 as the IAFP Foundation to help with public awareness; renamed in 1995 with a new mission of connecting financial planners with people in need through pro bono and outreach activities.

FPA, Financial Planning Association: Formed in 2000 from a merger of the International Association for Financial Planning and the Institute of Certified Financial Planners.

FPSB, Financial Planning Standards Board: Established in 2002, launched in 2004; controls licensing of CFP certificants outside the United States.

FPSB, Financial Products Standards Board: Established in 1984 as an independent organization, funded by the ICFP as a public service. Drafted guidelines and standards for structuring real estate limited partnership investments, mutual-fund, and oil-and-gas industries.

FSI, Financial Services Institute: Created on January 1, 2004, as a membership association focused on broker-dealers.

IAFC, International Association of Financial Counselors: The original name of the membership organization formed on December 12, 1969, by Loren Dunton and 12 other colleagues.

IAFP, International Association of Financial Planners: The first name change for the IAFC.

IAFP, International Association for Financial Planning: The second name change (from International Association of Financial Planners) for the IAFC.

IBCFP, International Board of Standards and Practices for Certified Financial Planners: An independent certifying body created in 1985 to own and manage the CFP marks. See CFP Board.

ICFP, Institute of Certified Financial Planners: Founded in 1973 as a membership association by members of the first graduating class of the College for Financial Planning.

ICI, Investment Company Institute: A national association of U.S. investment companies, established in 1940 as the National Committee of Investment Companies, changing to the National Association of Investment Companies in 1941, then to the Investment Company Institute in 1961.

International CFP Council: New name for Board of Affiliated Associations adopted in 1994, along with a policy to promote CFP certification globally.

International College for Financial Counseling: An educational institution formed on December 12, 1969, by Loren Dunton and 12 colleagues, renamed the College for Financial Planning in mid-1970.

ISO, International Organization for Standardization: A Geneva, Switzerland–based federation of national standards bodies from 140 countries overseeing development of worldwide ISO standards.

MOAA, Military Officers Association of America: Founded in 1929 as the Retired Officers Association, changing its name in 2003, offering a voice on legislative activities and services to military officers and their families.

NAIC, National Association of Insurance Commissioners: Founded by state insurance regulators in 1871 to address the need to coordinate regulation of multistate insurers.

NAPFA, National Association of Personal Financial Advisors: Created in 1983 with a focus on fee-only financial planning.

NASAA, North American Securities Administrators Association: An investor protection organization formed in Kansas in 1919 with a focus on state securities regulation.

NASBA, National Association of State Boards of Accountancy: Founded in 1908 to serve as a forum for 55 boards of accountancy.

NASD, National Association of Securities Dealers: Created in 1939 in response to amendments to the 1934 Securities Act.

Nazrudin Project: A think tank founded by financial planners George Kinder and Richard Wagner in 1995 as a forum for exploring the concept of life planning.

NCLR, National Council of La Raza: A national Latino civil rights and advocacy organization.

NEFE, National Endowment for Financial Education: Created in 1992 by the College for Financial Planning as the college's holding company; became a private foundation in 1997.

PFS, Personal Financial Specialist: Credential established by the AICPA for CPAs who specialize in personal financial planning.

SEC, Securities and Exchange Commission: Born out of the Securities Exchange Act of 1934 to protect investors, maintain fair, orderly, and efficient markets, and facilitate capital formation.

SFCE, Society for Financial Counselling Ethics: Founded by Loren Dunton on June 19, 1969.

SFSP, Society of Financial Services Professionals: Founded in 1928 by the first graduates of The American College.

Society for Financial Counseling: A later name for the Society for Financial Counselling Ethics.

SRO, self-regulatory organization: A nongovernmental organization with the power to create and enforce industry regulations and standards.

Financial Planning History Center
First Completed Phase of the Master Vision Project

The Financial Planning Master Vision Project began in the fall of 2000. During the early period, many ideas surfaced on the possible priorities and phases of the project; it was then that the co-director of the project, Oliver Welch, initiated the idea of a Financial Planning History Center that would have the potential to be developed into a world-class institution. The idea was well received, and the project leaders began exploring possibilities.

In May 2005, Texas Tech University was selected as the site for the Financial Planning History Center. Texas Tech's Personal Financial Planning Division had grown steadily in both quantity and quality. Two of the leaders there had consistently been active in financial planning: Dr. A. William Gustafson, senior director of the Personal Financial Planning Division, and Dr. Vickie Hampton, program director of the Personal Financial Planning Division.

It has accumulated historical documents, which are available for public access. Donors include the Brandon Research Organization; Lee V. Bruner; Graydon Calder; Richard C. Donahue; A. William Gustafson; Henry I. Montgomery; Pennington, Bass and Associates (Lee Pennington); Gary Pittsford; Texas Tech University's Personal Financial Planning Division; and H. Oliver Welch.

In association with the Division of Personal Financial Planning at Texas Tech University, the Brandon Research Organization, and Oliver Welch, these six programs have been initiated:

1. Programs to further concepts, strategies, and answers on professional financial planning of value to the general public.
2. Development of recorded oral histories of pioneers and leaders in financial planning: oral histories recorded at annual conferences of the

Financial Planning Association (San Diego 2005, Nashville 2006, Seattle 2007, and Boston 2008), plus distance-developed oral histories.

3. Pioneers of Planning series. This is a series of brochures developed by transcribing recorded oral histories, interviews, and research. They are on file and available at the Financial Planning History Center.

4. The development of a CFP Alumni Department at the Financial Planning History Center. This department has developed a basic database of CFP certificants.

5. Reunion meetings. At the Financial Planning Association's annual conference in 2007, the History Center in cooperation with Brandon Research Organization created a pilot program, which brought together large numbers of the first 10 CFP classes.

6. A program to encourage and help chapters of the Financial Planning Association to write their own histories.

As of 2009, Texas Tech University's Division of Personal Financial Planning employed a full-time faculty of 11. The division was one of the first 20 university programs registered by the International Board of Standards and Practices for Certified Financial Planners (now CFP Board) in 1987. Annual enrollment is approximately 150 undergraduates: 6 students in a 150-hour program; 115 masters students, including students enrolled in a dual degree (MS PFP, MS/JD, MS/MBA, or MS PFP/MS Finance); and 38 doctoral students. Its program offers 25 undergraduate and 35 graduate courses, including 5 courses for non-majors to enhance financial literacy. The Center for Financial Responsibility complements the Division of Personal Financial Planning with a focus on research and outreach.

Questions, requests, or donations to the Financial Planning History Center may be directed to Monte L. Monroe, PhD, Archivist, Personal Financial Historical Archives and the Southwest Collection, Box 41401, Lubbock, Texas, 79409-1041. Telephone: (806) 742-3749. Fax: (806) 742-0496. E-mail: montemonroe@ttu.edu.

First Graduating Class of the College for Financial Planning

October 1973

David L. Allard
Kay Baird
James A. Barry
John M. Bulbrook
Graydon K. Calder
Charles F. Church
Colin B. Coombs
Lavell G. Craig
W. Paul Crum
Howard W. Dance
Joseph F. Dillman
Walter A. Durham, Jr.
P. Kemp Fain, Jr.
John C. Gebura
Jerrold Glass
Ruthe P. Gomez
Robert Hallum
Richard E. Hanson
John L. Hawkins
W. Robert Hightower
B.J. Johnson

Robert C. Kelpe
Bernard J. Kessler
Jordan Kokjer
Herman Kramer
Jerome M. Ledzinski
Ronald A. Melanson
William B. Moore
Claude Morgan
Bernice Newmark
J. Chandler Peterson
Shannon Pratt
George Ratterman
Joseph Ross
Gordon A. Shepard
Richard A. Stone
John Strutt
Richard Venezia
Lawrence Vukelich
Dennis D. Wielech
Larry G. Wills
Herman W. Yurman

Affiliates of Financial Planning Standards Board (FPSB)

Australia	Financial Planning Association of Australia Ltd. (FPA)
Austria	Österreichischer Verband Financial Planners (Austrian Financial Planners (AFP))
Brazil	Instituto Brasileiro de Certificação de Profissionais Financeiros (IBCPF)
Canada	Financial Planners Standards Council (FPSC)
China	Financial Planning Standards Council of China (FPSCC)
Chinese Taipei	Financial Planning Association of Taiwan (FPAT)
France	Association Française des Conseils en Gestion de Patrimoine Certifiés (CGPC)
Germany	Financial Planning Standards Board Deutschland (FPSB Deutschland)
Hong Kong	Institute of Financial Planners of Hong Kong Ltd. (IFPHK)
India	Financial Planning Standards Board India (FPSB India)
Indonesia	Financial Planning Standards Board Indonesia (FPSB Indonesia)
Ireland	Financial Planning Standards Board Ireland (FPSB Ireland)
Japan	Japan Association for Financial Planners (JAFP)
Malaysia	Financial Planning Association of Malaysia (FPAM)
Netherlands	(FPSB Netherlands) Financial Planning Standards Board Netherlands
New Zealand	Institute of Financial Advisers (IFA)
Republic of Korea	Financial Planning Standards Board Korea (FPSB Korea)
Singapore	Financial Planning Association of Singapore (FPAS)
South Africa	Financial Planning Institute of Southern Africa (FPI)
Switzerland	Swiss Financial Planners Organization (SFPO)
Thailand	Thai Financial Planners Association (TFPA)
United Kingdom	Institute of Financial Planning Ltd. (IFP)
United States	Certified Financial Planner Board of Standards, Inc. (CFP Board)

Recipients of the
P. Kemp Fain, Jr., Award

P. Kemp Fain, Jr., was the first to receive this award in 1993 in honor of his years of service and dedication to the profession and the CFP mark. The recipients who followed Fain were selected for qualities and contributions that demonstrated superior professionalism.

1996: John T. Blankinship, Jr., CFP
1997: Loren E. Dunton (posthumous award)
1998: Henry I. Montgomery, CFP
1999: Charles G. Hughes, Jr., CFP
2000: No award given
2001: No award given
2002: William L. Anthes, PhD
2003: Richard B. Wagner, JD, CFP
2004: Alexandra Armstrong, CFP
2005: Colin B. Coombs, CFP, CLU
2006: Bill E. Carter, CFP, CLU, ChFC
2007: E. Denby Brandon, Jr., CFP, CLU, ChFC
2008: Don Pitti

Notes

Chapter 1: A New Profession Emerges

1. Rich White, "A Preliminary History of the Organized Financial Planning Movement Part 1: (1969–1974)," *The Financial Planner*, September 1979, 17 et seq.
2. The International Association of Financial Counselors later became the International Association of Financial Planners, and then the International Association for Financial Planning in 1982.

Chapter 2: Building a Profession

1. For a complete list of members of the first graduating class, see Appendix E.

Chapter 3: Growing Pains

1. *Southern Insurance*, August 1985: 4–5.
2. College for Financial Planning, Gail Quint, ed., *20 Years of Excellence*, June 1992: 28.
3. Ibid., p. 20.

Chapter 4: One Profession, One Designation

1. Bert Ely, "Savings and Loan Crisis," Library of Economics and Liberty, www.econlib.org/library/Enc/SavingsandLoanCrisis.html.
2. Catherine Newton, "Institute of Certified Financial Planners: 25 Years of Building a Profession," *A Look Back, A Look Ahead*, December 1998: 28.
3. Ibid., p. 29.
4. *Financial Planning*, September 1991: 12.

5. Catherine Newton, "At Long Last Unity: The FPA Story," *Source Book 2000*, December 1999: 18.
6. Catherine Newton, "CFP Civics: Nurturing a Profession," prepared for the Financial Planning Association, 2000.
7. "What About Bob?" *Financial Planning*, September 1999.
8. Catherine Newton, "CFP Civics: Nurturing a Profession," prepared for the Financial Planning Association, 2000.

Chapter 5: Responding to New Challenges

1. Shelley A. Lee, "10 Questions with Sarah Ball Teslik on Reaching Consumers, Threats to the Profession and—Oh, Yes—the F-Word and the C-Word," *Journal of Financial Planning* 18(10), October 2005: 10–14.
2. "Helping to Ease the Pain," advertising supplement sponsored by ING in *Money*, March 2004.
3. *The Age of Independent Advice: The Remarkable History of the Independent Registered Investment Adviser Industry* (San Francisco: Charles Schwab Corporation, 2007), p. 2.
4. Adi Ignatius, "Wall Street's Top Cop," *Time*, December 30, 2002.
5. CNN timeline: www.cnn.com/2008/BUSINESS/09/30/us.bailout.timeline/index.html.
6. "History of Dow Jones Industrial Average," MD Leasing Corporation, www.mdleasing.com/djia.htm.
7. Jeanne A. Robinson and Charles G. Hughes, Jr., "To Act . . . Like a CFP," *Journal of Financial Planning* 33(4), April 2009: 67–70.

Chapter 6: Global Expansion

1. "A Preliminary History of the Financial Planning Movement, Part I," *The Financial Planner*, September 1979.
2. Julie Bennett, biographical article on Gweneth E. Fletcher, *IFA*, June 11–17, 2007.
3. IBCFP annual report, 1991.
4. CFP Board annual report, 1993.
5. Laura Garrison, "Financial Planning History Made in Malaysia," *Journal of Financial Planning* 17(7), July 2004: 22–24.
6. "Regulatory Environment Comparison Table," Financial Planning Standards Board Web site: www.fpsb.org/CMS/index.php.
7. For instance, see Professor M.D. Nalapat's "Ensuring China's 'Peaceful Rise'" at www.bharat-rakshak.com/SRR/Volume14/nalapat.html. Accessed 6/8/2009.

8. For a convenient source of international GDP statistics, see www. nationmaster.com.

9. For a concise account of China's modern economic history, consult the 'Economy: General Considerations' section of the China article at www.britannica.com.

10. Sean Dorgan offers a nice summary of the Celtic Tiger phenomenon in "How Ireland Became the Celtic Tiger." www.heritage.org/research/ worldwidefreedom/bg1945.cfm. Accessed 6/8/2009.

Chapter 7: Theory, Technology, and Process

1. Sharon Hatten Garrison and James L. McDonald, "Computer Communications: A New Tool for Financial Planning," *Journal of the Institute of Certified Financial Planners* 5(3), Fall 1984: 187–192.

2. David Huxford, "Running Your Office with a Computer: An Overview," *Journal of the Institute of Certified Financial Planners* 1(1), July 1988: 6.

3. Ed McCarthy, "Keeping Pace with the Web, Windows, and What's Ahead," *Journal of Financial Planning* 9(3), June 1996: 44–46.

4. Nancy Opiela, "The Internet: Can It Reach Out and Touch Someone?" *Journal of Financial Planning* 12(7), August 1999: 64–71.

5. Nancy Opiela, "What Does the Future Hold for the Financial Planning Profession?" *Journal of Financial Planning Source Book 2001*, December 2000: 14–24.

6. Ed McCarthy, "Tech Tools for Disaster Recovery," *Journal of Financial Planning* 20(2), February 2007: 28–34.

7. From Harold Markowitz's autobiographical statement on the Nobel Prize Web site: http://nobelprize.org/nobel_prizes/economics/laureates/1990/markowitz-autobio.html.

8. Ibbotson Associates, a registered investment advisory firm now wholly owned by Morningstar, Inc., holds annual conferences on topics of interest to financial professionals: www.ibbotson.com.

9. Lisa Holton, "Is Markowitz Wrong? Market Turmoil Fuels Nontraditional Approaches to Managing Investment Risk," *Journal of Financial Planning* 22(2), February 2009: 20–26.

10. Lynn Hopewell, "Decision Making Under Conditions of Uncertainty: A Wakeup Call for the Financial Planning Profession," *Journal of Financial Planning* 10(5), October 1997: 84–91.

11. Shelley A. Lee, "The Journal's Journey," *Journal of Financial Planning* 17(6), June 2004: 46–56.

12. Ibid.

13. www.bankrate.com/brm/news/sav/20031230a1.asp, December 30, 2003.

14. Roger Gibson, "The Rewards of Multiple-Asset-Class Investing," *Journal of Financial Planning* 17(7), July 2004: 58–71.
15. William W. Jahnke, "The Asset Allocation Hoax," *Journal of Financial Planning* 10(1), February 1997: 109–113.
16. Yesim Tokat, Nelson Wicas, and Francis M. Kinniry, "The Asset Allocation Debate: A Review and Reconciliation," *Journal of Financial Planning* 19(10), October 2006: 52–63.
17. Shelley A. Lee, "10 Questions with Daniel Kahneman on Humans and Decision Making," *Journal of Financial Planning* 17(8), August 2004: 10–13.
18. http://nobelprize.org/nobel_prizes/economics/laureates/2002/kahneman-autobio.html.
19. Nancy Opiela, "Rational Investing Despite Irrational Behaviors," *Journal of Financial Planning* 18(1), January 2005: 34–42.
20. Michael M. Pompian, "Using Behavioral Investor Types to Build Better Relationships with Your Clients," *Journal of Financial Planning* 21(10), October 2008: 64–76.
21. Dick Wagner, "Integral Finance: A Framework for a 21st Century Profession," *Journal of Financial Planning* 15(7), July 2002: 62–71.
22. Richard B. Wagner and George D. Kinder, "Tales Will Tell," *Journal of Financial Planning* 9(2), April 1996: 30–31.
23. George D. Kinder, "The Seven States of Money Maturity," *Journal of Financial Planning* 9(6), December 1996: 36–37.
24. National Endowment for Financial Education, "Practical Applications of Life and Retirement Planning to Financial Planning," 2002, www.nefe.org/Portals/0/NEFE_Files/Research%20and%20Strategy/Personal%20Finance%20Papers%20white%20papers/09Practical%20Applications%20of%20Life%20and%20Retirement%20Planning%20to%20Financial%20Planning_Nov00.pdf.
25. Ken Rouse, *Putting Money in Its Place* (Dubuque, IA: Kendall/Hunt Publishing, 1994).
26. Lewis J. Walker, "The Meaning of Life (Planning)," *Journal of Financial Planning* 17(5), May 2004: 28–30.
27. Roy Diliberto and Mitch Anthony, "Financial Life Planning: Navigating Life Transitions," *Journal of Financial Planning* 16(10), October 2003: 26–29.
28. Carol Anderson and Deanna L. Sharpe, "The Efficacy of Life Planning Communication Tasks in Developing Successful Client-Planner Relationships," *Journal of Financial Planning* 21(6), June 2008: 66–77.
29. *The Age of Independent Advice: The Remarkable History of the Independent Registered Investment Adviser Industry* (Charles Schwab Corporation, 2007), Chap. 5, note 3, p. 146.

30. Ibid., p. 146.
31. Ibid., p. 5.
32. Catherine Newton, "Institute of Certified Financial Planners: 25 Years of Building a Profession," *A Look Back, A Look Ahead*, supplement to the *Journal of Financial Planning*, December 1998: 10–39.
33. Ed McCarthy, "Financial Planners Flock to Asset Management: Are We Losing Our Bearings?" *Journal of Financial Planning* 9(1), February 1996: 38–41.
34. M.P. Dunleavy, "Coaches for a Game of Money," *New York Times*, New York edition, December 12, 2008: B6.
35. Pride Planners, www.prideplanners.com.

Chapter 8: The Quest for Professional Status

1. Catherine Newton, "CFP Civics: Nurturing a Profession," prepared for the Financial Planning Association, 2000.
2. IBCFP *Information Update* newsletter, December 1987.
3. IBCFP annual report, 1991.
4. CFP Board annual report, 2008.
5. College for Financial Planning, *20 Years of Excellence: A Look Back*, Gale Quint, ed., June 1992: 10.
6. Charles G. Hughes, Jr., "Financial Planning Needs a Conscience," *Journal of Financial Planning* 1(2), October 1988: 104–107.
7. IBCFP annual report, 1991.
8. *CFP Board Report* newsletter, October 2008.
9. Catherine Newton, "Institute of Certified Financial Planners: 25 Years of Building a Profession," *A Look Back, A Look Ahead*, supplement to the *Journal of Financial Planning*, December 1998.
10. *IBCFP Manual*, 1987.
11. Catherine Newton, "Institute of Certified Financial Planners: 25 Years of Building a Profession," *A Look Back, A Look Ahead*, supplement to the *Journal of Financial Planning*, December 1998: 10–39.
12. Jeanne A. Robinson and Charles G. Hughes, Jr., "To Act . . . Like a CFP," *Journal of Financial Planning* 33(4), April 2009: 67–70.
13. P. Kemp Fain, Jr., "Unifying and Professionalizing the Financial Planning Segments of the Financial Services Industry," whitepaper, 1987.
14. *CFP Digest*, February 21, 1979.
15. Catherine Newton, "Institute of Certified Financial Planners: 25 Years of Building a Profession," *A Look Back, A Look Ahead*, supplement to the *Journal of Financial Planning*, December 1998: 10–39.
16. IBCFP annual report, 1991.
17. FINRA Web site: www.finra.org/index.htm.

18. Richard B. Wagner, "To Think ... Like a CFP," *Journal of Financial Planning* 3(1), January 1990: 36–41.

19. Catherine Newton, "Institute of Certified Financial Planners: 25 Years of Building a Profession," *A Look Back, A Look Ahead*, supplement to the *Journal of Financial Planning*, December 1998: 10–39.

20. Duane R. Thompson, "Living in a Glass House: New Disclosure Standards for CFP Stakeholders," *Journal of Financial Planning* 13(10), October 2000: 24–26.

21. Jonathan R. Macey, "Options for Future Regulation of Financial Planners, Part I," *Journal of Financial Planning* 15(6), June 2002: 92–99.

22. *IBCFP Manual*, 1987.

23. CFP Board annual report, 1993.

24. Shelley A. Lee, "What Is Financial Planning Anyway?" *Journal of Financial Planning* 14(12), December 2001: 36–46.

25. Shelley A. Lee, "'Making of the Profession' Roundtable: The Public's Memory, the Public Benefit, a Profession's Foundation—and Where You Go from Here," *Journal of Financial Planning* 20(2), February 2007: 22–27.

26. Jonathan R. Macey, "Options for Future Regulation of Financial Planners, Part I," *Journal of Financial Planning* 15(6), June 2002: 92–99.

27. Norman M. Boone, "My Plumber Is a Financial Planner?" *Journal of Financial Planning* 13(1), January 2000: 30–33.

28. Tom Warschauer, "'The Role of Universities in the Development of the Personal Financial Planning Profession," *Financial Services Review* 1.1, 2002: 209.

29. Ibid., pp. 205–206.

30. Jonathan Clements, "Due Diligence: The Five Key Rules to Heed When Choosing a Financial Adviser," *Wall Street Journal*, May 31, 2006.

31. Jane Bryant Quinn, "Planners Wanted ASAP," *Newsweek*, March 3, 2008.

32. Financial Planning Association, "Consumer Attitudes and Awareness of Financial Planning: A Telephone Survey of the American Public," conducted by Opinion Research Corporation, February 2006.

33. "Investor and Industry Perspectives on Investment Advisers and Broker-Dealers," LRN-RAND Center for Corporate Ethics, Law, and Governance within the RAND Institute for Civil Justice, 2008.

Chapter 9: The Next 40 Years

1. Bloomberg, February 2009, www.bloomberg.com/apps/news?pid=newsarchive&sid=a60APVwmz01g.

2. Bureau of Economic Analysis.

3. "Workshops Raise Consciousness About Money," *San Francisco Chronicle*, March 2, 2009, www.sfgate.com.
4. Deena Katz, "Financial Imagineers," *Financial Planning*, December 2008.
5. www.longtail.typepad.com, January 9, 2005.
6. U.S. Bureau of the Census.
7. U.S. Bureau of Labor Statistics, "Spotlight on Statistics," July 2008.
8. Alicia H. Munnell, Anthony Webb, Francesca Golub-Sass, and Dan Muldoon, "Long Term Care Costs and the National Retirement Risk Index," Center for Retirement Research, March 2009, www.crr.bc.edu/briefs/long-term_care_costs_and_the_national_retirement_risk_index_4.html.
9. Center for Retirement Research, www.crr.bc.edu.
10. Employee Benefit Research Institute, as reported in *U.S. News & World Report*, August 2007.
11. Center for Retirement Research, www.crr.bc.edu.
12. Yankelovich, "Monitor Minute," Generation Ageless study, 2007.
13. *Investment News*, March 26, 2009.
14. Moss Adams LLP, "Uncharted Waters: Navigating the Forces Shaping the Advisory Industry," 2007, www.mossadams.com/publications/financialservices/uncharted.aspx.
15. See note 8.
16. Rick Adkins, "Facing Our Profession's Transition," *Journal of Financial Planning* 20(7), July 2007: 30–33.
17. "Suddenly, Life Insurance Is Cheap," *SmartMoney*, April 30, 2007.
18. "Rethinking Retirement," www.agewave.com/research/SchwabAge WaveRethinkingRetirement071508.pdf.
19. "Americans Take Stock and Reinvent Themselves and Their Careers in Retirement," *Business Wire*, August 27, 2008, www.allbusiness.com/population-demographics/demographic-trends-aging/11495902-1.html.
20. www.agewave.com.
21. Ken Dychtwald and Joe Flower, *Age Wave: How the Most Important Trend of Our Time Can Change Your Future* (New York: Bantam Books, 1990).
22. Ken Dychtwald and Daniel Kadlec, *With Purpose: Going from Success to Significance in Work and Life* (New York: William Morrow, 2009).
23. "The Future of Age Never Looked Better," *Orange County Register*, March 9, 2009, www.ocregister.com/articles/dychtwald-work-says-2327303-boomers-success.
24. Mitch Anthony, *The New Retirementality: Planning Your Life and Living Your Dreams . . . at Any Age*, 2nd ed. (New York: Kaplan Business, 2006).
25. Mitch Anthony, "Maslow Meets Retirement," *Financial Advisor*, January 2008.

26. Cynthia Wagner, Aaron Cohen, and Rick Docksai, "See the Future Through New Eyes," *The Futurist*, November/December 2008.
27. "When Nest Eggs Change Colors," *New York Times*, April 4, 2009.
28. Moss Adams LLP, "Uncharted Waters: Navigating the Forces Shaping the Advisory Industry," 2007, www.mossadams.com/publications/financialservices/uncharted.aspx.
29. "Alumni Statistics," www.cffpalum.org.
30. William E. Thompson and Joseph V. Hickey, *Society in Focus: An Introduction to Sociology* (Needham Heights, MA: Allyn & Bacon, 2005).
31. Population as of 2004, U.S. Census Bureau.
32. Shelley A. Lee, "10 Questions with Sheryl Garrett on Why 400,000 Planners Are Needed . . . and Where They'll Come From," *Journal of Financial Planning* 21(3), March 2008: 16–19.
33. John Rogers, Jr., Charles Schwab, and Mellody Hobson, "The Ariel-Schwab Black Paper: A Decade of Research on African-American Wealth Building and Retirement Planning," October 2007, www.ariel.com.
34. The Ariel/Schwab Black Investor Survey: Saving and Investing Among Higher Income African-American and White Americans, www.ariel.com.
35. National Council of La Raza, *2009 Policy Agenda: A Public Policy Briefing Book*, www.nclr.org.
36. Ke Bin Wu and Laurel Beedon, "Hispanics 65 and Older: Sources of Retirement Income," *AARP*, November 2004.
37. Shelley A. Lee, "10 Questions with Louis Barajas on Returning to the Barrio, Changing Cultural Beliefs, and Helping with *El Camino a la Grandeza Financiera*," *Journal of Financial Planning* 19(6), June 2006: 18–22.
38. Shelley A. Lee, "Be Careful What You Wish For: Large-Firm Financial Planning in the Wake of Court Ruling," *Journal of Financial Planning* 20(10), October 2007: 28–35.
39. Financial Services Institute, www.financialservices.org.
40. "Calling for Financial Advice . . . and Reassurance," *New York Times*, April 2, 2009.
41. Ayco Financial Network, www.aycofinancialnetwork.com.
42. Jim Pavia, "For Advisers, Technology Is Not an Elective," *Investment News*, April 2009, www.investmentnews.com/apps/pbcs.dll/article?AID=/20090419/REG/304199991/1008.
43. Bill Winterberg, http://fppad.com/2009/03/15/adviser-use-of-linkedin-may-violate-sec-rules/.
44. Generational Advisory, www.generationaladvisor.com.
45. Angela Herbers, "The Great Divide," *Investment Advisor*, February 2005, www.investmentadvisor.com/Issues/2005/February%202005/Pages/The-Great-Divide.aspx.

46. "Young Advisers Face Longer, Rockier Road to Ownership," *Investment News*, January 4, 2009.

47. www.aycofinancialnetwork.com.

48. "Experts Urge Greater Regulation of Financial Markets," *Voice of America News,* October 22, 2008, www.voanews.com.

49. "Fiduciary Issue Attracts SEC Interest," *Investment News*, February 22, 2009.

50. Letter to the *Wall Street Journal* from CFP Board, FPA, and NAPFA, April 2009.

51. "Hope, Greed and Fear: The Psychology Behind the Financial Crisis," *Knowledge@Wharton*, April 15, 2009.

52. Robert Shiller, "How About a Stimulus for Financial Advice?" *New York Times*, January 18, 2009: BU5.

Appendix B: The History of Financial Planning Timeline

1970s Flashback: www.1970sflashback.com.
1980s Flashback: www.1980sflashback.com.
1990s Flashback: www.1990sflashback.com.
www.thepeoplehistory.com/2003.html.
www.infoplease.com/yearbyyear.html.

Index